Karl,

my brother
in arms!

E

one-of-us

The Reluctant Goldwyn

by

J. Elliott Goldwyn

authorHOUSE
1663 Liberty Drive, Suite 200
Bloomington, Indiana 47403
(800) 839-8640
www.authorhouse.com

This book is a work of non-fiction. Unless otherwise noted, the author and the publisher make no explicit guarantees as to the accuracy of the information contained in this book and in some cases, names of people and places have been altered to protect their privacy.

© 2005 J. Elliott Goldwyn. All Rights Reserved.

No part of this book may be reproduced, stored in a retrieval system, or transmitted by any means without the written permission of the author.

First published by AuthorHouse 09/16/05

ISBN: 1-4208-4656-6 (sc)

Printed in the United States of America
Bloomington, Indiana

This book is printed on acid-free paper.

"I am here, writing this, for one purpose only. So that you might understand who I am, for if there is an i, there are others who feel like i and struggle with the same sorts of things that i do too. Some in more one way or the other, and others in less this is true (no doubt) but we are all the same. It is important for me to know who i'm here with. Therein: one may begin to know one's self, and my work may begin. My life is about helping, if I fail to assist where I'm able then I am no one. Today, I choose to belong and believe. That, may be the great struggle... but also the greatest reward."

Table of Contents

Forward 1

Joe: book 1

Begin 6
Twice? 14
Firsts 26
Firsts #2 30
Teenage reflections 32
Egypt! 34
Misery? 36
Spain 37
College 39
CDI 42
Prom time 44
Smokin' cuban 53
QU.1 (quiz unit one) 56
City of the stars 62
Only prayers 64
Mark 66
Spirit 69
Light 75
Although 81
Magick 93
A Glimpse 98
Body 3 105
Reality? 107

Book 2: (Elliott)

Elliott	112
Church?	115
Jail	118
Frustration!	119
Motel goddess?	121
My mom?	122
Ride!	125
Respectable?	127
Rachel	129
Guilty?	130
Menage a trois!	131
Entertainment full tilt!	135
Problem solved?	136
Achieve esteem!	138
Sabrina #'s 1&2	140
Hope!	142
Big toe?	144
Mexico	145
Lori lost!	146
Cocaine needle!	147
Lesbian love?	149
I can gamble	150
Love basis?	151
Lesbian vengeance!	153
If you can!	155
Over our heads!	159
Tale of Two Blondes	160
Hit no one!	162
Kari	164

Book 3: (Daddy?)

A cry to heaven? 170
Lesbians in charge! 171
Saint or sinner? 172
seems perennial 174
All alone? 177
Myself! 179
The future? 184
Hypersensitive? 187
Dreams 189
Writing/Talking? 194
Debra 195
Circles of light! 199
Worry too much? 206
Bright eye! 212
Debra's needs -or- Desire too! 217
Sara! 218
Climb so high? 220
It's a matter of trust 221
Can I trust him? 223
Permission finally? 226
Out of touch? 229
Not anymore! 237
love love love 238
Body and soul 239
All the above 241
My big day? 245
Sara understands! 246
Life's operating manual? 247
The age is dark 249

Two cats in my crib? 250
Lying eyes 252
Heaven -or- Hell 253
Let things slip 257
Endless war! 259
"Super-physical" 263
No free rides -or- law 'n' order 265
In a nutshell 267
Rape? 270
Sometimes 272
One word 275
The end? 277
Follow? 279

Book 4: (Questions)

Reflections? 284
Barrel time! 288
Sin? 291
The kids? 293
Bullshit? 298
Are you? 300
More? 301
A part? 303
Help? 307
We let them? 309
The devil? 311
A third choice? 312
Stand and state? 315
My train? 316
Limited society? 319

Growing? 322
Perform magick? 323
Doubt? 325
who's responsible? 326

One of us: Book five, answers -or- the beginning of the end

Forward 328
Las Vegas here I come! 330
There was more, ... 334
1st beginning 338
The big day 341
The video tape 344
The first end 346
Michigan 347
A letter 350
In the eye 352
Within six months 354
Jeff's Parade 356
Clouds do disappear 358
Lightning strikes twice 360
Criminal Sexual Conduct 363
The Confrontation 365
As if there could be a good part 367
Just one night 369
The present day 376
Children 377
Church 382
School 386
Responsible Reality 388

Soul versus Brain	391
Love	393
Responsibilities	397
Mom and Dad	401
Evil	403
Genocide	405
skimming off the top	408
Ya know	411
From Iraq to North Korea	412
about an hour and a half later	414
Breaking it down	416
With all due respect:	421
one of us	422
"...and sleep"	425

Forward

I've always been taught that the best place to start is the beginning. The start, for me, is where the trouble begins. There are many beginnings and all with their own ends, each containing subsequent social, mental and emotional lessons. So I've decided to separate those lessons into separate chapters as best I'm able.

In fact I'll assign the first chapter to my childhood which began Jan. of `63 and had it's end when I became the man of the house (my dad needed something he couldn't get at home). Because in or around 1970, my dad moved out.

Unlike most people, I was subjected to a second childhood at the age of 22. My second life began after a motorcycle accident which left me paralyzed, comatose and with a traumatic head injury. Unfortunately or fortunately, because of my 'near-death' at 22 my whole life was erased and I had to begin all over again. All social, mental and emotional lessons were gone. Because of a childhood at age 22 I believe I have an ability to explain the how's and why's said lessons effected me, hurt me, and scared me to death. All I wanted to do is love but the world had different plans for me... both times I've found.

Although, the events of my life which took place between the ages of zero and 22 are in this dream like fog now, sort of. All I have is memories mostly of good, pleasant things. The bad stuff or mistakes I've made I have trouble recalling.

Fortunately \ unfortunately, I have (because of divorce) many sets of parents who remember those times Joe failed and feel the need to inflict guilt on the remains of Joe. But, I do apologize in advance for any memory of mine which is not quite accurate concerning such things as names and dates but I'll do the best my head trauma handicap will

allow. The entire book of Joe is skippy and non-fluid due to the effects of a coma and subsequent amnesia. So please just bear with me. This entire work took me over eleven years to grow confident enough to go to print. No one but I has touched the direction or composition of this novel. No one but I has corrected grammar either (thank God for spell check!) so please keep that in mind. If there is ever a question you might have as to my meaning about anything I might have said in my book, ask me. Just me. No one may say anything about my life's meaning to me, but me... dig?
    me@one-of-us.com
   So when I say, "God helps those who help themselves" you'll know I really mean it.
   This first book will end there. The second book will begin with my second life.
   (Which did not begin right after the coma, but please don't jump ahead to the bloody part because the foundation of my soul is important too!) I believe that true intelligence is shown by learning from someone else's mistakes rather than having to go through the horrors of life twice, or once in each life at least. I have made many mistakes, so... all you smart people might just learn something as I struggle with my broken brain.
   If there would have been someone else honest enough, I would not have gone through each lesson two times. Although, since this life is full of prophets for profit I'll find out why I wanted to sell my soul in commercialistic California. There is a good side though; Now I know those lessons well... and just how much my soulfulness is worth.
   My full name is Joseph Elliott Goldwyn. At 23, or so, I stopped being a Joe and I no longer wanted to be Joe again. After a while (a long while), with time spent in personality

reflection and reformation, I slowly began to reject the name of Goldwyn and what it connotes to many of the others whom have played a role in my life and I in their's.

I hope you enjoy what it is you may read, and if it helps you I'd like to hear. If it just entertains you, good, that's what I'm here for.

I am Elliott, no more... no less. And now I'll tell you why:

Joe: book 1

J. Elliott Goldwyn

Begin
* * *

Michael Anthony Marine was born on the 27th of January in 1963. I don't know if he ever even touched his mother's outside, suckled her breast or looked into her eyes. Mike had other parents but he had not even seen them yet. The world had other plans for him. It might have been for the best, but Mike was taken away from the only person he had grown to love for the first nine months of his life.

("The Handmaids Tale" comes to mind.)

I was born in Los Angeles under the name of Michael Anthony Marine. I had no mother to speak of and a child with no mother often dies. Although, I was adopted a short while after my birth. I was a choice baby for adoption or otherwise, blond hair, blue eyes and male. Even though the best of the southern California life was going to be my oyster (with many pearls) it was my incubator that was my jail, my own private hell. Which explains my own fear of hospitals.

Coldness and loneliness is how my life began, and I've been trying to avoid just that since.

There is nothing as sad `n` heartbreaking as a child separated from mom or dad and then placed into solitary incarceration. Like a zoo animal, fed, watered and a keeper to clean my cage (my crib). But it was worse than that. There were hospital employees to poke, prod and examine me - keep me alive.

No one to love or love me.

Although, what is life without love? Hollow empty existence.

That was just my first week. The world, God, the Goddess, or the great mystery of which no one really knows anything about, brought me to live in a human form so that I could bless a married couple who could not achieve pregnancy or be parents any other way - but adoption. Although that was only one of the many, many reasons.

At my tender age, everything affected me, especially the "guardian angels" who became my new parents. They took me out of jail, touched me and the most important gift of all - loved me. Even though they were not my parents mattered little because of the attention I received.

On Valentines Day, 1963, I became the legal child of Mr. Alvin Morton Goldwyn and his wife Florence Betty Goldwyn. My new name was the same as my dad's father, Joseph Elliott Goldwyn. I was free to love and to bond with my guiding lights, my new mom and dad!

My childhood was planned so that very little could go wrong, as everything in suburban Ca. should be.

Smog free Orange County. Beautiful (country-like) tract homes, each a little different from the other (sort of). Some had pools, still others had beautiful yards with great big avocado trees. Those trees helped support all my ten year old cravings, which became twelve or thirteen year old debauchery. Every house looked slightly different but what you can see can also be controlled.

Picture perfect 60's suburban "town and country" living with the grocery store five blocks away... and a fruit tree orchard in between. I was living in a plastic world where children are toys or pawns on the great chess board of success in life with material gain seemingly the only 'checkmate' in the middle class "American dream" game. (Game ?) Yes, a game. People spending a lot of time at work, to build a better picture perfect place where kids are cute at the cocktail party. When I stopped being cute we got a maid.

(Is that the second time in which there seemed to be some transference of responsibility in the rearing of Master Joseph?)

Of course I received more love and attention that anyone else and I deserved it. I was godlike. I was the one thing this spiritually split (Jewish/Baptist) young yuppie ever so nuclear family couldn't buy themselves at a department store.

Flo was not producing eggs (wow... young and barren).

I wonder what that's like, and does it explain her first reaction to my own partner's news of pregnancy? But then I'm rushing the story.

I guess the ability to procreate is not a given. Too bad for father, two strikes, two wives and four daughters (no boys). It seems both mom 'n' dad had done the marriage thing already.

Adoption was the only answer. I'd always been told that I was not mom `n` dad's natural born kid, but I was probably even more wanted because dad had to pay for me.

A truly wanted baby. A baby with purpose and many new things to experience. I was already in the vehicle best suited to examine much of the life that is very different. (I've been alive before...)

Male and female - female and male - we make a circle seemingly, but we are individuals with many potential circles from which to choose. Although, I was taught many things by society and life, and the most anti-social of them was to disregard that which I always knew to be true - lucky me. I was born to truly appreciate women, I was just not taught how to appreciate because life in society did not want me to know. Seeing as I was raised to be a provider, bread winner and guiding light through the horrors of reality, I really had little chance to think beyond the fact that women were here to make babies and keep us men content with our various needs met. (Boy, did I have a long way to go.)

I was not enrolled in the great class of gender relationships. All I knew was that dad was always gone but mom is here most of the time. Just because she was there more, I became bonded to her; after all... the ties that join mother to son do not have to be a result of a prenatal physical connection.

I led a life of luxury. I believe every child does until he or she is maligned by mass materialism. For some it's clothes, others it's toys, or there is something different for each individual. My life was perfect because it was, but it was also all I knew. Although there was more I needed to learn, so let me go on...

The first time I felt for a woman, in ways which no preschooler can explain, had an appearance in the first child taming structured environment I was subjected to. I fell in love in Kindergarten, with Sandra. My parents remember my infatuation. I liked the way "Sandy," rolled off my tongue.

I was an only child of a woman who could not get pregnant and a son to an aging (40ish) Jewish man who could only produce girls. I have four older sisters from my dad's first marriage; Terry, Linda, Jan and Kathy-Jo. Sisters were a big part of my life, and I feel therein lies my fear/love of women. It turns out dad did various things for me he would not do for them just because of my gender (or so I was told), and... I was also hated/envied/loved/feared and loathed by my step-siblings just because of how I was born.

On the surface they all treated me nicely enough, but a baby (because of its innocence) can feel things which are not spoken only because that is the only way for a baby to communicate. I was more than, therefore to save their (sis's) own "faces," I was made less than.

The challenge was made. I, the only child of a "goddess and god" decided to meet the responsibility placed at my feet.

Success, success in school is what mom and dad wanted. It was my duty to give it to them. In a small way repaying their being saviors of mine. (Ever see the movie, "Oliver"?)

School was fun, with everything we did being social in a communicative and imaginative, expression based, no winner or loser activity. Participation in class was non-competitive.

I was no longer alone! There were many people to play with my own age, my size and the other kids in class hadn't been effected by commercialism yet. I hadn't been either, and I didn't want to. Because the "keep up with the Jones'" race was not worth running. No winners, only losers! I was not taught to play that way by any teacher, but... dad did go off into battle daily.

I just wanted to do what I wanted to do and have it be of some value to someone so that I may use my skills in trade for what I need to survive. Of course, those were thoughts of a four or five year old. (Plato-like thoughts, remember this point.)

I was four when I was introduced to the most beautiful and the most horrific of ideas. Sandy, the shy five year old red head I had feelings for in preschool, introduced me to love. Or as much love as a kid can feel. She was beautiful. Sandy was special, I liked her because I couldn't understand her. In love at four, with an older woman. (She was five.) I felt like a grown man in a child's body. I wanted to say things I couldn't, and that hurt.

Love is a great thing to find it at four. Guilty, in someway, someday, someone will hurt me because... love hurts, or so life keeps telling me. That's a hell of a four year old revelation. (Life's hardest on the children.)

I also became aware of guilt when I was four. The beautiful place called church (looks/deceiving equation), where there were clean happy people who came bright eyed and bushy tailed to hear how they've sinned all week long. (The 2 things I learned were: love and guilt... so far anyway.)

A person should hurt no animal, no man, woman or child, except to save or sustain one's own life, right? From the mind of a babe? It made sense to me and still does. The same is true about respect.

If anyone wants respect - just give it and ye shall receive. (From me and my heart.)

But, No. I was taught and trained many great things in church, although I was told doing anything human was a sin. That's not fair, is it? To make almost everything human against the rules. And church had a cruel vindictive God that WILL send me to burn in hell for eternity for what's been done in a mere human lifetime. I'm not sure. (More later...)

Didn't the big man with the cool collar and bible just tell us that the "God" thing was all powerful, all knowledgeable, all loving AND all understanding? Didn't the most religious man in the room tell us that any other version of the bible or name for god was wrong and "they" were going to hell? That makes them bad people, people to argue with, fight with, and... kill.

(Right?)

I know this is an extreme point, but it is true that most all of the world's battles were "religious" in nature. Even the Crusades. Many people died in the spreading of Christianity, and some still do!

The preacher said God put our souls inside our human body, which is just another animal, and that we need to ignore the body's strong mental, emotional, and physical needs in order to reach a pinnacle existence, heaven. I felt this cannot be true, all these 'adult' people cannot be duped by this shell game... can they?

There is plenty of time for holier than thou in heaven, or what ever you'd like to call it. The Goddess doesn't care, she understands.

We were put here, or we wanted to come here, to live in tactile bodies. To feel, to sing, to touch, to be touched, but of course only with someone who wants to be.

In my short life I felt many things, sang many songs, touched a few and a couple have touched me. I've felt what I've needed to, mostly. In my short life I've felt every thing I could feel; love, hate, disgust, envy, with a couple of speed balls thrown in.

Singing in a band appealed to me, so I did that for awhile. As a matter of fact...right up until the very end. (Pardon the rush.)

Twice?
* * *

It was useless for me to stand up for what I wanted to believe in, for the day had come for me to be a big brother. So, now the spotlight shines somewhere else. Al and Florence adopted a baby girl when I was five. My sister was also something which mom `n` dad couldn't buy in a store, but "boy-o-boy" was she cute at business cocktail parties. I hated her. I loved her.

I named her Sandy after my first true love. Love can teach a person many things, like when to or not to touch someone, when you should or shouldn't offer a hug, or if you should lift up a li'l girl's skirt and when you shouldn't (everything's relative). I've kissed many girls and a few boys in my life, and have come faced with my share of rejection. Although I have never been slapped because of social ineptitude. During most of my social lessons I paid attention.

Sometimes I felt if I hated Sandy long enough and hard enough, she would just blow away. I was either wrong or I didn't want it bad enough. Or, maybe she had a purpose in the future? I never spent much time with her because she was different. Sugar `n` spice, wore different clothes and played in different ways. That's what I was taught, by my mom and dad... sort of.

Me and Sandy-"fanny farkle face" had a very unique relationship. I think that was due to the fact that she was there one day, but the day before she was not. No nine months of pregnancy to prepare me for the complete and total change that was to come. My life was no longer the same, I was not the pride `n` joy anymore at home. School was a different story. In school I was the best Joe there was in my seat and in my shoes. My only competition was with myself. There was no dog eat dog survival technique class in school for me to learn the lessons that were to come. Although, in school there was this competition in between students to see who could wear cooler clothes and who had cooler stuff. (This happened later, not in the beginning.)

I was enrolled into El Dorado Elementary School for the gifted child. When I was five

I tested very high on an IQ examination, so I went to a special school on a short bus.

A short school bus means two things to every school age parent, retarded *or* private school. It didn't matter to the cruel neighborhood children. Either way it went, short bus means moron.

I wasn't friends with any of the neighbor kids. The guys on the street would, if I gave them the chance, chase me down and "pants-me". (It only took once.) Even though I was demoralized and humiliated I was taught to "turn the other cheek." Because boys will be boys. Although, if I were a girl there would have been new bracelets all around.

I hated boys, and I hated "turning the other cheek." (Still do.) I never did much with my fellow street dwellers. I went to private school for seven years but somewhere in sixth year... I was told, or learned about it somehow, that the perfect marriage between Al and Flo ("until death do you part") was over.

Everything I've been shown until that point was perfection, so when the picture perfect pasteboard walls came tumbling down reality was impossible for me to comprehend, only because I was in a bubble surrounded and protected seemingly by money. Even though it takes money to raise a family, it also needs a lot more, but... money's nice. So, reality was not something I wanted to look at. With reality came mom, or dad. There was no more mom and dad.

I was asleep in my room, and it must have been 2:00ish in the morning when my mom came bursting into my room, the first time I remember seeing her drunk, stinking drunk.

I accepted that alcohol is an allowable adult avenue of actuality avoidance... and all the social games that ensued became devastating. She said, "Your father, that Bastard, left the Party with that Mexican Slut!" (Plus other 'man anger' stuff I'll not repeat here, so just imagine it.)

Two questions came to mind:
   1) What do you think my picture of alcohol was?
   2) What do you think my opinion of men was?
      (Dad was?)

Let alone I was feeling scared, because here`s a woman who looked like my mom, acting crazy and saying terrible things about her "life long partner." (My dad?)

Is everything disposable? Spouses, cars, homes, careers and children? Especially adopted children? What was safe?

Life's a joke, Right? We're all living in a cartoon. (Ever feel like that?) Seeing's as I've always been told that television was fantasy, with "safety nets" like a stand-in and second takes, but here it is happening to me right now and I can't change the channel or wake up. Even though everything in my life was hell, it was a hell that worked. It had to, I had no choice.

It was meant to be. I couldn't have become who I am without having exactly the right environment in which to mature. I made an incorrect correlation, divorce and subsequent hell = reality. I was young but old enough to lose all respect for men and the reality that men teach..

My father was "the knight" who saved me and now he was gone. The house was different, felt weird; no matter the reasons, remember I was only seven or eight... My dad was dead.

Sure, he'd come every other Sunday to take Sandy `n` I to do his laundry. Do the wash with him and his bimbo. Bimbo was mom's word for the home wrecker.

Her name in America is Felicia, I think it's the same as that anywhere else too. She was kind enough, but she sparked my curiosity by being so secretive. Dad was also, was this "Mission Impossible", or is all this just some more of that reality shit? I was confused.

I was getting older and I had my first paper route but that was too hard for the money so I gave it up. Piano looked good and dad enjoyed playing (Sandy's still too small) so we got one. But that too was too much work for a nine year old, so in a month I stopped trying. I just no longer saw any purpose in starting a life long practice if they could end in a moment's notice.

Being honest and "secret free" was no longer important to my parents and step-parents... so I gave them up also. If I am disposable, so are they! (Labor and parental honesty.

It seemed the only rules in life are the one's of lies and the telling thereof.)

There was a guy down the street who owned a camera. A nice camera and I wanted it, so I took it.

My first crime. See my eight year old logic? Marriages are forever? Ownership is forever? (No, not anymore! If everyone else endeavored in escapades contrary to their statements, then I should to... right?)

I got in trouble for that. I wanted attention and the only way to get any was to make trouble. See, if you did something good, then fine, because you are supposed to do good. I didn't get much positive reinforcement because both my parents were head strong and stubborn because of divorce. There was no emotion left for the kids.

My account was bankrupt. I was getting very little love.

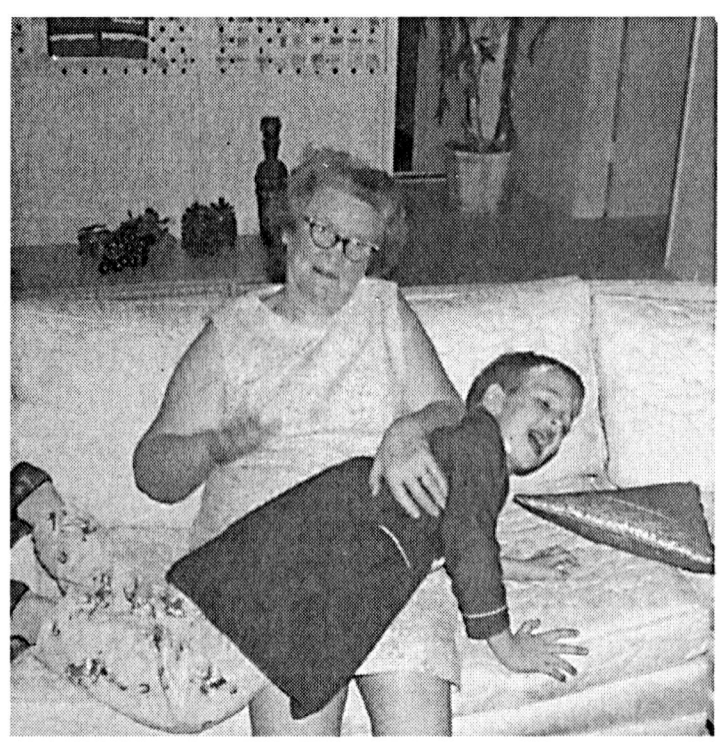

one-of-us

Most of that love came from grandma Clara, bless her. So in the end, I had very little love to give. Clara was always there, to visit or call on for love and entertainment. I have very dear memories of her and Paul.

Grampa Paul was quite a man, as grandma told me; Paul was a drinker, and Clara worried something terrible about him... so, one day he just up and quit. Twenty or thirty years (or longer?) of drinking were over.

Paul was a Mason. Even though at that time I had no idea what a Mason was, I idolized him and what he stood for. (I have his Masonic bible today, and there is much knowledge inside.)

When I started writing there were two memories which I could still see clearly from my childhood. The first was of me, grampa and grandma at Buena Park's "Japanese Deer

Village" as I recall. I don't remember anything about the place itself, only what happened there.

I was going into a petting zoo section for kids, so that I could touch and feed the baby animals. Before I went inside I was given a bag of peanuts from Grampa Paul to feed the animals; this happened when I was four or five, so I was very excited and nervous because of the tremendous size of the llamas.

Small deer and squirrels surrounded me. All the animals wanted my attention, so I gave them all an equal amount. Although, one older llama had a problem. He, or she, wanted all my attention. That damn animal put his nose in my face begging me for more food, which is love to a four legged creature. That llama put himself between me and every other animal, maybe he was hungry or jealous, either way I tried to ignore him. He had other ideas; when my back was turned he grabbed the bottom of the bag of peanuts and tore it off, spilling the contents of the bag on to the ground.

Feeding frenzy, and there was no more need for me. I'll bet the tears were welling before the last peanut hit the ground. By the time the other animals had pushed me out of the way, I was bawling. Everything was shattered, all was gone, my acceptance was through. I turned to leave with tears flowing freely, and there was my Grampa Paul waiting with his arms open for a reassuring hug.

Oh yes grampa with love to give and in his hand was another bag of peanuts, which told me that when my bank account (bag of peanuts) was empty, he was there to make a deposit. I loved my Grampa Paul, and still do.

He died when I was six. My second childhood memory is at his funeral. My mom and dad made me kiss him goodbye. Even though I was told he was gone to heaven, I had to kiss his shell bye-bye.

I don't mean to show disrespect to my grampa but I didn't want to kiss his dead body because I knew at that time I loved HIM, not his body; Paul was in heaven, not in his lifeless body.

I have done a lot of traveling with my dad on camping trips, business trips and to Chicago to see my father's side of the family when I was just a boy. I made some connections with my cousins, the girls mostly and aunts and uncles. Unfortunately when dad left mom, Sandy and me, didn't the rest of his family go with him? So, I missed out on half of the family.

Pretty juvenile you might say. Well... I was only seven when everything changed, and my heaven became my hell. Mom `n` Dad, up to the separation, were very untruthful to each other. Mom sent away for an illegal drug identification kit. What for? Are you saying dad's a junkie? "No, but he comes home kinda loopy and doesn't smell of alcohol."

Let's recap for a moment:
Seven year old genius with an education in drugs. Volatile if I do say!
The second:
While traveling with my dad on one trip we were driving somewhere from somewhere else and I was playing around with cards, food and other "in the car" stuff. Being curious as

dad drove, I looked inside things like the glove box or other storage places. I found pens, change and a cool wooden box. A box that looked like one of those trick boxes that take any person a little time to open it. So I did.

I saw joints. Many joints. I knew because I'd seen them in mom's I.D. kit for drugs.

I told Dad, "Look dad, Marijuana!"

Dad said, "Those must be the maid's, she probably left them in here when she cleaned the car." Now maybe dad thought he was dealing with a moron seven year old but I don't think so. What he told me was that drugs are okay, but you have to lie about them and hide them. It was very hard on me and it put more distance between us. He had asked me to look the other way for police and he pretended to throw them out the window but I saw he did not.

How could he outright lie? If he told the truth, things might be different, but he didn't - so they're not. I never smoked with my dad in America, we waited until we traveled into international waters. I was fourteen when Felicia, Dad, Sandy and I went to Spain for a cruise around the Mediterranean Ocean. On the planes we took, and through all the border patrol checkpoints dad carried his money and I carried the pot. Welcome to international crime, my son. (But, I'm getting ahead of myself.)

Mom `n` dad were not together any longer. So when I had turned ten or eleven (or somewhere in that age bracket) my adoptive parents sat me down and tried to explain the structure of divorce and its effect on me.

What they said hurt me. How they felt about being together and apart, how Al still loved Flo and vice versa and how they still loved me.

I wondered and asked them, "how can you say you love each other and sleep with other members of the opposite sex?" If that's love well then I'll serve up love as mom `n` dad taught "what love is". At a tender age I'd been pushed into a hole.

Love has/is a switch, to be turned "off" or "on" as we see fit. Love is lying, falsehood and deceit. (Oh what a tangled web!) There were no such things as value or morals, my parents were saying one thing, but doing another. (A reoccurring parental scheme.)

I started talking about drugs in a curiosity way, and dad said,"If I want to try it (smoking pot) then he could get some." Since I was being led astray by Dad and Felicia, and Mom and Jerry, I got interested in this secret game that was going on... the adult/child - deceive/drug game.

Jerry was the father replacement that my mom picked up along the way. He seemed nice enough. So I began investigating and I didn't have to wait very long. I looked in secret places and found many things. I was learning about my environment and my step-parents. As to who they were and what they were doing to my mom `n` dad.

Plastic toys, rubber toys and vibrators. But that's not all. I also found prescription drugs. Cocaine, heroin and pounds and pounds of pot. Thai sticks up the ass.

Mind you that I was told all my life that drugs are very, very, very bad and here are my parents doing them (gasp) but lying about it (double gasp). It was soon after that, I tried some. (No need to gasp.)

Before my thirteenth birthday, my good friend David spent the night. David was fourteen already so he was more learned than I as to the ways of the world. "Wanna smoke some pot, Joe?" That was my first time. I was doing grown-up stuff. I enjoyed it. Pot took all the load off my shoulders.

This happened on the night before my friends had plans to go to Magic Mountain with me for my B-day (which was still five days away). All my friends were older than me, but up to that point I didn't care. (Although, I soon would!) Magic Mountain was about one and a half hours away from where Mom, Sandy and I lived in the city of Orange, CA.

550 Wellington Rd. to be exact. Me and Dave had planned it all out along with the other guys. We would go inside the park until my Dad left with Walt, who was the husband of half-sister Linda. Then the guys `n` I would go into the parking lot to get high. We lit up behind a motor home and before we could get two hits we were rushed by private police. They busted us royally. They took us, after they caught us all, (no easy job!) to the office and took all our names, ages, and phone #'s. They tried to call everyone of our parents but no one was home. (What do you think they were doing?) Five kids, no parents, the private pigs' hands were tied.

J. Elliott Goldwyn

Firsts
* * *

So, me and my "gang o' criminals" were sent to jail.

They put us into a holding cell and one by one the cops took everyone out of our cell. (Our cell!) Pictures and fingerprints. When the police were done with them, (my friends), they were transferred to a main jail cell. That process happened to everyone but me. In a strange way, I equate how it was I felt with abandonment. In a perverted way... it was.

I was too young to go to jail. I was only 12 and it was painful for me to wait alone in a holding cell while my friends are together somewhere else. Solitary when I was twelve, two days short of thirteen. I would have given anything for two days.

After eating my jail meal, (I won't say food, that would be too kind), I heard a song on the radio playing outside my private hell... "Do you know where you're going to,

Do you like the things that life is showing you..."

No I don't (thank you very much)!

As one is reading this he or she might see a problem beginning... but I beg to differ. Just look at my growing environment. I didn't see much action or groundwork to raising a child whether it be happiness, healthfulness or honour. (And aren't those important?)

Parents who do drugs have kids who do drugs. (And go to jail!) By not being truthful, my parents told me that life is a game. Lie, cheat, steal, and do any drug you want. (Just don't get caught!) So, I did. (And I don't have a drug charge since... that I remember.)

one-of-us

Now, I don't want to be all condemning, because my parents taught me many valuable things, just like church. Most of those things varied but one aspect stayed the same. They were all social keys to interaction... but interaction inside my plastic bubble.

I feel if mom or dad would have explained to me that pot was one more thing for adults only, much like alcohol, maybe things would have been different. But no, my life was just beginning. My mom was still living in Orange in the old house, while my dad moved into Felicia's house in Anaheim, which I guess was more conducive for their relationship.

Up until then, dad was staying in motels and such but I now had a home to visit my dad in, Felicia's place. Which was nice, until I started hailing questions.

Sex was the first topic of my queries. Mom did not have answers (how do you explain the toys I found to a twelve year old? So I never asked.) or she didn't want to give any. By that time I turned thirteen, 1976 was going to be a year full of lessons. My questions about sex made Flo very nervous.

So, she sent me away. First summer camp, then to dad's new house in San Clemente. I moved into dad's condo before school started, and when it did I enrolled. San Clemente High was okay to begin with but pretty soon I started to see through the other student's (and a few teacher's) plastic California facades. The first semester was all A's or B's, the second semester... continuation. (Which is where you go in school when no one wants you anymore.)

I had everything I could want or thought I did, living in escape from the hell of reality. Living on the beach and me with a waterbed, so... the fun had just begun. I didn't do well in school socially... so I just no longer went.

Me and my friend Greg from San Clemente, traveled in to see my mom and the Orange County crowd. I found out on that trip inland that it does matter to people where you live. My friend Cindy, who lived around the corner from my mom, came over with her friend Cynthia to see me and meet my surfer friend Greg. It wasn't long before Cindy, she was 17, started teasing Greg so much and so hard that Cynthia `n` I decided to give them privacy. We left them, petting kind of hard, in my old bedroom in mom's house.

Cynthia `n` I were going to go out for a walk. We got to the front door and I said, "You know, we don't have to leave if you don't want to." (Mr. Smooth) Maybe those were the best words I had said in my thirteen years of life! Cynthia went back to my room while I went to the front room to tell mom and Jerry, "we would like to be left alone for awhile." Mom was not up for that but I'll always be grateful to Jerry for cooling her jets. (Thank you Jerry!)

I went back to my old bedroom and there she was, tall, dark long hair and two years older than me. Cynthia was 15.

(Happy happy joy joy)

A fantasy for any man, whether he be young or old. Quickly I pulled out the hide-a-bed, from underneath my other bed... hardly disturbed Cindy or Greg. All the while trying to remember everything I had ever read about "How to's" in Playboy. It didn't fail.

It was over pretty fast (Go figure!), and as all four of us were getting dressed Cynthia told me something which would shape me sexually for the rest of my life... "You were pretty good!" That may have been a lie, but I didn't care.

(Thank you, Cynthia!)

I wanted to be older. I wanted to escape. My logic at this time was: youth in reality, sucks! Nothing was/is as it seems. I was living my life in fantasy. I was young and loving it. Only the way I found out what was really going on with my parents, destroyed any hope for reality. My plastic bubble was smashed. So, I made my own world.

Joe's World. (Excellent)

Firsts #2
* * *

I remember being the outcast at San Clemente High School because I did not have any roots from which to draw upon to define my own individual personality. I could be many things, but not myself. The mall told me what I was and what I was to be. Before I could become what surrounded me I had to see it and live in it for awhile. (The social chameleon in me.)

Beach activities started soon. Beach harassment started soon after that. On one hand I admired their "belong to the clique" mentality. On the other hand the beach was one more place I did not belong. I wasn't having good luck with acceptance and started to doubt myself. I did not choose my friends. All us outcasts were just thrust together to band in brotherhood and survive. Food chain full tilt! I was forced to survive in a socially restrictive environment. I learned to surf, but... never was accepted.

I tried really hard but that didn't matter as much as something I just did not have. Maybe it's in the blood or something else I could imitate? Well... it is and it isn't.

I could do it well enough but it just wasn't me. I surfed California and most of Baja Mexico, but I was not a surfer. It's one thing to "do it" and another to "be it", (as with every other "hat" I've worn in life).

Funny, life's sometimes the biggest puzzle. Well, it was one more existence experience for me to enjoy, and I did, from the outside. I learned a good deal from the sidelines. How to, who to, what to, when to, and... why not?

The time was right. I was young. I was alright looking, had a little money, and there was no such thing as AIDS. Even though there was less stress, there was less (a lot less), sex for me. I didn't fit in to the mold they had for me with their beach mentality. I needed a girl from somewhere else.

Then I met Kathy in San Juan Capistrano. She's from Chicago! We dated for awhile, then something broke us up. (Slut!) Well, his mom did own a corvette. A lot of wonderful stuff happened that year living in the plastic bubble of a So. Cal. suburb. I hate this, but I love this. So much eye candy in fantasy land, USA. Everything happened so fast, one moment to the next... bang, bang, bang.

I need a person from somewhere else, again. Not Chicago again. Kathy came from there and she was rough. I wasn't sure if that's everyone from a big city (roughness), but I knew I didn't like it. I would love to meet someone from the Midwest. Where people are real. Although Kathy `n` I were not done yet. I would see her once again but that's for the future. Besides I was getting my first car soon and I had an idea of what it was going to be too.

Dad's mid-life crisis survival transportation vehicle was perfect. A sixteen year old boy with the machine to make his getaway. The boy, me, now drove a rocket, which was the first of many. A 1975 Pontiac, 454 Trans-am just for me.

Things had become far too complex for me to ever attempt rationalization. All the justification was there and the only thing for me to do was get out, and get out I did. Everywhere I went I went fast. That's why I died, but that too comes later.

There seemed like no time left, I had to do it all now before the clock ran out. (tic-tic-tic)

Teenage reflections
* * *

See, everything my parents taught me was really a lie. Religion and monogamy or being just `n` true was all a fallacy. All that and more was going on inside my head. Around that time mom had moved to Palm Springs. Dad shipped me off to mom's soon after I came home early on a day that dad asked me not to come home at all. I did though, because I fell into a muddy patch on the field while we, Greg `n` I, were playing in a game of football. I was not asked to leave because I came home early (I don't think dad found out) but I engineered an exit as soon as possible after all was said and done...

When I came home dripping wet, dad's car was there. I set up a ladder and climbed into my 2nd story bedroom window. I had changed my clothes and was ready to leave the same way I came in when I realized that I was home for another reason contrary to clean clothes.

I looked over the railing and down the stairs. I really couldn't believe what I saw.

There was dad dancing with another woman (not Felicia), and she was black. (Gasp!) Let me explain the reason that the woman being black was such a shock to me. It was because of how he (dad) treated my older sisters Linda and Janet. Those two were dating black men. I've known that fact for quite some time, but it was not mentioned because I did not see how it mattered... although it did to dad. Dad was very vocal about his dislike of said relationships and the bad mark that they gave to our good name.

Our good name? ha! Now which good name would he be speaking of? Would that be, The Pot's, or The Kettle's?

I think watching my dad with the woman who had "taboo" skin color made the scene perfect for me to doubly lower my respect level for my father. What if I had walked in on my dad cheating on my mom? I would have been totally shaken, I might have killed him.

And the hell he put Linda and Janet through for doing the same thing that he was. Life's just not fair, it seemed, unless you got lot's o' money.

Money, and the power that people give to it, seemed to me to be nothing more than the ultimate game, where winning is "THE ONLY" solution to the hell which this commercial society was imposing on me. Dollars and more dollars made all the problems go away. Only to make more problems, which I found out soon enough on another day.

The disrespect and mistrust I was feeling for my father drove me away (slowly but most definitely surely), and I returned to mom's house in Palm Desert.

Before I left, I had learned to take care of #1 (Me). To get anything I needed, which I couldn't get at home, I added one more defect to my personality. I sold my body. Sure, I was used and abused, all the horrors were there, but I went more places and did many more things than anyone I knew. Many men thought they could, or at least wanted to own me; even though they did for awhile, I received more than just rent ($).

Prostitution gave me power that dad's money and last name didn't. Respect, honor, love or what I thought love was, and hard drugs. It made me feel important. (Too bad huh?) I don't know about that.

I was a survivor and survive I did.

I want no one to misunderstand me, I just had rich boy friends (2) some call them sugar daddies, but let's face it... they were just regular johns.

Nothing more & nothing less than memories.

J. Elliott Goldwyn

Egypt!
* * *

Dad told me that we all were going to Europe. It turns out he won some bonus sales trip(?) to the Mediterranean Ocean on a cruise ship. We left California for New York soon after his notification as I recall. Spain was nice, beautiful in fact with so many gorgeous Spanish women in high heels and short skirts. Me with long curly blond hair, looking every bit the California surf punk. I had barely got off the plane when Andy Warhol's famous quote, or what I remember it to be, came true.

"Everyone's famous for 15 minutes." My fifteen minutes, in reflection, has been more like 15 years. (Of course fame is individually relative.) We boarded another plane to go from Madrid to Barcelona. It was there that we went aboard our ship, the S.S. Italis. Tremendously huge boat. I think at the time it was third biggest in the world still in the water. There were people from all over the world on that cruise, and the first night's captain's cocktail party to welcome us on board was a blast. Remember my international smuggling ability? Not only that, but I could drink and gamble now too... while the ship was in international waters anyway. I fell into infatuation with the Latin girls which has haunted me ever since. Which is also a reoccurring theme for me. (You'll see.)

While we were on the ship, we went to Greece, Italy, Turkey, Malta, Israel and Egypt. Of all the things we did and everything we saw, not always together, I only have one very strong memory. (Beyond all the women.)

The Great Pyramids. I can not say it long enough or hard enough; There is something in Egypt we're NOT seeing. (Pity!) I felt knowledge, I felt safe and I felt the most extreme spirituality.

one-of-us

Misery?
* * *

In the time we spent in Jerusalem, Israel, I felt some spiritual power there but it was all because of the people who thought that that's where it all began. All those religion's and religious people were right. It is where guilt giving, masses controlling, first originated in the form of organized religion. Spirituality does not control, religion does.

The way I thought was this, church was getting in between me and God, NOT bringing us closer together. The time I spent touching the Great Western Wall, or walking Stations of The Cross were like, to me, walking around any old city and touching any old building. I'm not trying to say anything derogatory, because many people choose to believe but... I'm not them.

Misery loves company, but the church's misery is not going to get mine. I don't need to deny myself anything to go to the white light (heaven?). I must be clear on one sixteen year old point for me, what I mean is this: I will do anything I want, (free country, right?) but hurt no one and show no disrespect to anyone else, including myself... Unless They Show It First.

Spain
* * *

While I was on the ship I fell in love many times with almost everything I came in contact with. People, places, and all the things which are not in America. The history is what really grabbed me. I had a real drawing to museums (I still do). With all the time I spent in the museum in Madrid (The Prado), I did fall in love with one man's brilliant works, Mr. Claude Monet's. My father had to drag me away from his exhibit but that's okay, I take him with me everywhere I go.

When we had returned to Barcelona, I hung out with this guy who I met on the ship. He was another American who's father had moved the whole family overseas to Spain because of his job. I don't remember where exactly we went to, but that's alright because we only spent one night on the streets seeing sights. Not like a tourist, through the eye's of an American / Spanish local. I was able to afford it with the money my dad had won. He won the big ship's bingo, and I was given a percentage. My new found friend and I went to a street where all the action was.

Before I left that street that night, I had purchased an ounce of premium hashish. If I could smuggle for father I could do it for myself too. I must have known that I was going to make that purchase, because while I was in Turkey I also picked up a "Marrakech" pipe. I now put it to very good use.

The family and I only stayed one night after the cruise abroad. It seemed as though dad needed to get back to work in the states. To make more "love" which means money to him? (Now why was I asking that question? This _is_ America.) I could not blame my father.

J. Elliott Goldwyn

When I had returned to the states, I found everything to be different. In some way I had grown or something had touched me, and I couldn't tell you what did. Although I do know where it happened:. Egypt. More specifically, I had been given an understanding it seemed while walking around inside and outside the Great Pyramids. I don't know if it was the shape of them, or the location or materials used. Or rather everything we do know, and yet don't. The Gods and Goddess which inspired them may not want us to know, only because we as humans are not yet ready to know. (Remember... This is only a theory.)

College
* * *

I got out of school early because I took the high school proficiency examination. It was such a simple exam that I learned all the material I needed in elementary school. Back in the days when I paid close attention. I had a hard time remembering those days, only because those times were false or unreal. I wanted to forget the days and years in which I was misled. Force fed a fallacy. I was living a lie and I now wanted to live in reality.

Reality, the place with crime, prostitutes and heroin. Well maybe not that reality, but something close; like, jaywalking, one night stands and mushrooms. (Yeah!) Once again I had the world at my feet but every teenager I knew thought just that. There was so much to do, to try, to turn my back on... and forget.

I enrolled in community college because of all the pretty girls that went there. There were classes to keep me entertained with while the weeks passed. Winter vacation was just around the corner and there was this skiing vacation in Utah (where I really learned how). I went with Valerie. We shared the tour bus ride, the slopes, the drinks and a bedroom. She was a very proper li'l girl and I had to use the proper approach. All week long I only rarely placed my lips on hers. We were friends not lovers, (at least not yet).

I was driving a '75 Volkswagen Rabbit then. I had through various mechanical transplants built it into a monster which only the son of a rich man could afford. Because I had homes all over Southern California and friends - fans - and fucks all over the place in between them, I also got to drive a car which would take me from A to Z and anywhere/everywhere in between. But still, I wanted more.

I wanted to be recognized as the god I was. (Or thought I was, like most people my age.) I wanted to hear applause and my voice with accompanying punk music. I had something I needed to say and say it now. So I started going where those dreams come true. I became more involved in what it was "punk" music was saying and saying loud and clear to me. Greed for attention was taking over.

At the same time, there were all these pieces of expensive "cheese" just aching to be taken. (Remember them?) And I must admit, I chased after every one of them. I wanted "the car", I wanted "the girl", "the job", "the money", blah blah blah. I got that `n` more, and things were good. Sort of.

I was out every night, spending more money than an eighteen year old should and loving every minute. My schedule was full. I was either taking pictures for a college class, going to see a show, or falling in love. (Go figure!) There were many things to do, and I wanted all of them. I did go to a lot of parties, I had to, there were so many people to impress.

I lived for challenge. I was always taking on more responsibility than my scrawny shoulders simply should sustain. Not because of a need for power or money, but because "they" (the challenges) were there, and therefore... to be conquered.

CDI
* * *

When I was attending my first of many trade schools, Control Data Institute in Anaheim, California to learn the trade of computer repair, I was fresh out of my sophomore year at high school. Ready, willing and able, almost eager to start my life as an adult. I didn't know what lay ahead of me, and/or underneath me. Still... ready to take on the world.

I moved out of my father's condo and into Clara's apt. She, if you recall, is my mom's mom. I guess I was about sixteen years young/old and sixteen years stupid. God, I had fun.

I met a lot of people and proceeded to perform everything which Mom `n` Dad taught me to. All the stuff they never said. (Although, It worked and worked well!)

Everything went along just fine until my first test in computer repair class. We got to see a sample of the test, and I knew nothing about anything on it. I panicked, I went to study hall (did a lot of praying), and it paid off...

She was beautiful and she had a brain. Her name was/is Lisa and the "she-devil" knew everything I didn't.

As I remember it, Lisa sold me the information I'd need to pass the test. Made me smoke my last joint with her for that Knowledge. She told me the name of the guy who could give me every answer to every question, to every test - ever! It was when we got up the next morning that I saw how thin the line was between bitch and goddess.

Lisa and I spent many a night in conference. She had a bigger set of experiences than I. She was older (seven years older), but that wasn't what "hooked" me. Lisa listened to me and was always quick to draw out her opinion, which would leave me licking my wounds. She demanded respect but before she did I'd already placed it at her feet.

Lisa was the first woman I respected. Therefore, the first to share love with. I wasn't ready for love and she knew it. (She's always been smarter.) We did spend days `n` nights together talking, eating and loving until the world decided it was time for us to go our separate ways.

The school itself was another thing all together. It was like having to crawl through the sewer. I didn't feel much guilt from always cheating and I did graduate with a 93% test taking ability. Which didn't mean shit in the real world.

(But the ability to cheat did!)

Not long after C.D.I., I found out that the school taught me how to repair an outdated computer. It was like going to class to learn how to administer medical attention to dinosaurs. The school was teaching me things that were obsolete, on computers that were made in the dark ages for the most part anyways... (main-frames) Apple or PC repair would have been a better choice.

The only good thing that the school introduced me to was/is my friend (to this day)... Lisa. ("Hi girl.") Although, we have not spoken in quite a while. Where are you anyway?

Prom time
* * *

I was climbing the ladder and I was having a good time doing it. Southern California Fast Paced Life! I cannot begin to explain without completely incriminating others. Who could be where I am today, and who am I to take such a learning experience from them? No one! Besides... I'm no rat. Although, there's a time or two when no change will be made to protect the guilty (after all, I **did** already give you my full name).

I needed a new car to keep up with the image, so I got an `82 Rabbit Convertible. Almost at the same time I had met this real tight body (first impression) with the name of Eileen. Eileen, I think that's what she said.

She walked up to me at the bisexual club (I cannot remember the name of the trendy L.A. dance hole) at the border of Hollywood and Beverly Hills... on the corner of Santa Monica and Beverly, I believe. Eileen impressed me and asked if I'd like to dance.

Yes... and we did for a couple songs. I must have passed the "dance test" because when I asked if we could go outside for a cigarette or fresh air, I really don't remember which, she answered with... Yes.

(Let the games begin!)

I didn't expect anything but what I was told almost blew me clean off. Eileen didn't bring the Benz, or was it the Ferrari, because it's in the shop. (Right!) And she's a very busy girl at B.H. High School, (sure!) now that her dad is mayor of Beverly Hills. (Right!) What I'm thinking is: "Bar

one-of-us

talk". We've all heard of people like this but she did have long legs and a cute ass, so I took her phone number.

I'm sure she loved my car. Somewhere in the night we visited it, or maybe not, my money (same night, spent some) and my name. Somewhere in that ill fated night, I had mentioned it.

Eileen and I talked on the phone a couple of times. She lived miles away so that made her more attractive. She lived in the L.A. area. The land of dreams. The home of hard drugs! (But that comes later.) We made plans.

I was working on the side for my father's insurance corporation. After all my college classes, I had been promoted. I was no longer a delivery boy but now a full fledged bookkeeper with a gasoline credit card to prove it. That's not the whole of the equation of Joe. No, not hardly. Everything was falling into place. As long as I didn't get in the way.

When Eileen and myself first went out, I was to meet her at her house in Beverly Hills (Right!). I had high hopes of meeting the "king" of Beverly Hills and maybe kissing his daughter but then again I really did think her whole story was nothing but "Hollywood talk". If someone took the time, I'm sure they would, could and should (?) meet all the nearly famous people in and around Hollywood. I know... I lived there. But that will happen many women and years later. Did I say Calif. would be my oyster yet?

So I was riding north on Highway 101 through Hollywood and I exited onto Santa Monica Blvd. Eileen said her street was off S.M. Blvd. I drove slowly so as not to miss her alley

J. Elliott Goldwyn

way, or did she really live on a street? I didn't know. Really I didn't. I just kept driving right through Hollywood.

Elm, the street was nowhere in sight, and here I am going into Beverly Hills. (GASP!) Elm was right where it should be, across the street from the city hall in B. Hills. (Double GASP!) But even that did not prepare me for what was to come. As I pulled up in front of the address she had given me I could see she had fibbed about nothing.

The cars were all there in the long curvy driveway, obviously for show. Or so that the news people (network news ABC, NBC, and CBS) could film them along with her dad giving some political speech. As I walked up the drive, the gentleman who was being interviewed put out his hand to me to shake and he said, "You must be Joe", (yes) "Eileen's waiting inside for you."

Eileen 'n' I went someplace, where really matters little, to perform more of the human mating courtship dance routine. I must have done something right, because the flirting got fairly serious. Me, the naive Orange County boy. I was a little impressed, not by people but rather by their things. Didn't last long, things got boring... but she was threatening me with a visit to their beach house. Which was a hide-a-way apartment in vast ocean metropolis of Santa Monica. (Oh, I'm scared!)

Nice place, all a bachelor could want. An oven, a fridge, ceiling, walls and the biggest bed a man could believe. She took me there but the "taking me there" was not a gift she was giving me. It was another test to see if I was worthy. It was like she was setting up a hoop for me to jump through. She, on the other hand, was like the animal trainer just going through the motions.

one-of-us

Eileen kept me happy, well fed, well entertained and very satisfied. Even though I had many hoops to jump through, I found it so easy that I really only did it for the spiffs and not the acceptance which never was fully given by her. I always had some aspect of my personality I needed to prove over `n` over again or adjust in some way. (That got old.)

Sex was not a gift until one night about two months later. Eileen's parents and younger brothers had gone to sleep early as did the household maid... or did we come home late? When Eileen `n` I came home from the party, we were all alone in her parent's home for all intent purposes. She `n` I nearly took the fabric off the furniture and pulled up the rugs. God, what a night.

About two days later Eileen asked me in her cute little matter of fact way to her high school prom. She also told me about her acceptance into Arizona State U. Since Eileen would be gone in a couple months, and I did like her a lot...

"Sure, I'd love to go." I was a very happy boy. Eileen and I were getting along famously. Everything looked great for now, for the future and for me.

It was the eldest of Eileen's brothers on the phone (I do not remember the boy, that is now a man's, name). He had bad news, and he told it to me straight. Straight from Eileen's Dairy...

She was not patient. She couldn't wait until she was going to leave before she said goodbye in a sexual way, to her male best friend. See, It was like we had an unsigned agreement to not sacrifice our monogamy, which I thought we had, before the prom.

I understood that she would soon be "setting sail" for other schools in other lands, and 0I had grown comfortable with that reality and that any sexual stuff with others would wait till after the prom. But now the boy, Eileen's brother, had something to say. Something so important that he called me.

Telling me all, and that made me aware of two things:

1) Patience is gifted to the poor, because the rich have instantaneous gratification.
2) Eileen had shown me ultimate disrespect, or about as ultimate as a teenager can get.

I was not sure that what her little brother said was true or not, so I asked Eileen to meet me half way between her house and mine. We met at this park in Orange, CA. We talked about "it"; about how "it" was a spontaneous thing. How "it" was gonna happen anyway. How "it" shouldn't hurt.

I answered with, "I'm sorry, I'm hurt. I really no longer want to go to your stupid prom!"

"You stupid, stupid man", is what my head kept saying all the way home. "It's the biggest, best prom anywhere! It is The Prom that the T.V. says you gotta go to if you're cool!!!!!!!!!!!" (I called her as soon as I got home.)

"I'm cool", or so I said to Eileen. "I'm sorry, but I was hurt, although I still would love to go to the prom with you." I didn't want to let an all expenses paid trip to the Beverly High prom slip through my fingers. Even though we were going to the dance together, we didn't spend much time

one-of-us

together until the prom. Thinking back on it, I'm not sure we even saw one another before the dance.

All of the intricacies were worked out by her. Eileen chose our limousine, our prom flowers, our 'party favors' we would be enjoying all night and to top it all off she paid. She had decided to share our limo with her best friend Kathy, and Kathy's date. The table we would be sitting at was also chosen by Eileen. And yes, it was the same table as her male best friend. (Are you able to see my position yet?)

I was confused, because I did not have all the answers I needed. I had no one who could understand with which to talk to, so I just let the whole "prom thing" happen. I just showed up, shut up and got in line. The prom was as boring as other dances, although there were many things to look at.

I was feeling no pain when we left the prom, with Kathy and her guy, to go to the first "after prom party." The party was fun. The girls had changed their clothes and I was enjoying all the beautiful night had to offer. We had barely settled in there, when we, the four of us were whisked off to another party. Somewhere in that time Eileen said something to me which made me feel like a man, a good man.

"You know, Joe, I *am* having fun with you tonight". I felt like once again everything was falling into it's very own slot.

I felt that way again after Kathy said to me somewhere in the shadows of the limo, "You know, Joe, I'm sorry about what happened."

"So am I", was my reply. (We were talking about Eileen and her affair I figured.)

"I would like to do something to make you feel better", she cooed. (Did anyone else hear "the wheel of karma" spin?) Kathy was the most beautiful, powerful woman I've ever dated. Her dad owned a bank, or something very "Beverly Hills Savings and Loan" like that.

(Did I say many pearls?)

"We" started our dating right there, right then. We left the after-after prom party in the limo and Eileen holding

one-of-us

the bag. (Thanks Eileen!) Let's not forget Kathy's date, even though we did... no wonder I don't remember his name. He was another pawn to help my new Queen Kathy move into position. His job was to bring the woman I was going to leave the prom with. (Thanks partner!)

While I write this, I can't help analyzing who I was, where I was, what was to come and... what I was to become. We still have quite a long row to hoe!
(So, buck up soldier!)

Lie, cheat and steal. The three rules to life I was taught. Not through books or school teachers, but rather, by people's actions. (I pay attention!) It was simple for me. A young adult. Just beat the world before the world beats you. By eighteen, I knew that the amount of money, sex, and/or drugs you had and did was not dependant upon the social class in which you live. Unfortunately, the downward spiral staircase I was on was still pretty close to the top but it was going to take me to the valley (San Fernando valley) to meet the girl of my dreams. (Wet ones.)

Angie, was the girl I'd always dreamed of, almost. She was beautiful, she was sixteen and seemed ripe for the plucking. I met her at a party. This red head I'd met in San Clemente was throwing it in the valley city of El Monte in southern California. The valley was usually "Verboten" to an "upper crust man" like me. (tee-hee-hee) But since I met the red head at the beach it was okay... and ever since that redhead earth shaking blow job, it was **really** okay! I had nothing to lose, right? There was food, beer and naked women below the water line in the Jacuzzi. A typical So.

J. Elliott Goldwyn

Cal. party? Yes. What more could I (or any self respecting lesbian) ever want? More teenage girls? I think not.
   More time maybe.

Smokin' cuban
* * *

There she was, giddy as she could be in her skimpy little bikini. Bouncing this way, then that way. Definitely using her body to get my attention... she did. I was still seeing Kathy, but Angie was giving me all Kathy could, with none of the bureaucratic red tape bullshit. (Bye, Kathy.)

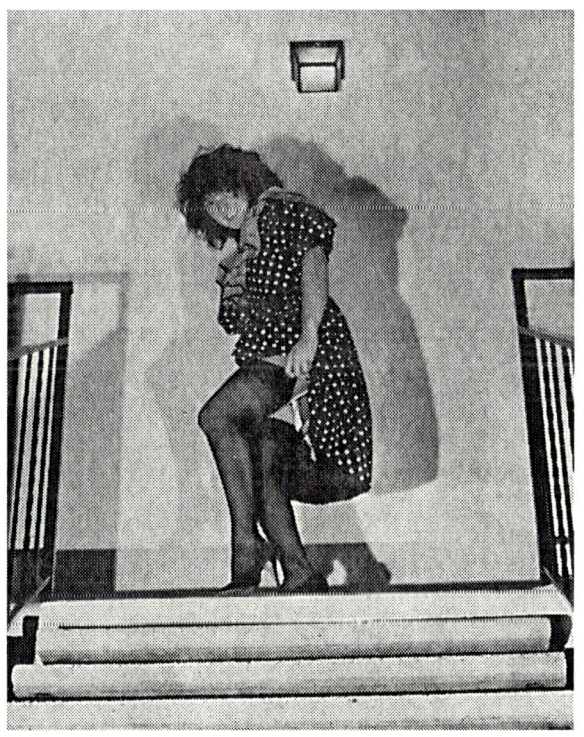

I took Angela back to my dad's condo in San Clemente. She was impressed with my car, my dad's beach house, and my beach-ability. I was still surfing, and Angie wanted to be included in the surf trip I was planning on the coast of Baja CA., Mexico. So, we went. It was nice to travel in Mexico with someone who could speak fluent Spanish (Angie's Cuban). We were able to go to places and do things most tourists don't ever do in the southern north American country of Mexico; like... get out of jail.

Like a kid in a candy store was how I felt in Mexico. Surfing, music, beer, sex, guns and drugs. (Not a good combination in a foreign country.) The Federales* took me away. I don't remember the crime or the small town I was arrested in, but I do remember the cell. Inch deep water (?) on the floor. Bugs `n` rats crawling on the walls, and the jail cell I was in was used in the off season (Off season?) as a butcher block room. You could smell the death in that place. (I kid you not.)

I could hear Angie down the hall screaming at someone in Spanish. And I thought that this is how Mexico got it's money. Holding hostages and receiving ransoms.

Simple equation / simply hell. Within an hour, I was outside, ("Born free...") because of what Angie said. That woman could do amazing things with her mouth.

I know I talk a lot on sex, because it's fun and I was taught nothing less of the social connection between men = money and women = sex. See... it works like this: man who equals monies gives/spends some on a woman, who then give him sex (or maybe not). I've been taught just that all my life, it's not who you are, but rather what you do, what you drive and where you live... that's what makes the man. And I usually did not go out with the 'maybe not' girls more than twice.

I know today that that game plan was incorrect for me. But then no one, not even the women tried to show me different at that point in my life. But that's alright, because I know more today through my life's experiences and my one death experience. Oops, I'm rushing again, that comes later.

I have more to discuss before I find my "first love".

*Mexican police.

It's that way with love, you never know what will effect you and what is only another ship passing in the night... Until, you speak and subsequently discover and explore an underlying attraction if any exists

J. Elliott Goldwyn

QU.1 (quiz unit one)
* * *

I bought my first motorcycle (legally) around that time. I also moved into my first apartment in Garden Grove, CA. The apt. was in one of my father's buildings. I believe I took Kathy to my new place once. Nothing spectacular happened because she was nothing but an "impress me" sort of girl. It's not my job to impress anyone. Besides, there was nothing spectacular about her, Kathy had served her purpose. Eileen lied to me about the "best friend", so her other "best friend" and I made a new lie. Other than that, Kathy was a subject of irrelevance to me. Just like, I'm sure... I was to her.

Angie `n` I traveled to L.A. to visit the club scene and enjoyed it all. My good pal Mike, who I met in Palm Desert, (we kept in contact, he will play a major role in the future... just like now), wanted to take me to photograph this band at a club in the Valley. I almost didn't go. I thought I'd gotten everything I wanted from the Valley. (I was wrong.)

Tom Neale played lead guitar while Patch played the electric bass, but I hadn't met the drummer or vocalist yet. The drummer (who's name I'll never remember), was supposed to bring the singer, but he didn't. A band without a singer is like a race car without a driver. It may look good and sound great but it's going nowhere fast. (In my humble opinion.)

Tom handed me a play list, and the microphone and asked, "Can you sing?" (Yes) So I did. I didn't know any of the words or any of the songs, so I just made stuff up. People were just looking at me funny, until Mike (god bless him) jumped out on to the floor and started to move to our beat. ("Our beat!") That's all it took because the rest of the crowd joined in. People clapped and people cheered.

one-of-us

Some people wanted more and no one knew I wasn't the usual singer. I didn't care, I was a star. Or thought I was. Stardom is individually relative, so I guess I was. Did I say fifteen years of fame? I was wrong.

Well that's punk for ya! I had injustices to speak on and the crowd joined in. I shared the mike with Mike. He sang a couple and I sang a couple. We both were hooked. We both were offered the job, we both tried out, we both worked hard for it, but I won. Pity, because that was the first thing that came between him `n` I. We had two very different paths to follow, and mike became Michael much earlier than joe became an Elliott. (A whole lifetime earlier)

It seemed mike got Andrea "pregger's". He had to grow up, so he did, or tried for awhile. Andrea was his girl, also for awhile. But the baby was his child forever.

I was the best man at his second wedding, and yes, I had an affair with the maid of honour, (story book stuff) but that's a terrific tale for another chapter yet to come.

Alright, let's come back to the story at hand, and recap a little:

Eighteen year old male in California (So. Cal. blond and blue and surfer too) with a bookkeeping job for a corporation, my father's. I also had a job in the mall selling cameras and other photo equipment. And I was the visual and vocal aspect of an almost hard core punk band. There was only one thing left to do.

Move to Hollywood. But where and with whom did I want to live? In the end I choose Angie. I didn't like being alone. Being alone made me look at myself and reflect straight to hell.

I have a habit of being my own worst enemy, by being two different people and always hating the other personality.

Corporate Jr. executive by day \ Anarchistic punk at night.

(Volatile combination: social outcast **and** access to money.)

I know all my own weak spots, or "buttons" (if you will). I've always tried to sabotage myself and so far I've done pretty good. Although, I've also been the one to put myself into positions, good ones, from which I was able to move my life from comfortable surroundings, to sleeping in my dirty clothes underneath a freeway bridge while it was raining.

It all started on my ride home from a rehearsal at some studio downtown by the river/sewer in L.A. I thought we had a great sound check for the show tomorrow, and I did have a little money. So, I stopped for a beer at some corner mart at 2nd ave and Los Angeles blvd.

There was this guy standing down the street on the other side who was trying as hard as he could to blend in, and then disappear. But, reappear to talk with every tenth car or so, for about a moment. (Hmmm....) I looked at my European model Honda Interceptor and thought on my options. I did not have to think for very long.

What went through my head was, I'm singing feverishly at night about what it was I was doing during the day and how it was against all forms of humanity and growth therein. I needed escape, big time. I didn't really "know" the L.A. street drug scene, but I was certainly curious in a "stupid" sort of way.

I got on my motorcycle, started it and thought about my curiosity in connection with respect for him and his obvious

one-of-us

business. Seeing as there is very little that scares me, I went right up to him, a small mexican guy and asked, "What's up?"

"Cheva", he said while looking at me. "Heroin, my friend." "Brown tar, do too much and you'll O.D.!" He sang that to the theme from The Beverly Hillbillies. (Everyone in L.A. is a star!) He knew I didn't know Spanish fluently. Probably from my look when he said, "Cheva". Either way... we made our deal.

Just because I'd never "main-lined" before (and this was all far too easy) it was one more thing I needed to try. It's like climbing a mountain, "just because it's there". I got started packing for the trip up the face of the crested peak (speaking in analogy), and someone sells me a twenty dollar rocket ship trip to the stars.

How could I refuse? Fuck the mountain, just call me "Rocket Boy"! My only question was: "With who, where and when do I (or we?) blast off?" That was a simple answer, whoever was the closest and right now. Jeanette, was a friend I'd made back in the Saddleback College days. She was from Texas but moved out to CA. for school. We got along great in the photo class we were in, even worked together a couple of times. Jeanette and myself knew a few things about each other. And, I knew she would at least be interested in a curiosity sort of way. (Much like me.) Whichever way she might feel about hard drugs and the use thereof, I knew she wouldn't throw me out. And she did live the closest!

"Yes, I did buy enough so we can share." When I said that, you could feel the adrenalin in the room rise like before a simultaneous orgasm. It was like the room had it's own theme song, "We're gonna get high, we're gonna get very, very high!"

Those were not the words I wanted my fiancé, (Angie) to hear. I had to keep up a false front to her, I shouldn't let her know about IV drug use. (In the deceive/drug game it's a need to know basis for the sharing of information, and our games were just beginning.)

The only thing I can compare heroin to, is sexual orgasm. The only difference is that heroin lasts for six hours straight, and makes you feel like doing "it" again and again... just like sex. That is the reason, I feel, many people give up their lives, their mate's life and their children's also. That's heroin for you. All consuming, engrossing and destroying. It's devastating in the long run, it always is, but I've just started and to me it's heaven. (Or, at least the best I've ever felt.) Yes, even better than sex. (Which *is* the reason to stop.)

Although, life as I know it now has just begun to evolve... (Dissolve?) I did make up my mind to move into a house owned by the manager of Van Halen. (Remember them?) Angie thought that would be nice. How could she not? Beautiful place, great yard and it's own swimming pool for us to play in. Before we moved in we had our share of up's `n` down's with credit cards, fantasies and their realization. I've always been able to get what I want, and if I don't "get it" then I didn't want it bad enough.

Not always did I work hard for the things which accessorized my life, many of the most beautiful (wine, women and song) came up to me, and poured themselves down my throat or out my mouth or down my pants. In no way did I lead anything or anyone on, because of who I am and what I say about who I am. It was plain and obvious to me that I made no promises, so I'd break none. (I was young.) But this young warrior had just begun his study.

12:00ish is when I'd say I'd be there, if... I was supposed to be there by noon. Ten minutes pro or con, either way the world will continue to spin. There is too much stress in the world (on your wrist) and I combated it with drugs, women, drugs, money and more women. Angie didn't like that very much*, on or about the fifteenth or sixteenth time I was caught in bed with someone else (young/eager thing) (young/stupid me), she put the law down in black and white. There were too many female fans of the band, and I had little in the way of self restraint...

Diamond ring, she wanted marriage, to me? Wow, what I thought about was just what drew me to her in the first place: She was cute, had very shapely legs and a beautiful ass but now she wanted a ring. (We had typical 19/17 year old relations.) Okay, I'll do it.

I had left the camera sales position behind because it didn't give me enough money, and it was not close to where I lived. So I started my own business with my name.

---

* Although, it was her who brought 'girlie magizines' to bed, so not to have to wear shoes or stockings. I thought: well, if you don't want me to bother you with my desires... it's okay because there are a line of women who would willing wear whatever I want. That confuses me, when someone (male or female) works hard to win the 'prize' but not to keep it... and then complains after the prize is gone to some other winner!

City of the stars
* * *

Angie had been working for an apartment owner/manager (slum lord) down the street from the apartment we eventually moved into in Hollywood and I used that to open an apartment repair/maintenance co. called, Goldwyn Maintenance. Even though every building I was sent to make repairs was close to total condemnation, I enjoyed it because of the constant challenge and all the friends I made... and a lover I'll not soon forget.

I remember one job (in particular) where there was water leak damage to the ceiling in the kitchen and when I started to pull down the rotten wall-board an avalanche of cockroaches came down on my head. They went down my shirt, shorts, and socks. I just stood there, bewildered, while wondering "why me?" (Did I say, "Mr. smooth" yet?)

That's when I realized what employees are for, the shit work. It was also the first time I'd ever utilized the great "boss power" I had since the day I had hired my first employee. I had almost forgotten how good it feels to be in control.

Even though I'm the kind of boss who would not ask anyone to do something I'm not willing to do myself, I HATE bugs. Not spiders though. In my early years I had an honor / respect for spiders, especially black widows. After my second bite the honour / respect thing was kept at a safe distance.

Most people learn their lessons the first time around. (Like hell!) But I needed to learn said lesson perfectly, so I went through the pain twice. (Ofttimes more.) I feel that one should give to others what they give to you (on an individual basis, not on eye color or something stupid like that.) Either that, or I cannot give a person less than a second chance. "A person only gets the treatment he or she gives to others." Now there are too many exceptions to that rule. People who are there only to make life difficult for others. They have no goals, no dreams and nothing behind their eyes. They are hollow people (H.P.'s). We have all met H.P.'s and we all deal with them in many ways throughout all our days. Some even have more money than anyone should. Sure wish they'd wear name tags though.

Although, none will admit it because that would be like declaring you're a communist during the McCarthy Era. It's an Us/Them world, Police/Citizens, Men/Women, Have's/Have not's and what I believe is of the most importance... real/hollow people.

In my set of experiences, of which I've already had a few (the best is yet to come), I've worn very many hats which have their very own set of values, morals, successes and failures in conjunction with their own set of spiritual higher powers, or lack there-of. A person could be from any nationality, of any sexual description or design, and be real. And I see that there does not need to be the restrictions or ramifications that our Us/Them society inflicts upon us. (Or, maybe there does?) (I'm not sure.)

Only prayers
* * *

Higher powers - God - Goddess - Allah - Jehovah or merely a light bulb, is a very powerful (life, and personal will erasing?) subject for discussion. Religion is supposed to be the bringing together of a faction of the masses to train them to follow after something which is in each and every heart. Inside each and every human body, sometimes. (I ask, why would anyone need to be trained to be like they were when they were "childlike"? Remember your childhood, before you were shown to hate or despise another race or class or followers of another form of spiritual belief? Although sometimes there isn't anything inside that body human, that's why we'll never forget about hollow people. H.P.'s have their own set of spiritual values which I've enjoyed but refuse to follow.

To some organized religion is the true way to follow God and for them I have only prayers. Others worship hard drugs while a few more follow the very selfish road in search of the hollow money god, (therein... may be no hope). While still more give away their own beliefs to someone who will "choose" their higher power for them. They preach to me, "Follow God's rules!" That sometimes feel right, but sometimes they don't.

(Not wrong, they just don't "feel right".)

Of course this line of thought is an application of So. CA. survival was in the mind of a twenty-one year old (drinking age), (oh no), white (not a supremacist theory, just the facts), male, not bad looking, blond `n` blue too, and I did have an idea of the theory that there is a power granted "only to women".

one-of-us

All women are born with the possibility of fertility but only some (most?) of those women are blessed (cursed?) with parenthood.

Which opens a "new can" all together. You see we have all heard of the horrors concerning possible parenthood, and there's more in that can than most of us can imagine. (Do you like Stephen King?) My adopted mom could not bear children.

There were pregnancies along the way in my life, but I was never included in any of the decision making that followed the "bed bounce". I do not feel that is fair to one half of the lie down equation.

Although, I see the unequal division of immediate parental responsibility but I ultimately feel it's a partnership decision. Not to be made without the others consent, and all concerned should have a complete understanding of everything that's involved. There should be no hidden agendas in parenthood.

(But, that also comes later.)

Mark.
* * *

I was installing a water heater into a cleared out firetrap of an apartment when I noticed Siouxsie Sue singing a song I've heard before. The same, yet different. On my lunch break I did my interpretation of a curious kitten.

Quiet and cunning, but with a level of curiosity which far "out-weighed" any inherent four legged feline killing machine ability. I believe, the day a kitten becomes a cat is on the day of it's first purposeful kill. And I, in no way, wanted anything to die.

The music was coming from the corner apt. downstairs. The door was wide open. It was a tape of "Siouxsie and the Banshees" on video. A concert that was obviously an imported large screen video view. Hard to miss. Quick look, a once over. I made a first impression call. The renter of the apartment was a man and he was gay. It was a nice place, functional, tidy, crisp and inviting.

My eyes returned to the television and then a man came from the shadows. He had been watching me. I felt foolish, like I had just been caught trying on my mom's underwear. I lowered my head as I apologized, "I've never seen this video before, and..."

"It's a limited edition... She gave it to me the last time", he whispered.

"Sorry I was peeping, but I wanted to see." Something like that is what I said. "Sure", he said, "I was hoping to gain your interest."

I was interested. I accepted his offer for some coke, or was it ecstasy? We had similar interests. We talked for awhile, and I spent the night. His name was Mark as I

one-of-us

recall. It seems as though our short relations in time were impressed by a future mishap.

He was a dream to me, he liked me for me. (No holds barred.) Mark was always very secretive, I believe his job or profession demanded he was. I asked no questions.

I didn't care, I was happy. I am not homo, hetero, or bi. What I am is sexual. I admit, I had the best of both worlds. Mark in one home, while Angie was in the other.

I knew, or thought I did then... Mark was on the surface, a make up artist. That may have been a cover for his real job. I'm not sure. I like to romance the small memory I do have. I had seen Mark until the very end. (I think I loved him)

It's hard to say. The amnesia of my life is strongest right before the accident. That's unfortunate. Because I'd love to tell you about our outings, Mark's 'n' mine, to various clubs on Sunset or Melrose in the detail which they deserve. But, my memory is still very much in a fog.

We did have a running theme though.

We used to go out, just not together. I was twenty one and my body still had not assumed any male bulk of brawn. In jeans and a tee-shirt I was a boy. In a short skirt, stockings and heels, I was something else. When I wore a wig and nails with one of my many bimbo outfits, I did look pretty good. And after Mark applied a professional make over to my face, I was a lady, and a very good looking one at that! (Or... very expensive!)

I would take a cab to some straight club, already agreed upon by us both. Walk in and every single man (some married) in the place wanted to know from where I came.

After I charmed drinks off all the boys, at least the ones who had the courage to approach me... in walked Mark.

To save me. The cheerleader, the secretary, the stewardess or the damsel... who was in no distress whatsoever.

We definitely had fun together. I enjoyed not only his car, I enjoyed his money, drugs and body. I enjoyed him, and what Mark was/is... Trouble!

(Good ole American trouble!)

As I've said, Mark liked me. Not my name or my motorcycle or anything else, just me. I needed that and so did he. I loved him for everything, especially everything. He was such a good driver, not crazy, only proficient. When Angie told me of his car crash, I could not recall him or even ever living in Hollywood. If me being comatose had anything to do with it, I'm sorry. I miss him. But again I rush.

Mark was more than gay, he was real. I was much more than being gay with him, I was being loved. I felt special. I already knew that I was found attractive by some members of this society regardless of gender. But I felt comfortable enough around him that I wanted to look good for him, not just to him.

I hope you are able to understand this point: "I'm not gay," I just liked Mark. You see, my desire to be appreciated and to go where that occurs is not gender specific. I just love... period. It's like a law, love is. Now that I'm seeing things a little more clearly,

I know Mark would never drive his car into a brick wall at 100mph+ like Angie said. (Unless... he wanted to.)

Spirit
* * *

I make all my decisions. No... that's not quite true, there are a lot of decisions which are best left to others, or so the world keeps saying. So I learned to follow my heart, which I might add is not always an easy thing for me to do. Our brain was trained for survival not love. That's emotion. An entirely different function all-together. Our brain is like the "Warden" of our body, which is like "jail" to our souls. I can NOT allow anything to tighten the spiritual chains connecting me to god or the "En-sof*," or a 60 watt light bulb somewhere in Deadwood, S.D. (That I'll visit soon enough.) Or, "Y H V H", who I, lowly I, will be seeing sooner than that. (Read on warriors, and listen.)

And now the question of hollow people. In discussing HP's we must also explore the concept of layered lives. Reincarnation, however believable, says by mere intention alone that there is a profound reason for every individual soul to learn, experience and enjoy. (Hmmmm...)

And if that's so... then maybe the first time a soul exists ever in a 3-D animal organism, "it" needs to go through life on a journey in which all lessons, feelings and emotions can be experienced along with the physical and tactile environment. We are banded together through sheer cohabitation in the maternal 3-D plane. I, for one, have never had such dramatic difficulties as when I followed my brain. Which I believe controls the body on a 51% brain / 49% soul guidance at the very best. And that may explain something...

* the correct spelling I am unsure of... the meaning is: limitless void, in effect/affect.

"Why do people of 'the cloth' make the most maladjusted mistakes?"

When I can, I try to avoid stress in every "thing" that may enter my life. This is accomplished when I listened to that soft purr of a voice I hear, when I meditate. When I pray to God, I talk to god.

When I meditate, I listen to God. She/he/it has kind, caring things to say.

I've had other gods. Applause and laughter were my first addiction. I still enjoy making people laugh. Next, I guess it was money and it was followed subsequently with success. Then it was women... or were "the women" always first? Girls, Girls, Girls! (With a capital "G" - spot!)

I'm only alive for the circle that "can" be made. Not everyone can find the other half, and they may be looking too hard. There are many people, I believe, who can serve as the other half of a partnership or relations of any kind. If you find a person with whom a "complete circle" is made, magick happens! (Chemistry kids, chemistry.)

All things fall into place so that growth matched with communication, certainly foster unique arrangements. Remember, the best relationships are individual in nature. While a complete circle is built out of a combination of two separate complete on their own pieces (people), which joined together (not always a perfect union because opposites attract), the pieces create a circular form filled with wonder and adoration. Not always is the fantasy of bliss realized. There is truth to the horror that crimes of the heart can be very cruel!

From a very early age I was drawn to dramatics. I watched a lot of T.V., saw all the movies and even liked a

one-of-us

few of them. I knew all about special effects and people's need to be fooled and pay money to be.

I guess, much like the next guy, I've seen a whole lot of ways to kill a man, woman, child, small farm animal or how to wipe out a whole city block. If you pay close attention in the movie theater, you know too. They can only show so much on television so there's big screen theater for a juvenile to see killing, money, risk, honor (or lack thereof), drugs, women, fast cars, boats, and airplanes with more fast women... and some people have to wonder why there is so much violence and crime in real life. Don't wonder, it's all in the brain.

Children are trained for war. Boys mostly. (Because girls are saved by the boys.) Or rather, boys are shown tactics for survival in a world in a time where there is a need to compete with other humans for existence. To be believed a hero is paramount for many, me for sure. Someone who says they have faith in me is what I've been looking for all these years. (Maybe?) Someone to say, "You're okay, chum... you're okay."

I've had friends who have helped me through life and almost the same number who hurt me somewhere at sometime.

My first mom `n` dad left me. My parents said in effect, "We're done with this `till death do us part' shit. So, deal with now being an unwanted accessory."

My first girlfriend decided she liked another guy the day after she said, "yes". Then every girl in between my first and my prom date left me after declaring temporary unity, but

I've already talked myself dry on that karmic wheel joyride. But that brings me back to the point of crimes in the name of love. In the movies those crimes can be horrible but there are some things going on which can't be used in movies. Life is stranger than fiction! And sometimes quite perverted.

While I lived in Hollywood I tried everything that would have been a taboo in suburbia. (Not really taboo, but that is only how my mind worked, as a child I believed in T.V.) How can a boy or girl choose a way in life without first looking over all the alternatives? It's one thing to take another's word for the horror contained inside any given experience. Although that is the easy way, if... you're a trusting "not get your feet wet" kinda girl or guy.

(Or, would that be intelligence?)

I'm not that way. I never was. I needed to see hell for myself. The road to Satan's home is paved with misleading mortar. Which just happens to allow me to travel on my motorcycle at 135 mph, or charge ridiculous amounts of money for one half an hour's use of my body... then injected into my vein to escape this horrible life at this horrible time. I was a realistically informed punk. (Death-wish included!) This is the future where the social system has been rearranged to fit the desires of a selectively privileged percentage of our (pitifully) fear controlled lives. The greed involved is in almost complete world control. Greed is unique in formation and expulsion. (Greed implodes.)

Like a black hole which, (you may know), has such a strong gravitational pull that not even light can escape it's undeniable irrepressible draw.

Money is that way, it has no choice. It's one of the material items which are food for the financial murder

one-of-us

monster known as "love for money", or greed. That whole arena of conversational topic has many avenues ready and waiting for unhurried exploration. So, for the moment I'll avoid most philosophical arguments by side-stepping their introduction. Because, once someone decides to sail that lonely sea do they begin to understand that it's a long, long way to the end of the voyage. With more hard work than ever the whole trip long.

Basically it comes down to this, it takes money to make money today. (Just like yesterday!?) Only today it's not an expanding market. In yesteryear, anybody with a wee bit o' money and a strong back could follow a basic set of guidelines and be a success. In the days my parents were growing into their parenthood, the market financially speaking, was growing along with them. But today, as I grow into self sufficiency, the market's back slide was obvious. On a horribly clock-work fashion. The 5:00, 7:00, 10:30 network television prime time newscasts.

As I was growing, I saw the groups of people coming together to socialize. Now I see people who always wear a "walkman" on the street. (So they won't have to say "Hello" to another person?)

Often I read the papers and other printed periodicals. I need well rounded wealth of information. I see we the people will have "cyber-stuff" to entertain ourselves with soon. We won't need "us" anymore. Scary thought! (Divide 'n' conquer?)

Back to the point, today not as many people are middle class as back whenever (50's, 60's, 70's), which means there is less money in circulation, because while we have less middle class we have an expanding lower class. Sure, the stock market is doing great... but are you?

The economy is falling, slowly but steadily. We the people see our strong country shake and quiver under the after effects of the weakening economy's depressing oppression. There's no longer any pre-approved plan of attack for acquiring monetary fulfillment. In plain english: People do more drugs and other vices to escape reality today, because there is more "crud" to escape from. That, and some people are weak. Sometime's life is easy, you got a little brains and an evil smile to charm with.

Work the room, work every room, every chance, everyday. Work, work, work, a boy's got his jobs to do! Always on, never let up because there are people out there who need to know me as is... Joseph Elliott Goldwyn. Pure Joe. Joe surfer, Joe baseball, Joe skateboarder, Joe stoner, Joe "mama" - and -when he wanted to: Joe brilliant, Joe inventive, Joe demanding, Joe success, Joe impress, and... Joe the beautiful!

(Which is a wide variation in social activities?)

Maybe. Maybe not.

Eclectic job search of choices to incorporate in the shaping of who I am and what I stand for as a human. A human who is in control of himself. Not my car. I try to do most repairs, not my loved ones (they can do their own repairs), just me. Not other people, places and things. I am never really in control of them. I might write their pay checks, but I'm not in control.

Light
* * *

November 5th, 1985, was a day I really don't want to remember, but I must. Go over it relentlessly with reflective direction, and an open mind. Great things are what I see, and with constant introspection new truths are shown to me.

But let me retrace my steps with the assistance of a police report, what people have told me, and the admissions form to the hospital:

The morning was like every other morning, sex, heroin, and do what ever I needed to do for my final curtain call. (Little did I know!) I think I got money somewhere, probably illegally, and I purchased some heroin. People said I had a habit, and I believe them. The police report says I was running from them. (Go figure.) An illegally imported European model Honda motorcycle and a pocket full of controlled substance moving a wee bit too fast...because when the man in the car tried to make a U-turn...

My motorcycle hit his door at 75 mph. (police report)
My body flew probably a city block or so, landed on it's shoulder, and it's head slammed into the asphalt. (police report and emergency medical evaluation) My body was not wearing a helmet.

The lights went out.

My body slipped into a coma. My body started having seizures. My body's heart slowed, and the blood kept filling it's right lung along with the cavity for my body's brain.

I'm not sure when it happened, but the heart stopped eventually. No wonder, there was "nothing" in it left, nothing for which to hold on to and fight... (for life?)

There was no reason for anymore life in this physical 3-D plane of existence. I was done, everything went black. No... Dark, like you are hiding in a closet to scare mom `n` dad. Very dark, I couldn't see anything, although I knew I inhabited some space inside that total darkness, or corner of the closet.

(Words are so incomplete.)

Then as a warm feeling came over me, this light appeared before me, or what was left of me. I will not say I moved toward the pin-hole of light to join it's comfortable warmth or I drew "The Light" around me. Either way, it was a pin-hole one instant and engulfment the next.

The Light seemed to have depth, and I was traveling deeper inside. When the realization was made that movement and thought were taking place on command, I began to grasp the concept that no longer was I alone (in the closet), but I now stood in the heart of the party. (Belonging!)

I felt welcome. I felt warm. I felt whole. As if, I've just finished the best meal of my life and I was now resting with my loved ones by the fireplace. Sharing information about me and all the people, "real people" I've ever loved throughout my various 3-D lifetimes.

At that time, (there's no clock on the wall there), I felt a strong message penetrate my very being... "Welcome home!"

A homecoming like no other. Words cannot express my feeling of "belonging" there because words are so weak. I

one-of-us

saw no shapes, or forms from which to draw association with any loved one, or with whoever it was I was communicating with. Although, the conversation was extremely real. Information passed between me and The Light at such a speed. Realize, there was nothing to slow the process. I was a part of a bigger "brain" (per-ce). There was no need for a form of any kind to communicate with me. Because speech would be too slow, and there was so much for me to learn.

A feeling: Some people, I feel, need to see something they are expecting to see to quell their fears (?) that The Light might be hell. They might see Jesus, St. Peter, or... ? But, I saw none of that. I didn't need to. (I was home.)

I watched as a video tape (of sorts) concerning my life played, and I was shown why certain painful things needed to happen in my childhood... and throughout my life. I was beginning to understand. There was something transpiring before my soul that was very important, so as usual, I paid attention.

I'll pause here to let people "catch up" while I explain in words, what I was feeling...

The social traps which are inherent or implied, such as: ego, modesty, insecurity, need for jealousy, greed, superiority/inferiority, hate, bigotry, blah, blah, blah... (just to name a few brain powered/controlled activities), were no longer there. (They never were a part of my soul!)

Take a moment and think about all of the "I" which was lost. I became... "Us." I was one with many, a greater power. I was, ONE OF US! (Intelligence, knowledge, love and respect like I've never felt.)

In the grand scope of my experience I believe that for every "I" there is also an opening for that "I's" completely unique history. Think on it in this way; The White Light I was in was like a very large computer, which is forever, relentlessly in search of and welcoming all forms of information.

I, like everyone else, am nothing but a data base packed full of individual knowledge `n` information. Like... an arithmetic occasion equation..

(Experiences and the lessons learned inside them make the man.)

Maybe I should explain the mood of the Light and how I feel after having been there. There is a definite, very separate intelligence above and beyond our brains. (Gasp!) But survival skill is as important as our procreative abilities, which are equal to our mathematical understanding. (Nature is not evil.)

Those things which "I" lost in the coma were all a brain engineered experiences, abilities of value on earth. Pretty crafty animal, Joseph E. Goldwyn. I had become proficient at survival to the point of being invincible, and now I was dead. I knew I was dead, because the memory of the Light was nothing but familiar. I knew where I was, and even though I saw no faces or forms or angels with wings, I was never alone. I had no shape, but then I did not need shape, or a vision of something to comfort me because I understood everything. Feelings of complete comfort.

The first thing I remember processing was, for lack of a better descriptive term, a "thought message" from my grampa Paul, "Hello Joe, welcome home." I knew it was him, because the vibration in the thought (voice?) was so familiar.

And welcome I felt. Some amount of time passed (does time exist there?) feeling love from all and loving all. I was able to move through the Light and select information about my life, and things which happened in it. There was a reason for everything that ever took place, even if it was just too much or too little. I'm not human, I do live in a human body though. I'm not god, but I was transformed in some way. Everyone who has come into my life, in some way, is transformed. Unfortunately too few recognize it.

The problems of the world were shown to me through my many experiences which have already been expressed. (But nothing yet in depth.) My past was explained, but there were still questions as to why I needed to live the life of "I". Remember my relating some form of understanding of my life and it's purpose that was shown to me like a video tape? The recording of my life was showing me why certain things needed to occur. It played out right up to the accident... and then the future came.

There is a child in my future (a boy), and my son and his mother are faceless in this "video tape" of my life. (oh gosh...)"My tape," did not end on Nov. 5th of `85, instead it continued on into what would have been my future? Too bad. My future had looked good. Like it was my previous destiny. I was aware of the fact that this vision, being just another plausibility, was still a question mark in the hands of fate. (Hmmmm...)

While I was looking at my possible future, I may have seen faces and the locations, but I saw them in such a rapid fashion. Like the "tape" was on play and fast forward at the same time. There was a mother in my future, but I needed to work hard in finding her. Travel halfway across the country on my Harley, (which I had not even purchased yet). She traveled the other half so we could meet midway between the coasts in Denver, CO. (But once again, I rush...)

As I'm looking at this vision, which is like seeing something with your "mind's eye," a question was asked by someone or everyone, or something or nothing at all. "Well, what would you like to do, now that you've seen your future?" Because I was surrounded by All Knowledge, I had an answer.

All I was able to feel, was mom. "I want to be with mom."

In the watching of "my tape", I witnessed my life, and now I felt those years I thought were wasted... were nothing of the kind. But now I had seen mom, she was out there somewhere, waiting. The choice was mine, and it was made at the instantaneous speed at which All Knowledge is shared openly and with total respect in the Light.

Although
* * *

There is another side to this story happening in the Intensive Care unit at Hollywood Presbyterian Hospital. Joseph Elliott Goldwyn is dead to the world. His name is now John Doe #243. John has a punctured lung, bleeding on the brain, a paralyzed right half of his body, and John was in a coma for days (five of them) before he became a Joe. (Joe coma!) At the time of the accident I had no identification at all on me, and my motorcycle was an illegal vehicle with no registration or plates.

I was a non-person, with a very small chance for survival. I had appointments which Joe did not make that day, because I could no longer open my eyes. All I could do was be John #243 and hold on till some member of my family tracked me down.

My mother found out where I was first, and she was soon by my bedside in the hospital. The outlook was not good, and no doctor had an encouraging word. They had informed her that I, eventually, was going to die. (I already had, so it's just a matter of time.)

My Mom, (adopted mom, Flo) was there, pacing, on the phone with the 700 Club, while crying all the while because her son is lying on a hospital bed with all kinds of tubes in him but very little life left. Doctors and other staff were running around to make sure his heart (my heart) continued to beat.

One more thing: The blood test had come back. My mom was about over the 'hump of depression' when the doctor informed her... "That's right HIV positive."

"Yes, he has signs of being a homosexual (Mom knew about bisexuality), but Mrs. Goldwyn... he also came in with a good deal of heroin in his body." It's a good thing the floor was carpeted. She had fainted. It's also a good thing there was a hotel next door because my mom didn't leave, and mom's need sleep too. Day turned to week. Week became a month, and still nothing. That's a coma for ya. All the while I'm slipping away, two pounds here, two pounds there until I weighed in at 117 lbs. The lab people ran a second HIV test which came back negative, and that gave my mom all the light she needed at the end of the tunnel in her mind. And soon, after six and a half weeks of deep coma, my eyes opened.

Now this is where what I have to say is very important.

I need for my readers to understand where that human body that everyone called Joe was at. A skinny twenty-two year old male physical form, with the brain of a newborn. Think of the brain as a blackboard, a slate of information on and about one's life. When I returned from being comatose, my slate had been wiped clean. Traumatic Head Injury (T.H.I.) full tilt!

I was a baby, (goo-goo). A twenty-three year old newborn baby with almost no chance for any recovery (boo-hoo). I was moved to a recovery hospital. And that's when some of my post head trauma's amnesia, like a dense grey fog, began to show it's "true colors".

I remember nurses with bags of stuff and tubes, lots of tubes. I was a baby, because every look, every person, everything was new. I remember a man who would often come into the room, like any other hospital staff. Anyway, he came in with three new people, weird people. Their clothes

one-of-us

weren't white. The man in white asked, "Do you know these people, Joe?"

"Uh-uhh", I could communicate yes or no with two separate sounds but not words. Severe learning disability. This was a strange time because my memory was so invalid, incapable of any recall. I couldn't remember anyone who I wasn't looking directly at, and I would forget people day to day or hour to hour.

"Well, this is your mother, your father and your fiancé."

Wow, I thought I was a baby! Things got weird inside my head. I already had a life? Which means that I'm already a person... and not a person "to be". I don't remember who I am, I do not remember those old people but she, Angie, was kind of cute.

Then stuff began to happen. I still don't remember much of anything, but I had friends, family and other people (the police, credit card companies, etc.) to tell me what an asshole I was! (Imagine parents telling their newborn baby he is shit, over and over and over...) I didn't remember all these things everyone said I had done, but I sure had to suffer through the hellish aftermath.

I was a ball of proverbial clay to be shaped and glazed, then placed into the kiln of life to become a beautiful piece of human pottery. (Like all babies are.) The son my parents always wanted, not the son he became... (I became!) I failed as a son the first time, but now my loving father `n` mother `n` fiancé had their second chance. I'm not sure who's to blame (maybe myself?), but my entire past life was erased. I was never told of the good things that happened (because nothing ever was?), but lectured on the horrors of my past.

Clothes were burned, pictures disposed of and all ties to my past reality torn asunder.

I started coming home from the hospital to sleep in my mom's house. For some reason my dad scared me. When I saw part or all of my future, dad didn't play a nice role. Well, that's his M.O.

Although, I believe that I can not at will recall information given to me in the afterlife... until it's time.

So we (you `n` I) understand one another: It's like I've been given time release capsules of information which open, sometimes fast, sometimes slow. These capsules of information allow me to have large moments of realization wrapped up in an incredible day long "De ja vu". I feel very powerful when that happens, and it does happen often, but like respect/love it can never happen too much.

But even though I was now twenty-four and living at my mom's house in San Clemente, CA., I had the life of an adult. I was married (not legally), and I was now going to a T.H.I. retraining program in a community college not too far away.

With more `n` more of my ventures into the outside world I met not with understanding, but rather... condescending belittlement.

I was less than. I needed help. I knew in my bones that I was very different, therefore an outcast to the fringes of this very cruel society. I felt alone. (I was alone.) No one could understand. No one wanted to understand that brain damaged man. (Who was now a stupid boy.) Angie tried

to help with my recovery by reintroducing me to pot, and in the end, by her allowing me to put a needle into my arm.
(Not much recovery there!)

It's almost understandable. Angie was engaged to a man (not a great guy, but a man none the less) and the man was now a little boy. (Who would not guess that a mental age of about seven or eight in no way could satisfy his twenty year old wife-to-be.) She was forced to (forced to?) have an affair. Serves me right, huh? All those times I hurt her, that EVERYONE said happened, but I did not remember. It was like I was in jail for someone else's crimes.

Angie was supposed to be at work and I was mindlessly (figuratively and literally) wandering the neighborhood when I saw a car parked in the distance (down the hill) with two lovers necking. Very soon I had this uncontrollable urge to get a closer look. (I still don't know why I got the urge.) I got about halfway to that car when Angie got out and started running to me.
It was at that time I wished they carpeted sidewalks. She destroyed the man inside the boy called Joe.
"It's the first time", she pleaded. (Yeah right!) "Really... ", she affirmed. (Yeah right!)
My only answer was, "goodbye." (Bitch!)
So the move out process began.
At that time, or up until then after the coma, I had been told of honor, love, and trust, and now I had seen the true nature of humans. (I was not impressed.)
I recognized that what Joe was, was just a collection of earthly survival abilities / tactics. Everyone hated Joe, or

one-of-us

what Joe stood for. He was a nonconformist. And, someone who follows nothing... is hard to follow.

Joe was too good. He made both mom 'n' dad, and most everyone else, swallow their own vicious actions and words they inflicted on who Joe was. Seems as though Joe made everyone eat crow.

Angie moved into her friend's place in Hollywood, Jeanette's apartment. Jeanette used to be my friend, but now I was very different - (weird). We saw each other (Angie `n` I) a few more times but I believe those times were to show her that I was still pretty messed up and to show me that I was pretty messed up still. I was not getting better, I wanted to grow, but I was only shown the ways to destroy any chance of recovery. Angie had reintroduced me to heroin and my dope times did make me feel a little better. Even though, after the Light, I was against all forms of vice; smoking, drugs, and stealing. But since we have the technology, I'll avoid the pain and begin to embrace escape provided by chemicals.

My elders (everyone was "older" than I), showed me how I could avoid the pain a person might feel (does feel) while working to better his... "broken brain". (I listened to S.N.F.U. before and after the accident. For those who don't know, S.N.F.U.'s a punk band.) The band S.N.F.U. had a song about just that, a man with a broken brain. The pain in their lyrics poured straight from my eyes. To only be able to feel and not think means I've gone insane I thought. Nothing I ever did was a success, or so everyone said. There was nothing I could do, to not be a failure.

While I should have been questioning "their" end goal result "they" had planned for me... I was doubting myself.

Me, the only friend I'm going to have through this recovery experience.

My parents saw their opening. With no protective fiance to look after me, (ta-ta-ta-ta) "let the brainwashing begin". They began by telling me complete untruths concerning that boy Joe. That I was going to be just like they dreamed, and nothing less. They dressed me in clothes I might wear on Hollows Eve, but not on the street in daylight hours. Although I was a little boy who need some guidance. I did not need to have a life thrust upon me. I didn't have a need for another completely different personality. (But then again, it could have it's benefits!)

While I was just beginning to become whole again, I had values and morals thrust upon me with infinite volume so that simple selection seemed impossible to my seven year old brain. My natural instinct was to love, believe, touch and possibly be touched was natural and normal, and therefore act on feelings rather than having to ask the brain for permission. The damaged brain I had was good for little of coherent decision making ability, so why should I awaken it from it's insanity avoiding slumber? This was the question I had to ask myself before I placed any prospective activity into it's mental molars for the subsequent smile, or regurgitation. For as simple as my brain was at that time, it still had 51% of the decision power as to whether or not I was going to play a role in any activity.

All that brain involvement hurt my head. There wasn't enough up there in the way of any knowledge or information to give me ground on which to assemble a rational decision upon.

After having to listen to mom or dad complain on how many people they had to pay off and how big the mess was

one-of-us

they had to clean up, made me pity them. It seems "Joe" left a whirlwind's wake wherever he had gone. (Only, "I" don't remember any of it.) Joe, was not me. But, if "they" are going to punish me (who "they" called Joe) for Joe's actions... then Joe is what I'll become. (To survive?) Yes!

There were all these hours mom `n` dad volunteered to spend time with me. The maid was hired to spend time with me when I was a lad. It was her job. But there were no maids now, I was twenty-four.

I should be able to entertain myself, right? Wrong. That's not the way it was. All the clouds inside my head had become very dense `n` dark. I did not need to have a life thrust upon me. Force fed existence is like prison for the free. Instead of doubting "their" dream of what I was to become, I was the brain damaged boy who could do no right, I began doubting myself more. Falling into the same holes I fell into before is what began to happen. "Do as I say, not as I do", is what's said. But unless it's said to the blind man, it has no value at all. (Especially to the boy who pays attention.)

What I heard was, "I'm not telling you to do this, but what I'm doing is how to survive in our world." (Your world?) Their words lie, they don't match the actions. (Hmmm...) I didn't like "their" world. The world I had just come from was like a dream, a dream of love, respect and knowledge. And now I had to survive in a world where I'm very different. (What else is new?) And I was not yet ready to give up on the "dream", but I was unable to capsulate, as of yet, the message inside my "dream"... The Light?

Time will tell as it often does, and it had quite a tale to tell.

J. Elliott Goldwyn

Most people can make a correlation between me and the state I was in with a normal 7 year old kid (who is nowhere near normal), in this way: I was a happy go lucky man/child who loved to play with crayons, painting, and splashing in puddles like all kids. (Not "all", but close enough.)

Then society began impressing me with the responsibility of being a consumer. I was shown many things: the value of being a young man, a white one, with a family with lots of money in CA. Very soon, because of constant repetition, I began to equate love with money. And, it only got worse. Thrust into life as an adult outside, in a body with the age of a child inside.

(Then the T.V. told me...)

There were other reasons for me to feel better than other people; class, sex, hair color or skin color. All of this line of crap was taught to my by people who say they love me.

I grew very confused. Knowing that a person is not his skin, or the color of the skin on the person's animal body he (or she) inhabits was more true than ever before. All of the people (souls) are a different color because every soul is a part of the whole. (We are all stars!) That is true in this way: "The Light" (which is white) is really just a collection of "all" colors combined. In the spectrum of Light, all colors make white.

3. Every man and every woman is a star.
2. The unveiling of the company of heaven.
1. Had! The manifestation of Nuit.
    (A. Crowley)

("The Book of The Law" (sic), is worth a look.)

Make not a comment until you understand his message, for ignorance makes a poor critic.

one-of-us

As a child (both times) my need to compete was founded in a desire to be "The King of The Hill". Not many can be a leader, even of their own selves. Society has a way of dismantling the weaker of the potential "king-like" candidates. If a leader of men (hopefully women also) rises above the cream in society, the "system" incorporates the leader turned teammate... so... the gag order to his/her brilliant philosophies can be enacted and enforced. (If you can't beat them, sign them up on your team!)

Change, and respect for change bringing a more tolerant outcome to our planet's fragile ecology (psychology?). (NO!) That is not what happens in the "real world". (Is it?)

I get up every morning hoping for a change, but every morning is exactly the same. Which is unfortunate, because of every day's goal is to be different than the day before, for me. Progressively, and when no progress is made an inhumane feeling comparable to stagnation occurs.

Am I struggling against an unmovable wall? (A psycho-roadblock, if you will.) Or am I wasting my time trying to educate others about myself, and seeing as my effort goes as unrecognized as one might be to their vacuum cleaner for sucking real hard.

Not noticing the inherent magic contained in a miracle device which sucks the dirt right out of our floors covered with fake grass (carpet) is due to man's weak memory of how life was before the invention of said magical machine. We've become complacent.

(News flash!?)

We're a society that believes a child should raise him or herself, and if individuality occurs (myself?), it was the child that failed (or so my parents said). I think Not. But let's follow that line of insanity for awhile shall we?

If a child is a failure, what does that say for the adult contained inside that child? Unless the child is insistent upon his/her belief in the self (or I'ness), the child is programmed to a life of potentially predestined successive failures... and the mood swings I've had for longstanding.

In no way am I trying to give guilt to my parents, for my childhood environment.

I thank them. For if I had found them perfect "parental units", what is left for me to improve upon? Because, to improve upon past behaviors is what being human is all about. (Right?)

For if the human drive to improve vanished, therein would lie complete complacency. It is often times a show of pure laziness to accept things (just as they are), when the affect would produce a more enjoyable result, rather than at-leisure acceptance alone.

There are things which are best left alone, other people, places, things. But the alcoholic / drug addict in me, has a problem with control.

Magick
* * *

Now I must write about what may be the final thing which came between what I thought at one time was my very best friend, and I. When I last saw Mike it was at his second wedding in Richmond, Virginia. When he invited me to his social arrangement (marriage) I was surprised beyond belief.

I was living in my own apartment in Santa Maria, CA, and taking classes at a business college (my father recommended). Soon I realized the school was far beyond my capabilities. Although an employment which transforms me into a self-supporting offspring, rather than a fully dependant brain damaged man, was all my parents really had in mind for me. I do not blame them, in fact I give more credit to my parents for allowing me to reject everyone of the possible personas that were offered. Although, just because my mom and dad allowed it to happen, does not mean they wanted it -or- accepted my choices when I made one. It was because (I believe) there wasn't any choice for anything that was different than the personas who mom or dad wanted me to be. They had to form me, make me into something I did not want to be.

I had to fight very hard to be an individual who forms himself from beginning to end. There were social manipulation games happening all around me, and I could not keep up with the ones going on at home (parents house) let alone the games at school. I had gotten a job to try out the computer information the Santa Barbara Business College I was attending had taught me, and the 'fun' (if I could call it that) of trying to remember what I couldn't.

J. Elliott Goldwyn

Like the child I was inside my damaged brain, I did not have the social tools to be able to alleviate the stress of the business world. Even if I did have the tools I would not know how to use them. I was living alone, and I began to drink alone too.

I could do nothing right enough. I made trips to find acceptance and found it in Los Angeles. I was reintroduced to heroin a while back, and now I had the money to buy some. The world did not want me any more... I felt. Only now my friend Mike wants me to come to his wedding. He wants me to be the best man, (but I was not a man nor was I best).

I should have declined his invitation, but I just could not. I would find out why when I got there. I took the train across these United States of ours and enjoyed it immensely. I met a few people on the Amtrak and they also could not believe the beauty of this country seen from a vantage point that a car never sees.

My arrival was one week before the leaves began their yearly color change in Richmond, and two weeks before his big day. The first of those weeks was spent at Mike's place. It felt good to be with my old buddy.

The second was also, only it was his new house across town with no heat, no electricity or running water. He had many things going on and I understand that, but I was very cold and lonely.

I had no car or friend to talk with anymore, and there was no phone. Down the street from Mike's new home there were a large group of guys that would let me hang with them after I bought some of their product. I believe that may have been the second thing which came between Mike 'n' I. (I regret that.)

I met a charming woman in the wedding and that may be another reason why Mike 'n' I talk no longer. Her name was Virginia, but she liked to be called Gini. She was the bride's maid and I the best man. Yes, it was very much like a Harlequin Romance...

We had both taken different trains into Richmond but decided to leave on the same one. Gini and I had quite the game of poker even though we had no money. We wagered other things. The only problem was the tiny size of the bathroom floor. To this day I believe that she threw that last hand just so I could win "all the marbles!"

Later I realized that just like Mike who asked for a "best" man, Gini also wanted a man. Although, at that time I could only be a child with the social skills of a child in a man's body. (An opportunity missed? I'm sure that it was.)

There was a great deal of time recognizing all my character defects and how I was "less than" just like everyone always said. All I wanted was to escape, but the paramedics had other plans for me. (All I can say to those "life savers" today is, "Thanks again!")

I nearly killed myself because I had become crushed by the pressure to perform socially in ways which I was unaccustomed to. I was lost into the dream of belonging to someone. At that time, I had no one who showed me any affection without alternate motives of some sort. But, here was the most beautiful girl (Gini) from New York city who liked me until I could no longer perform in a socially acceptable manner.

The problem in my not acting proper came from the memory loss, word find difficulties and mental slowness, which is often associated with retardation. All that was occurring in me as I was recovering from my head injury and aftereffects of the coma. It wasn't that I made terrible mistakes, but I couldn't handle the stresses which came along with life in society and escape therefrom. Everything happened TOO fast. I needed simplicity. My life was anything but. I could not handle living. I was subjected to intervention and deserved every bit of it, but what no one knew was I was having a problem with my broken brain and not the drugs. The chemical escape was wrong (I knew that), but it was the only escape that shut up my head. I was putting up walls between me and society, but that's exactly what I wanted to do. People, on the whole, in California were not very kind to me.

I needed to be alone, but I wanted to be together with someone else. (I had to learn.)

While inside the drug addiction wing of the hospital I came in contact with a psychiatric doctor who would talk to me. He showed to me a completely different view on the true origin of the infamous A.A.* Whether right or wrong, didn't matter because:

I finally had answers to so many questions. I had found that there was another view on the hollow religious answers to the spiritual questions I had in my life (a guided epiphany).

It was my will I needed to follow. Not the expectations of all the other people, places or things. I had been right all along, and now I had a direction for my individualistic tendencies to relax into. (But still I didn't want to be alone.) That is when my "true self" began to emerge and I noticed I had begun to follow my own true will, and girls began to look at me differently. I was becoming me!

*Before alcoholics anonymous, the A.A. is a magical fellowship.

This was a slow process, but the shocker in Virginia with Gini launched me on my new found quest to grow in all ways. (I did learn, and I continue to absorb daily.)

I have a self empowered outlook now because I only need myself, but myself does not need to be alone. I had been slowly mastering the tactics of getting closer to being a "real person". I now wanted to become a PERSON, and not just a shell.
But how? (prayer and meditation)
Time spent in reflective rhetorical rumination.

After a great deal of reading, research and re-introspection, I had found that not only does magick work, but it was nothing like people (the preacher) said it was. It just made so much sense to me. Another definition of magick is... LOVE.

How can love be wrong? (I'll let you answer that.)
Therefore my "first love" is magick, or should I say I love the Light which comes from it's study.

J. Elliott Goldwyn

A Glimpse
* * *

All throughout our lives we are all shown various things and therefore learned subsequent lessons. Although, seeing as we are a world of individuals, I see there being the possibility of as many individual interpretations.

Therein lies, unfortunately, some basic need for some members of our society to attempt to control my own personal interpretation of myself. Let's explore their need:

For another person to control my thoughts, actions and representations is a definition of slavery. As many people do, I have my own views on "slavery". Disgust and disrespect are two of them. It takes a hollow person to not be a leader, but rather... an owner of other people's lives. (Or even try.)

To be monopolist is the end result of mind control on the grand scale. (A monopoly is when you have no other choice.)

Rhetorical query time: Did you ever wish you had a third choice in every election, a choice which has shown consistently to reflect the needs of "you" a very real person and not the greed of big business or the self defeating "two party system"?

I've done many a thing (life threatening stuff/fun stuff) but not out of eminent insusceptibility or a core feeling of immortality, but the spurring of the grey cloud. That which christians and many others call, Armageddon. (Even sounds inevitable!)

From a early age I was shown how "we" as a people are doomed. Doomed in the beginning and unless very wealthy, or sometimes because of it, cursed by doom for years after your demise.

one-of-us

No one's free, living in a world where it's someone else's job to offer (or cram) the message of untruth down your throat until it seeps out from underneath your fingernails. This very capitalistic heaven, the earth, (not just America anymore) is only big enough for those with the ability (instability?) to sell out.

To offer an expression of said ability, I'll ask another rhetorical question, "How much value is any T.V. evangelist weighed against the amount of his wage or income?" Of course you can't really put a price on unlimited sexual escapades with the `Johnson's` teenage daughter or their five year old son at church summer camp, can you? Not all of "them" act that way, I know.

Although, sometimes only one can ruin the bunch.

The group of "them" I've just spoken on, follow a path which was written a long time ago and convince some of "us" into believing it's still true. It is, but not the way "they" preach it. They only tell us what they want us to know. Not the truth, because the truth is everything. (And we do not know that.)

The ends to the story are always catastrophic. Seems to me, that if I were to read somewhere that I were to die in a mishap in the sky, I'd rarely fly. But we read about it everyday, and we just keep repeating history. (pity) Shouldn't we just have planned to avoid this predestined date from the beginning? This Armageddon, this end?

Yes, we should have. Did we?

No. (Just like lemmings into the sea.)

Why? The T.V. can teach you to follow.

Are we not an intelligent race?

No. Not all of "us" are.

I'm not saying I know everything, in fact I know very little. Only I was given a glimpse, a vision on a whole level of existence reliant upon nothing but love. A tremendous love. A love so complete and yet completely limitless to my budding comprehension. I was overwhelmed. I "felt" like I was whole.

It was that love and so very much more. When I say "felt" like, I mean seemed like or felt like in my bones or soul, so to speak. I had no physical form in the Light. How could I "feel" without my fingers? (The same way babies communicate without words.)

My formlessness afforded me the sight of a singular being transformed, or rather evolved into oneness with many other former (or soon to be?) singular beings (stars). Once the many crystal-like colors of light are assembled together, "all of us" create the Light we are blessed to see when the body we are living in dies. There are many different views on life/afterlife, and I have only two things to say about that:

1. Everyone of "the views" is right.

2. Everyone of "the views" is wrong... as wrong can be.

Let me explore #1 - The correctness of that sentence resides in it's semantics. "Yes Virginia, there is life, and after life there is afterlife."

And #2 - If I had the technology and equipment to, I'm sure I could refract white light into as many different colors we humans could possibly imagine. Maybe even beyond. Surely as many different individual colors as there are individual life forms on this planet, and therein lies ground for infinite individual interpretations. Remember, we're all just stars. And being such, we all have different views which are "right" for us, but "wrong" for anyone else. This point is where acceptance should begin. (Unfortunately... most 'star-wars' do.)

In it's construction, there is one end of the light spectrum which could be connected with the other end (bear with me until I'm able to reach my conclusive ends) and in so doing it creates a true "circle of light". Which is a part of my circle theory.

All things to me have some point to call their own on some circle somewhere at all times. "And yes Virginia, not all things stay on only one, or need to be on only one circle at any one singular time." Therefore, I do not.

I need many circles of experience because I am a man of many colors, if you will.

I recognize all the many circles around me and choose to incorporate them... or not.

My coat of colors is made from fabric which I alone choose.

For all things have an opposition to all the other things, i.e. best/worst, soft/hard, up/down, in/out, or left and right, I've found that the law of opposition is as old as time. (In fact, time *is* opposition.)

"Unfortunately Virginia, this also is true. Just as completely as we win the race, we lose. As we progress, we also systematically decline. Evenly we share love with hate, peace with war, life and death, and always it's the two extremes in which we focus our attention."

On the day my son was born, I needed to share in the birth of his life with his mother and him. On my own I shed a tear in quiet grief in realization of his being born, predetermined one day far into the future (knock on wood) his life will end. I gave my son life\death, and everywhere in between them.

Examine there being basic personalities, or "auras" if you will, which have colors assigned to them and each with their own vibrations. We are all individuals with our own individual vibrations and colorful wants/needs, goodness\badness, life and death. And, because of our core uniqueness we will have different purposes than any other persona.

Exactly like the similarities and differences between each and every single individual color, in the color spectrum which contains no two colors which are "exactly alike". Colors that are close. But not a perfect match. A match, just not totally "exactly alike". Unless you'd like to talk about parallel existence?

(Maybe later.)

And born from different purposes are different needs/wants, good/evil, lives and deaths, successes/failures. Many need to live their lives with the acceptance of something more powerful, like a boss or a god. Acceptance comes in paychecks or in the belief that you are going to heaven or at best.... not hell.

There is only one spirituality, we evolved from apes, and when the evolution was complete enough our beautiful, color like, singular, separate souls began to live in them.

Evolution and creation together at last. Maybe the first "cave-person" with a soul was a man named Adam. I can see it now, the first human soul in human body... walking and declaring his right to be 'one and whole' like any two year old, by beating his fist and shouting his name like the god (lower case God), but a god nonetheless! "I Am Adam!"

one-of-us

A profound exclamation of Love, I exist!

There must have been some origin of omnipotent opening occurring!

There is only one spirituality, love. Which is "The Law".

To get into The Light, show love. However much you have, a little/lots/all or none. If you need to hate, then I suggest hating the terrible way we have been treating our beautiful mother earth. (Pick up one piece of trash on the street a day, I dare you!)

Very few will say, "Thanks." Because very few people care on the whole.

On a grand scale, of all the earth's inhabitants, the Native Americans lived in near perfect union with the earth, which is our physical representation of the mother goddess.

We are killing her. Slowly but most definitely surely.

We don't have to. Beings do the killing not machines, unless a corporation is a "machine". Beings can stop it. (But we won't... not yet anyway.)

Humans have a need to not believe in themselves. Humans need to believe in something more powerful being in control and being there to write the rules so we humans can break them. And why? So there is something more powerful (him, her, it?) we can disregard the power of? Yes, that and so much more.

Some humans have a spiritual light shining inside them. Some brighter than others. A few don't have any light at all, at least not one that shines. Some humans have a goodness inside them while others don't. The others are not evil, they just are not born with the goodness (a soul?) inside.

And if you, them, or anyone else thinks that a person who is not born with goodness inside should acquire it from society around them, is definitely not living in the real world. (Or... has great drugs.)

Kids today are capable of killing their own parents. Why? I believe that can be because the parents may have brought the kid into a life where the kid is an accessory. The child must love and respect parents (the world?) who neither loves nor respects them. You get what you give. If the parents wanted to own something and run its life, I feel they should have bought a hamster.

Similarly, I believe there are kids today having kids because they feel like owning something themselves that they can force to love and respect them. The kids having kids have no love or respect shown to them (on the whole) from the world. I ask, how can they possibly show love, or respect or teach it to their poor little babies? Little babies are like sponges, and with nothing there to "fill them up" the world is creating hollow people.

Fortunately, hollow people are less of a threat than evil people. Evil is made not born, and everywhere on everyday there are a lot more people out there who are teaching hate, bigotry, sexism or class-"ism" than there are people who are showing love, honor or respect to their fellow man, woman, or child. That does not mean to say it does not exist, it's just not prime time news worthy.

Body 3
* * *

I had regained much of my ability to articulate like a "normal" person. ("I, no longer... talked... simple no... more," like a two/three/four year old.) My parents needed to satisfy their own ego's and quell their fears about me never being able to be self-supporting and only being a four year old boy mentally, in the body of a twenty-five, thirty-five, forty-five year old man. Forever.

To escape that sort of social hell, of having a brain damaged son who would be a constant twenty-four hour burdensome responsibility, my parents made the very incorrect decision to send me to various "training institutions" before I had a chance to evaluate who it was that "I am."

The simple fact that after my "deep sleep" (coma) I didn't even know who my parents were is a direct result of not knowing who it was that I am. I was reset to ground zero, baby-like.

I have been reading in various medical information pamphlets, one such report was written by Doctors Robert J. Sbordone, Ph.D., A.B.C.N., A.B.P.N. and the University of California at Irvine School of Medicine, Dept. of Neurosurgery and Physical Medicine, and Michael E. Howard Ph.D., of the Dallas Rehabilitation Institute, Dallas, TX. also added his expertise.

The report suggests that a head injury patient should decide for themselves when it is time to begin school or retrain themselves in the abilities to hold an employment position, or the decision in which to return to work. Forcing retraining would allow said T.H.I. recipient to deny any and/or all of the subsequent character defects involved in the retraining process. Whether those difficulties are any combination of, or including all of the possibilities of mental, emotional, cognitive, or just an ability to label the feeling which the patient is experiencing, and to act in a socially acceptable manner. But the THI victim should be carefully evaluated as to the success or failure of said re-engineering, or if the 'time is right' or not.

Sometimes, I feel as though I'm still not ready.

Reality?
* * *

The need to escape this reality that I now was in so as to remain in the beauty (the unconditional love and understanding) of the "Afterlife" has never been stronger than when I look at men's and women's daily show of disrespect to each other.

The Light I went to after the accident had everything I have ever searched for and unfortunately been unable to locate here on earth. When others show disrespect I become angry and that line of frustration occurs when I realize pure "human to human" respect, or lack thereof, is taught not always inherent.

We the people learn to show mistrust and experience difficulties in relation to other people when we give trust and then have that trust violated. I have not only a theorem or a feeling but now a belief because I was shown reasons for the "day to day" difficulties involved in my very successful accomplishment of various responsibilities contained in the experiences of daily earth bound existence. Survival - 101

My belief is this: There are bodies on the earth which because of their existence we must interact with on an every day basis. (Some days more than others.) The people I speak of are, hollow.

Hollow in this respect: There is nothing behind their eyes, and because there is nothing behind their eyes there is no more soul inside their bodies than a pretzel or a hotdog.

(Food for thought!)

My logic is thusly applied: H.P.'s (hollow people) have no 3-D reality expressions located in the memory (core) of their soul (if they have one). And since all any persona is is just a collection of memory of their events, a soul with no wisdom from which to draw on has no reservoir of information with which to make any conscience based conclusion socially. So a "socially correct" decision may not be reached concerning a myriad of experiences everyday in every way on this beautiful planet. Without needed information H.P.'s are subjected to, and so are we, their own second nature "animal" impulses.

(Lucky us?)

(I think not.)

To fight or fuck. To better one's self by belittling the other, by gossip, slander, libel and other crimes against nature which in the long run hinder, hamper or just destroy any chance of success in completing all expressions of love, knowledge and respect. Life is not easy for us, because of them. ("Whew!")

It's an Us/Them survival arrangement. We (us), see ourselves helping another human succeed in their life. "Us" people do that.

Unfortunately there are a lot of "them" out there also.

This is very Pro and Con. I will explore that truth, but first allow me to expand further.

Question: Have you ever been held up in respect to the successful accomplishment of a goal which is good for all involved by someone who merely desired to frustrate you and make your existence more uncomfortable? This other person, who at first glance appeared trustworthy, who seemed to be real and have content to his or her personality? (depth?) But... because of their involvement in your life, that "H.P." has brought every laid plan to waste? (Double "whew!")

And why? Because of their loose moral foundation?

No, not because of a loose foundation but rather a lack of any assemblage of morals, values or a basic human characteristic of having a conscience which is supposed to be inside every human being's body. (Don't believe everything you've been told.)

I noticed at this time I had begun asking questions that no one seemed to have an answer for containing any common sense activity whatsoever. I realized that I no longer wished to be another "Joe" and confined to the limits of the personality contained within that restrictive pronoun. Everyone, my parents especially, had an idea of who "Joe" was... and I did not like their ideas.

All I wanted was to be free.

Book 2: (Elliott)

Elliott
* * *

And therein the problem lies. Society will not let an individual be just that... an individual. I am, but it *was* hard, is hard today, and will probably be even be more difficult tomorrow. Placing me into a schedule of events and experiences by my parents to produce the happy well adjusted money making conformist geek whom I had no intention of becoming. That would take large amounts of persona disallowance. (I am who I am, not who you want me to be.)

But you know, respect your elders. My parents had a life planned out for me.

I wonder when they had time to live my life for me. They made one thing perfectly clear, their love will be very conditional. Mom 'n' dad showed me the equation between my conformity and the love I might receive. If I was who they wanted me to be I'd get love 'n' respect. (Lucky me!)

No, I will not! The puppet they would love 'n' respect would not be me. My parents tried to dress and then control their puppet (baby joe) twice, before and after the accident.

Conformity can be misery, and like misery, conformity loves company. When my parents (and the world) started on that brain-washing routine to make me a bookkeeper / accountant, I felt at times like I was in jail doing "responsibilities" I really did not want to do... but I trusted my elders knew best. At times, I was being "raped" by a way of life which I hated deeply.

It was their fault and it was not their fault.

I did not stand up for myself, but I did not know myself.

I feel as though I was manipulated because I was a babe in man's skin who was not allowed to decide anything for himself.

When I was a child I believed my parents had all the answers. When I was seven, after my parents split the marriage in two, every answer I thought they had taught me about values, morals or ethics went right out the proverbial window. Just like my dream/fallacy of a loving understanding respectful family. (Unconditional love/belonging.)

Which brings me to a conclusion. Conformity which is applied by everyone needs to be replaced with understanding or acceptance if understanding is impossible. Understanding is not impossible, it never is. It is sometimes very hard work only to be accomplished by an open mind. Not all people's minds are open ones. You can't be friends with everyone and that's unfortunate for them.

I wear my hair a certain way (have for years). Most people wouldn't wear their hair my way but I don't even try to make them adopt my fashion. Why must I adopt theirs? Does it say I must somewhere in their Bible? Can't I be an individual with my own hair?

Besides, their bible is supposed to be the word of God, right? Wrong... in my eyes. (Great book, but...) Once the word of God is written by a human hand, it becomes the word of human. I believe that is why "their" God is so humanly vindictive, judgmental and condemning (which are not the only comparables).

My goddess is not, my god is not, human in any way.

He `n` She is all. Even more than the human imagination can dream, all love, all knowledge, all understanding and all... respect. He `n` She is not vindictive, judgmental or condemning. Because those are "human" traits.

Church?
* * *

The white Light is a heaven of sorts, and there will be no race war in heaven, no class war in The Light because those too are human traits. Therefore, how can you now say that you're close to God? Oh, so you go to church? Nothing could be further from God. Because there is no church which does not belittle the other churches. (That is anti-god!)

Every church is the "right" church, while all others (not just religious beliefs) are "wrong". How very unlike the all love, all respect, all knowledge and all understanding of God. (I use the word "God" because the masses who believe in a male god is who I'm trying to reach. God is not only male.) I'm not sure I'll be able to reach "them" because some of "them" need to go to church to hear about how wrong everyone else is. (They are?) In church wearing their Sunday clothes (and fake Sunday faces) they hear about how they are going to get the big "thumbs up" from God.

Hey kids, (god fearing people), realize your getting your "thumbs up" from another human (priest, rabbi, etc.) who is getting your donations (money) to tell you just that.

If god's all love, what's there to fear? If god's all respect, why don't you? If god's all knowledge, what's there to know? If god's all understanding, why can't you? (Just try!)

Maybe it's easier to follow a widely accepted entity rather than doing the hard work necessary to find your own answer to the spiritual questions most of us ask. To stand up for yourself takes a great deal of self-respect.

If you will not respect something then I feel you shouldn't have it. If you don't respect school, you shouldn't go. If you don't respect your partner, you shouldn't have one. If you don't respect your life or others lives, then maybe you should die. (And so on...)

A tiger does not respect our society, so we don't let them live in ours. (More later.)

It's not that people can't realize my emotional capability, but rather it's a matter of acceptance. To allow me as a man to have depth emotionally would be too much work or demand too much effort to understand my complexities. (Why have girls always left me?) My feelings are not wrong but I need to shut them down or so society tells me. I need to fit in, walk in the same direction and at the same speed as everyone else.

No wonder people sometimes explode on the inside. They can't fight their individuality expression anymore, so they strike out in anger. Anger, because anger is the emotional straw that broke the individual's back. Yet we as a people scratch our heads in wonder as another human breaks down and explodes (implodes?) under the stress `n` strain we as a people are born into. (Under?)

A race we have no choice but to run. If you don't finish a leader then society does not look upon you favorably. As if it's because you didn't try, when in fact the exact opposite is probably true. If everyone wasn't against everyone else there would be a lot more winners in the Rat Race. There's only so many slices of pie and some are so selfishly scared they will stockpile the seeds to grow the wheat to make the crust of the pie so you may never really taste any. (Let alone have a slice!)

The longer we as a people chase after the "pie-in-the-sky" hallucination, we remain slaves to those who eat the pie.

As long as we continue to follow the game plan (which is falling apart) we will continue to fall apart as a peoplehood. Peoplehood is not possible under commercialism, until it becomes the slaves against the masters. (Time will tell.)

We as a people are giving the government the reins more `n` more everyday. Upon research, I've found countless times the need for government to be:

Increasing the people's liberties.

Thomas Jefferson was not a stupid man and neither am I. He (T.J.) would say that's not happening today and neither would I.

You no longer answer to mom `n` dad, now you answer to "the man". (Unless you are one!) Some (police people), are the biggest criminals of all.

(Relax officers... I said "some".)

Although, the whole barrel is ruined by a couple well placed rotten ones.

(Their rotten ones have guns too.)

Jail.
* * *

As I sat in my cell, at Santa Barbara Co. California State Correctional Facility, I thought upon my options when I would be released. I had been in contact with a few different ladies across these United States of ours, and I was seeing this restaurant owners daughter named Sharyn.

By my release date I had accrued 200 hrs. of community service I needed to perform along with $2,000 dollars in fines which I could not pay. (I had the capability of a school age child, I could not hold a job and dad wasn't buying.) I thought about the lessons I was learning while incarcerated (jail is not nice, and doesn't teach nice either...), and I felt that I had paid enough for being caught at what it was I needed to do to survive. I couldn't make money, but I could drink and steal. (Which was a survival reality I needed to change.)

Jail allowed me the time I needed alone necessary to make an introspective journey which allowed me to correct the personality defects I had been acquiring since the coma.

I cannot hide behind the curtain of a high salary job, with which to protect me from the harsh realities of life within a culture divided by classes competing for control. Greed is an expression that can be associated with control, on both the individualistic or grand scale. When we follow after the money god, we are ignoring the reason for living in an animal body. (Which is not to work in competition always...but to strive to assist your fellow workmates while being in competition with yourself.)

Frustration!
* * *

To do better, to learn more than you knew the day before should be the only objective of any (real) person. To be superior against others does not make you better... you are who you are regardless of your superiority (real or imagined). On the whole, I believe we as a people know this. Only we go home from the commercial world where the underlying message is... there is not enough for everybody to be able to survive. The Information box (t.v.) says that loud 'n' clear everyday in so many obvious and subliminal ways.

Keeping up with the Joneses' is understandable. But trying to keep up with fantasy land (t.v.) for most of us is impossible. Which creates whole lives of frustration, which is borne of a social goal always left incomplete. So, my answer was to leave California behind. Because Cali. is a breeding ground for deep running frustration. (Not to mention police harassment.)

Although, I had a dream of what should be awaiting me as I exited my home (of sorts) for the last six months. Sharyn would be waiting in the parking lot... leaning against her Sirocco... dressed all in black with a black hat covering her eye... and a cigarette hanging limply from her mouth... waiting for me to light it... and enjoy. She was, and I did. (Although...)

All things had changed, I guess I expected nothing less. She's young, and it was foolish of me to expect otherwise. When you're eighteen and your friend leaves for six months things will become very different... and they did.

We spent a couple more nights together, but moreover... "it" was over. (no loss) And, I did need to get things started for my move anyway. (all gain) Things had become very different, and there's no reason for me to remain in the commercial kingdom that is California.

My father put me up in a hotel while I arranged my life so as to leave without too much stress 'n' strain. There was this night auditor at the hotel I chose who had the most beautiful eyes, and I told her so. She always wore a sweatshirt and baggy jeans but there was something under them I needed to see.

I assume she felt the same. Because on what was to be my last night there...

Motel goddess?
* * *

She (don't recall/name thing) could hear my sled (Harley) as I returned from a midnight A.A meeting... (yes, I was sober). She waved me over to the window, but as of yet I knew not why. The motel goddess looked changed from the shoulders up, but that was just the start. She wore a dress tonight, and told me it was just for me. (I hoped the heels were too!) I was not wrong. So I invited her up to my room. She giggled, and I smiled... not only on the inside.

Afterwards, she told me of her unhappy marriage... there's nothing but trouble in infidelity, huh? And I started to cry on the inside. Well, the grass is always greener on the other side. (bye - bye)

My mom?
* * *

Besides, there was this girl somewhere I needed to find. (Waiting for me?) Maybe her name was Fran. But she lived in Denver, and that's a long way away. But all I knew is that I had to find out, so I had a destination at the end of my slide (interstate ride/drive). What I knew of Fran was nice, and I'm sure it'll be a fun ride. Fran 'n' I had met on one of her trips out to Cali. She was a nice girl, and I wasn't nice... but I was perfect. Fran said she would "put me up" for awhile, and I knew she could. We had met at an A.A. dance a week before I went to jail. I drove my Sportster then, and she rode on the back.

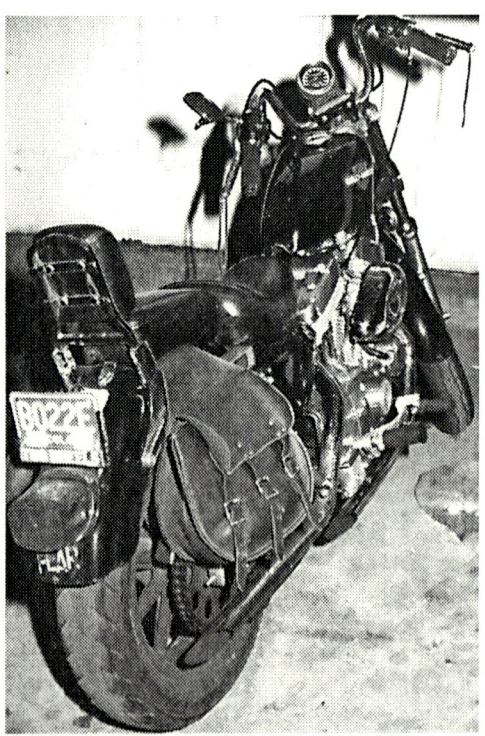

We drove down to Santa Barbara and spent the days together, we spent the nights together also. She was quite a woman, and she had (like all the others) the potential of being "the girl" of which I've always dreamed... (but only seen once in a very deep sleep.)

Every new person or girlfriend (especially the girls) are in the right place, at the right time and in the right way too. Because I never move down the ladder (unless I need to). Each lover is more correct than the last. Fran was now the perfect girl for me, she had everything I needed and was prepared to provide.

My father was against me leaving my legal responsibilities behind, but I did not have his where-with-all to satisfy my need. He doesn't look at reality anymore. Dad had caught his money god (lucky boy) and was able to easily stomach the amount he had to "sell out". I had a head injury that everyone, especially my dad, tried to disallow. There were financial responsibilities I'd never be able to satisfy on my limited income ($ 0.00).

My situation was like a person who does not even make enough to pay their taxes - let alone living expenses.

See, life is expensive in paradise and I couldn't even hold a 10 hr. a week job for minimum wage. Everyone said life will get better, but all I could see was my life going down the tubes because I didn't have enough money to afford it. And the system (which I couldn't afford) didn't want me anymore. So, I fled California, but California was not done with me...

It was raining hard the day I went through the hills.

I was on my way out of the state, and as I came out of a set of turns I lost control of my bike. My rear wheel began to slide out on it's own (I hit an oil spill), and I knew that I was gonna kiss the pavement soon. My fear was not of the asphalt, but of the truck coming right at me on the other side of this curvy two lane highway.

As the gearshift touched the ground I instinctively pushed the bike away from me, but at 50mph the bike `n` I were gonna be going in the same general direction, and we did. Right across the highway in front of the 18 wheeler (he wasn't that close) and off the other side of the road.

Ride!
* * *

I didn't see death coming, but I did breath hard. (I needed a drink.) Before I could do anything else, I needed help.

My leg needed attention, my motorcycle needed more than that. But... I guess if I can't ride, I can walk. Or, I can accept a ride from a total stranger who could call a tow truck on his car phone for my machine. (lucky me)

He took me to the cheap hotel in town which would save me money to spend on chemicals with which to settle my brain. (nice guy) The street where the cheap motels are is often the street where drugs are sold (or very nearby). I spent everything I could on rock (big mistake), and I was ripped off for everything else (bigger one). I stepped right into a situation where I could be mugged. (Which was the biggest of all!)

My escape from California needed help, so I called my dad. He could have wired me money but he needed to drive down so he could see me (laugh in my face) in person. He didn't believe in the effects of a head injury/coma. (But he did "loan" me the $.) The night I spent scared after my accident/mugging was sobering, and I safely made it to Las Vegas on the repaired bike.

It was a beautiful ride on a beautiful bike on a beautiful day. I was out of California, and that's a reason to celebrate in itself.

I may not be able to communicate this so anyone could understand it, you may have to have lived there (Cali) to fully understand...

California on the whole (not all) is a state driven by commercialism, from the corporations down to the individual. It's not who you are, but... what you drive - own - do for a living - how much money you make - what your name is - and what you can do for me - sort of scary social situation.

I saw it from both sides and I wasn't happy with either.

I guess it was freedom. I felt free. I was in Vegas.

Sin City (and I didn't sin). No drinking - no nothing (at all). (How unlike me.) I spent time with mom `n` Jerry both and they (mom mostly) told me of how wrong I was with what I was doing and how I was ruining my life. All the while I knew I could never explain how right all this felt. Surely she (mom) had done something "crazy" (or so other people thought) and would never change a thing because of how her "other people" felt, right? (Apparently not.)

Maybe Mom never had a dream to follow. So how could she possibly understand? She couldn't, so I didn't waste my breath. Maybe that's why she couldn't understand individuality - because she had none, or at least... no dream she had beaten down by the crush of societal peer pressure or be controlled by conformity to "social norms". Maybe she sold her soul to "fit in" and now it's impossible for it to return. (Maybe she felt it too much trouble to be unique.)

one-of-us

Respectable?
* * *

My stay wasn't long in Nevada, and I drove into Utah with-out a circumstance. I was in Red Rock Country when I realized I should keep my mind off the beauty of the terrain and watch my speed as I came off the mountain. (Or somebody else might!)

Someone else did.

When he first hit the lights I was maybe doing 90, I slowed down quickly and pulled over. "Do you know how fast... " he said.
"No, but I was **really** movin'... wasn't I?"
He laughed, and said, "No seat belt either, I presume."
I laughed. More chit-chat, warning ticket (in effect), and I was on my way into Colorado. (If you should read this, officer, sir... "Hello, and thank you!")
Colorado, Rocky Mountains. Boulder, where dreams are made. And Denver, where those dreams are smashed (but I didn't know that yet). I was welcomed to Denver with open arms from a girl I had seen/met over seven months ago. (Fran) I saw ulterior motives from the beginning. Her dad was the head sheriff, and I the most proverbial ("look who I'm dating dad!") bad boy.
I was just an accessory or trophy if you will. Things were not gonna last, but we did have fun.
She tried to change me into someone respectable, and I needed a good girl to corrupt. I wouldn't change and she was as corrupt as she could be and still live a life of A.A.
I needed more and so did she, but we needed it from other people.

J. Elliott Goldwyn

My new christian college student good girl type lived two doors down the hall from Fran. Fran didn't like that, but I'm not able to choose from where she came.

Rachel
* * *

Rachel was beautiful. Young curvy lady who hid behind clothes rather than them flattering her gorgeous body. I tried to bring out what I could from her, and she followed suit. She made me proud and proudness turned eventually to disappointment. Rachel was young and eager to learn what she needed to do to get what she wanted. In getting "it"... she lost me.

All this time I was going to what was turning out to be "my-restaurant", The Pegasus. On 13th Ave. on Capitol Hill in Denver. Everyone went there, so Fran took me to be the bad boy she was conforming. I went with Rachel also. Fun people worked there, and Steve (the manager) hated me... it couldn't be more perfect. 13th Ave. was the alternative street in town - music stores - clothing stores - bars - and people - and I lived just down the street.

Amy - Hope - Lori - Ami - Rachel - Fran - all beautiful, but I was the bad boy for them all. All my life it seemed to be a love\hate thing, but love\hate is better than no love at all. Each in her own way offered me a family to adopt, but the families wouldn't even take me in for dinner. I was different but I wasn't bad, or was I? Am I not what the constitution says is a free man? Able to follow his heart without opposition? Yes, I am.

Am I not what everything on television tells you is wrong with this society... individuality? Yes I am, guilty as charged... on both counts.

J. Elliott Goldwyn

Guilty?
* * *

Am I destined to live a life of condemnation? It seems that way. What it was I forgot about my life before the accident, was refreshed and revisited by both my parents. I'd never forget my mistakes. If it wasn't my parents it was "the man", "he" never forgets.

I had karma I needed to answer up to, or so they both said. I had spent time in death for my karma, didn't they understand? No they didn't, and mom `n` dad or the government didn't want to.

My hell was mine, all of it, I owned every last drop of it. (And it was never boring.) The Pegasus (13th's Ave. bar and grill) became my playground. So many people to meet and play with. My favorite waitress was a li'l girl named Debra. (My favorite because she hated me...I think maybe she's gay.) Every time I came in I'd play like I didn't know her name. She got angry, but she remembered me.

One day about three months after I moved on to The Hill... (Capitol Hill), I asked Deb if she would let me find out what the information was she had deep in her eyes (pick-up line, but the truth... which comes later) by having dinner or going to see a movie or whatever. That's when she told me directly about being a dyke and indirectly about how she hated men like me. (Oh good - another challenge!) Girls had been too easy anyway. (Girls hadn't really been too easy - I was.) Deb was gonna take time, and I had more time than money.

Menage a trois!
* * *

There were other people to entertain me, and for me to impress. On a night soon after that when I walked out of another bar there were these two girls walking toward me from down the street... whistling a song.

I'm not sure if it was my bike, or me, or both... which caused them to say "hello". So I took both Katrinka and Ally home. I thought that a threesome would have happened when I was in a band, but no. It happened now.

Oh well... I never dreamed that I could satisfy two at once, and I didn't. At least not at the same time like in the pornos, but I did try - it was just too fun, too nice, too perfect and over too fast. (Go figure) I was not in charge. I didn't need to be. In the moment after the first or second kiss, Ally had taken control. She undressed us (Kat 'n' I) by command, it was nice to lay down the reins for the night and morning also (the dark had become the light). Although, preferably... I should have been with the girls singularly before both together. Although that's just what I want. I wouldn't change one single moment because if it wasn't supposed to happen that way - it wouldn't have. (Goddess bless.) And besides, I was not supposed to be the "giver", it was mine to "receive".

(Pan blessed me also!)

Somewhere in that time period I was living with Amy. But I'm positive it don't matter anyway. Amy, although, had a very scaring role in my life, let me explain:

Amy `n` I were living together on Bayaud St. in an apartment that was a performing arts theater in it's self. I lived there awhile with Rachel (good li'l christian girl) but that was no more.

A man by the name of Richard (hey Ricky-boy!) of "soon to be fame and fortune" (or so he always thought) lived across the hall of this two floor building with four apartments total.

Rick loved Amy. Rick loved Rachel. Rick loved Fran. Rick loved every girl he saw me with (everybody did). I may be a very unique one, but I'm drawn to beautiful women (in one way or the other) and I guess by their response I don't smell all that bad. Rick `n` Fran loved each other for a night or two but that's a story only they can tell.

Amy an I lived `n` fucked together sometimes good, sometimes great. Looking back I feel some things should not have happened while others ("our end") should have come sooner. Although, we did have some fun together. She was a "working girl" and could not turn off her "on the make" attitude while we were together.

(Which was both good and bad.)

I guess that's where it all began and where it all ended. Amy drew me in with her eyes - tight li'l frame and her legs -shoes - lingerie - ability or "D." - all the above. She lost me in about the same way on two different occasions. I came home one night to find her and some boy in my apartment. (My place because we had no agreement, and I paid the rent). I asked him to leave and yell turned to push, push turned to mace. I didn't get hit in the eyes so I grabbed a bat and went after him. I was temporarily disabled and I lost him on the street.

I know it didn't matter anyway, if I caught or naught... because that was a temporary pain (mace in face) and

I knew he wasn't a break-in so I should not go to jail for hurting him.

(The cops already hated me.)

Amy had to answer some questions, and I certainly was not asking all of them. The answers didn't matter, nothing does to Amy.

Amy `n` I went dancing one night at a club (Rock Island) in Denver and two things happened while we were there on this night.

1) Amy was working the room in high heels. (lack of respect)

2) Some bar employee (a girl) was giving out coupons for free Jagermeister shots and she gave me ten, or so.

The result was a firecracker with a lit fuse.

(I exploded)

Nothing mattered and I wanted to leave, so, I left.

Amy came down the steps after me and I should have paid her "no mind", but I could not. She wanted a ride home. And I said, "get on." Off we went... like a shot. Into a curb. We went to the hospital together... yet separately.

The hospital stitched up my eye, and I walked back to my motorcycle and begged her to forgive me. (I'd swear she didn't want Amy on her, so she threw Amy off in the best way she could as fast as she could.) Motorcycles are ladies too, but my Harley was my mistress, my lover and my whore bought `n` paid for.

I had insulted her (Sarah, the name I gave to my sled), but I believe she forgave me only because of all the memories we had to live together in the future (and she had shown herself to be a dedicated trooper/warrior).

My baby had bent handlebars and a scratch or two but that was about all the damage she sustained. I straightened the bars but left the scars on her. Scars are memories, and how could I take her memories from her?

A quote:

"The only thing I have is memories - the only thing we can be sure of. Anyone who tries to rob me of my memories attacks me in a very real way. Everything is memory and aesthetics. Those are the only things that matter."

(Anton LaVey)

Amy `n` I were launched at about 35mph after she (my baby Sarah) hit the curb. But Sarah was made of steel of American descent. Sarah suffered less than the two humans.

I'm not sure what happened to Amy. She moved out of course and stayed with my neighbor John who owned Polly the pig. (miniature potbelly) I'm sure John-boy became bored with her (Amy) after awhile because that's how long she stayed. He was a methodical man, and John-boy loved the arts. I liked him - he was wise, and John lived in art whenever he could. He would reenact Civil War battles that were very colorful, very real, very respectful and very artistic (in my opinion).

No one liked her (Amy), not even Deb at the Pegasus... "She's a whore", were Deb's words. (end of story) Things were not working out where I was living, and I became bored there and with the people. I didn't know Deb lived around the corner with her lover, but when they broke up somehow I knew. (Another one of my feelings.)

Entertainment full tilt!
* * *

Deb had been single awhile so I asked her out, she replied with a hearty, "I'm a Dyke". (Wow, I was right... but I better think fast or this might be more work than it's worth)

Although what I said or how I asked was, "you know there is something in your eyes", she knew that, "and I would like to find out what it is and learn." But now I sorta knew. She had laid it on the line (with a body that could fuck me into next week). Oh well, ya can't lay them all... overnight. (Might take two.) There was a bond, undeniable yet unspeakable.

I needed to move from where I lived because of my boredom, and I owed the landlord a few more dollars than I had. I'd been to the owner's house (to smoke and buy drugs) on several various occasions and knew they wouldn't suffer, but I was going hungry. (So I did my best interpretation of Robin Hood.)

I lived away from Capitol Hill to begin with (where all the daily "good" eventful stuff happened), so I moved there. I found a great apartment on Pearl St. in between 10th and 11th. I was definitely going to be entertained there.

As my friend Wes and I unloaded his truck with my belongings I noticed one house two doors down was doing lots of "business". (I'm not stupid.) The look of the "customers" patronizing something from the house's inhabitants told me of it's illegality.

I guess it was our shaved heads which incited one (customer-type) gentlemen to put a gun in my face and ask, "Whatcha lookin' at?" "I don't know yet," was Wes's reply.

(I was right... entertainment full tilt!)

Problem solved?

* * *

It was while I lived there that I met a girl who lived nearby who wanted to learn of magick. She became important, she was just the girl I needed. I owed a lot of money to the courts and my freedom was threatened daily, so I worked ritualistically... sexually and perfectly. I'm not in charge of how the problem gets solved, but it does.

Afterwards I jumped on my bike, she left to go to her "sugar daddy." I went on my way, around the corner and down the street.

The lights came on... slowing me to the curb and of course the cuffs were on in minutes. I had this feeling I was going to pay my debt to society behind their bars. I was sitting in my cell from 11:30ish p.m. to 12:00 midnight. Then I fell asleep.

I awakened at 5:30ish and was shuffled off to see the judge. I was the first man in the courtroom, so I felt I was gonna be first to stand before him. (I was wrong.)

I watched as the court room went through each and every suspected criminal. Losing confidence all the while and certain the old man's gonna be angry by the end of his list. He'll probably throw the book... and my name was called when I was the only target left in the room for his anger to "strike out" at. I felt doomed, and I swallowed hard and concentrated on the work I had completed only hours ago (with that young lady who's name I cannot recall).

"Well, Mr. Goldwyn... case #1104253, it says here you owe the court $758.00. How would you like to take care of this...Mr. Goldwyn?"

"Your honor, I have $22.53 on the books (in my pocket when I was arrested), and I'd like to put that towards the money I owe and serve off the rest at $50.00 a day in jail, if I could, sir."

He replied, "Okay Mr. Goldwyn, case #1104253, that's $22.53 off your total and the rest... (This is when I became worried.) ... the rest is... time served. You'll be out in 2hrs, give or take... after paperwork red tape." (Magick has a way with moving red tape.)

"I thank you, sir", was all I could say. $700 (approx.) in less than 12 hrs... not bad. The money I earned went right into the hands it should have. The circle was now complete.

(Goddess bless.)

I received what I had worked for. There are many examples of just that so far in this story, and I hope you're paying attention. Even the times of hardship (especially then!) or incarceration (is there any doubt?), I got not only what I had asked for - crime/time equation - but also the time alone with introspection one. I began to see how I needed direction to follow. Up until this time it was my brain that had taken control, and I needed to return control to my heart.

Magick, which had at one time relieved my desire to drink can only remain effective if I am consistent.

The struggle between the opposites (brain vs. soul) doesn't need to be, but it's my conscience which often times takes the back seat... only to suffer along for the ride. As with most people, if the brain\soul conscience control competition goes unchecked it's my brain that assumes the monarchy.

Achieve esteem!
* * *

I only saw the "no-name girl" once again, we talked about how it all worked for the both of us. Seems her man offered her a condo and gave her a Volvo, and we both gave thanks. I hope she is well... to this day I do.

I noticed I was drinking more and doing more coke than anyone should, when people really started to bombard me with requests for my time and attention. I am a giving/receiving man, so I gave. I was going to regardless of the possible benefits.

During one of my nightly excursions I was introduced to an interesting lady named Lori. She had a power all her own. I'm not sure she ever gave up even a little of that "guarded Lori" she kept hidden from most. It was Lori who drew me in, she had a friend of mine (sort of) bring me to her. She was a frightened girl, and I slept two nights just lying next to her before any real intimacy occurred. There was very little of that intimacy, but it did happen...

This is where I need to explain my needs as a human:

My desire to achieve esteem through intimate expression was not only real, but valid and strong. My need for closeness may be borne from many different sources, but where it came from is less important than the honesty involved. I never ever in my life hid behind the shroud of distance on the personality communication level with any lover in my life, especially with Lori.

Lori had a need to hint at and promise satisfaction of various sexual enterprises which began, admittedly, with my fantasy. I wanted her tight li'l back door. This, along with other requests are variable to this extent, any relationship is a two way street, if one says "no" then no is the law of the land. (My body my rules... her body has hers.) She didn't say no, she bought the K.Y. That was as far as that went.

In that week (of coke `n` women), my friend Ally brought over her friend Ami. Ami was bountiful. Her position was assured, but Ami asked anyway. We were at it in hours, and the train didn't even slow. I don't believe I introduced her to cocaine, although she says I did. She enjoyed it far too much for a beginner... Ami was a pro.

She even said, "Ahhh", when I pushed the needle in. (Can be taken either way.) I not only had my anal fantasy fulfilled, but new ones... which I'm not sure I had the time to enjoy the way I should. Before complete realization could occur I had become her protector in her prostitution.

She was sleeping with men to get us the drug she wanted. That's what broke Ami `n` I up - coke. We both watched as the "we" that was, become an "I"-sore. We didn't even separate correctly, but there are many splits that aren't quite right. Don't get me wrong, the split was right, it's just the way it came about. She was dragging me down, and I wanted out.

J. Elliott Goldwyn

Sabrina #'s 1&2
* * *

I was banking at a local branch of some larger establishment, a place where I was able to satisfy my need (desire?) to give my money to some sexy teller-type. I went to that bank often to see my very favorite teller of the day, Sabrina. She always worked a half day at the drive-up. Lucky me, she got to see me on my Harley the first time we locked eyes, and I knew she was soon mine. (for the night) Sabrina worked part-time at the bank, and the rest of the time at a club (I could never get into) and in a bathing suit covered with mud. I'm sure any gentleman with the correct amount of money could have chosen from any number of fluids for her to play in. She was certainly a plaything.

In the back of my mind was an unfinished bond with a dyke supreme who served me, and all the girls I was with.... coffee. Even though there was disgust at my exhibition (parading) of the daily/nightly/weekly women in front of her. I spent a little time wondering if there was any of the butt I brought in which Deb found attractive enough to go home and think about while touching herself. And if that was true, did she think of me also... of what me and whoever would be doing when I took them down the street and into my home. (my web).

The funny part is that I often thought of Deb, maybe love denial, maybe... self-imposed of course. I guess the challenge of it all drew me in, and Deb's eyes had their own voice, and to me they were screaming. She had softened into inviting me to attend a gay bash of her's...

I accepted her invite, only to not show because of my need to speak "one on one" first (and a small fear of straight bashing).

I knew one other "gay" woman. She was a witch supreme, only I could see she had spread herself thin (life has that effect). Her name was Sabrina (Sabrina #2). Although, when that name vibrates inside my ear, I dream of her (it can't be helped). Sabrina was an exquisite individual vision of a woman, maybe she stood 5'4" with a light inside which I can still see in my mind's eye.

On the night she allowed us to practice together, is what my memory of sexual equality is of.

Music was made by our own sounds mixed together, as instruments mixed with a movement creates an orchestra all it's own.

Although, just a couple days later I was in another accident on the motorcycle with Hope (another girl) riding on the back, that was to bring me money... even though I wasn't aware of my need (in the future) to get out of the state. The police were getting angry with me. It seems as though I "shut-down" two crack houses just doors away from where I lived.

(Which I admit was no easy task.)

I lived there, I was not gonna put up with the insanity that goes along with crack cocaine in my neighborhood. I had guns pointed at me, knives pulled, but I must be blessed because the only thing that ever came of such an assault was a torn shirt.

(I liked that shirt damnit!)

So there were people on both sides of the law not happy with my behaviors, but I needed to survive in this world that "is"... not a fantasy where there is justice to keep the common man safe.

Hope!
* * *

There are people out there who could have earned a couple of rocks (cocaine) by killing me, and cops out there who gladly would have bought the bullet that left their gun and entered and ended my life. The cop wouldn't get a couple of rocks, he would get more (but that's a 'buy the cop' reality I don't know). Maybe a two week suspension with pay, which is a paid vacation. It's a no win situation, so what's a guy to do?

Buy a gun, simple enough. If no one listens - speak louder. I got arrested one hour later, maybe I'm not supposed to own a gun (right now). I had more important things to worry about. I'd gotten a few thousand from the insurance co. the other driver in the accident I was in with Hope happened to have (yea!), the wreck was all his fault. (Double yea!)

It all went down this way:

I was riding across Colfax Blvd. (in Denver) headed toward home with Hope after we went to the employment department in search of a job. I had the green and started across... when in the last instant before leaving the intersection another motorcycle (a fuckin' Honda) ran the red and rode his huge "Gold Wing" into a direct broadside with us. His front tire slammed into my engine casing at 35mph (approx.) crushing my foot between his bike `n` mine.

My motorcycle (and Hope `n` I) were lifted into the air and thrown about two lanes of traffic over and came down on her side pinning Hope's leg under the exhaust pipe. My whole steel toe on my right boot was bent down across my foot to what looked like I'd have no right toes left.

That... and the pain I felt didn't matter, Hope was my #1 responsibility.

As people stared at Hope while she was screaming, I jumped to my feet and picked up the motorcycle like it was made from balsa wood... then fell to the ground screaming too.

Big toe?
* * *

My foot was not well, but that's me and I always heal so my worries were not on me. Hope was paramount, and I breathed easier when she told me of her being shaken but not beaten. Off to Denver General Hospital (the gun and knife club) to repair my wounds. They cut off my boot and gave me a Codeine #4, (yeah, it hurts like a headache... assholes!) but they couldn't do any more till they saw the x-ray. When the tech. came back with the film there were five or six doctors with him - shaking their heads, frowning, talking, more shaking, then they all pulled apart so I could see the picture of my foot.

All looked fine, except for my big toe. The second bone looked changed, like an ice cube in a plastic bag crushed with a sledge hammer. At that moment a nurse with a needle came into view, she looked like Angie coming at me with the pre-sex syringe filled up. All I could muster was to pull up my sleeve. Before I went to doctor administered drug heaven, someone asked if they could amputate. I said, "What!"

"Me `n` big toe have gotten kind of used to each other, dude." I woke up with my big toe attached and in effect the money was already on it's way. Lori `n` I bought plane tickets to Mexico, to try again. I had fun in Puerto Vallarta and Lori did too... I'm sure. Only we didn't have the best time together.

Mexico
* * *

While at a fashion show (in P.V.), I "cat called" this one spanish girl a little more than I should (always the case - death by extremes). I slept alone that evening. Although we "made up" we really did nothing of the kind. I believe Lori gave me many memories, I had seen her work for the Denver Post (photography) and even helped her arrange products so they would look good on film for the advertisement she'd been hired for. They used the shot I arranged! Lori didn't ask me anymore.

I even danced in a club that she had managed at one time, Rock Island. Lori told me of how the club used to be different. A much better establishment in fact. Not hard to believe. The Rock had the feel of a "one time great place" that had begun to go square, and Lori could be a very powerful woman who could do very powerful things. The word "could" was/is the operative one. It seemed to me even though Lori had fire in her eyes burning very bright, she fought fanning any flame by feeding it fiction. She never used her own powerful imagery to the extent I would.

For flights of fancy very seldom occur without imagination to ignite and burn as the needed propulsion to carry the second dimension through our third and into the fourth or maybe fifth. It was like Lori has used her innate power incorrectly, in this life or another, and she's now destined to suffer alone in someone else's fantasy. The company she kept was "just so." I on the other hand, hope I left her with stories to tell her "thin upper crust" friends. My job was done with her, and she knew it too.

Lori lost!
* * *

Well, not quite. Lori was bringing me groceries one night that Ami (not Amy) had stopped by, chaos ensued. Ami was famous for laying it all out in the open (sort of), by the time she reached the bedroom, she had stripped to the typical stockings and heels (how shocking!), and I being the typical man, jumped head first full force through her proverbial "hoop". Ami brought powder to numb the brain and lube to ease the pain.

She wetted up her second hole after our first bang and said, "please, please... Elliott please!"

There was only one thing missing from this made in "Porno Heaven" dream cum true, and Lori walked in as if on cue. "What are you doing? I've been watching! What are you doing?" She screamed on, "I've had it with you!" Lori threw down what she was caring and stormed out the way she came in... alone and in a hurry.

Ami became excited after our confrontation with a jilted lover, and we continued on to the end. Debra didn't like Ami and voiced disapproval, "she's a whore too." I wonder to this day if that didn't turn Debra on... she the dyke, and me with all the women. Who was I? (The giver, when I receive.) I'm a mirror to the emotional effort enacted, no feeling shown means none returned. It's one thing to "do" another (no emotion), while the opposite is to "give" to the other person (full feeling).

If you "do" me, you'll be "done"... but if you "give" unto me than "ye shall receive".

one-of-us

Cocaine needle!
* * *

I broke off with Ami because I didn't want all the hell I'd surrounded myself with to be so constricting. I wasn't eating like I should (powder after effects) and soon Ami was gonna come home with a real killer load (HIV). I rode down to "Mary Lou's", which is a café where a good "trip" buddy of mine, Zoja, works. She always reminded me of my sister. No, never incest. She's just a close chum.

"M.L.'s café" (the restaurant) is where I met many people, sold many drugs, and made fast friends (tee-hee-hee). I met Hope there. She worked right next door at the import movie theater (The Mayan) and lived across town from me for a couple of weeks -then she moved into my building right upstairs. (Way before I had gone on my cocaine cruise.) She hated cocaine, everyone did. Slamming coke is close to sex in enjoyment in most ways, some better, most too costly. (Cocaine moment, bear with me...) It was to be my last, and I need to relive it:

Cocaine is a mistress, coke will always be there and always perform, if you have the money. I had the money and I was gonna have the best "drug sex" ever. It was hard to compete with a drug habit and I had decided to reach an extreme.

I loaded my point with twice as much coke as I'd ever done and asked Lori to hold my hand or beat on my heart if needed. She didn't want to but she agreed to (if needed). Lori was once a lifeguard... as I recall.

As I slid the needle in I saw lights on the walls (my imagination?) telling me, "no, Elliott please don't". So, I did it all.

A wave came over me. As I laid there on my bed my foot began to shake, then the other, then my legs `n` hands, arms... It was closing in on my heart and Lori began to cry. I had begun to leave my body and watch myself die. I looked down at that poor tired body shaking because of drug induction. And grew angry because of all this looked/seemed like a cheap made for T.V. "after school special" and I really didn't like the outcome of my role. So, back into "that" form we go and fight for life. I watched Lori's tears slow and a smile form on her lips after I mouthed the words, "That's it, I've taken it as far as it can go."

She saw my seriousness and enjoyed it also.

(To this day I'm still serious)

Back to "M.L.'s café": A day or so after Lori's definite "break up" with me. While sitting in the café, a friend of a friend introduced me to Lucretia Madden. A dear woman, who through the ways `n` means at her command (very witchy woman), convinced me that there was "no other" for me for a week or so. Tia `n` myself were working on an intimate friendship and going somewhere with it when something inexplicable happened.

I was with a group of friends (4 or 5 girls) at the Pegasus, for coffee and cigarettes afterwards, when it struck me to ask Debra out on a date again. I'm not sure where the courage came from.

(Maybe it was the mushrooms?!)

one-of-us

Lesbian love?
* * *

"I've just gotten a new car, see... (1963 T-Bird across the street through the window), and I was thinking I'd love to drive you home, say tonight?"

"Sorry, I rode my bike", she answered.

"Tomorrow night?"

"Sure", but you could tell she didn't really think I'd show.

So I did.

11:00 straight up, just like promised. Deb was shaken, she wasn't expecting me to "really" show up. Not only was I waiting, but definitely ready and willing.

Although, there were a couple of hoops I needed to jump through. Her best friend Kiersten approval was my first hoop. Tough nut that girl "K", but a few well placed words and Deb 'n' I were on our way downstairs (same building) to her place. She shaved my head (which is an intimate and spiritual experience for me), and we talked about stuff that we both found important and I became frightened. I had little to fear before Deb kissed me, once our lips touched it seemed, "all over".

I was in serious trouble. Many are lucky to find one bond in life in which to explore all the emotional avenues contained therein and I was blessed\cursed with two.

Their names were Lucretia* and Deb.

---

* Her nick-name is Tia.

I can gamble
* * *

Tia was "there", although immobile. Deb on the other hand would come with me if I decided to leave the police state of Denver, CO. So Deb `n` I moved into South Dakota. S.D., because I'd been there to visit a girl who'd come down to Colorado to meet me.

(I felt like something was awaiting me in the southern of the Dakota's) Dixie was brought down to thank me for the good pot and acid deals I'd given to her friend from S.D. a long time ago. Dixie was nice but unfortunately very misled. (I ended up spending the night in jail for that girl, but that comes later, or maybe not.)

When Deb `n` I drove into South Dakota we only had $50.00 left and we needed money for food, gas, and a room. She couldn't find a job that fast, but I could gamble.

So I won enough to put us up for a week or so, only Deb `n` I had other problems. When we fell in love I was Elliott, (I'll always be), and Elliott was in love with another. Tia had been enchanting. Something about her charmed me. The talismans, her own practice, her hips, her feet, her long blonde hair... or "F"- all the above and so much more.

Tia had a problem that Deb didn't (at least not yet). Tia would spend too much time in the day correcting me. She could have taught me so much if she would have led me down the path of knowledge by the nose or like most men, by some other phallic object. Although, what Tia did was drag me by the neck to go down "her" paths of knowledge, because Elliott's paths were all wrong. So I needed to conform.

(tic-tic-tia)

Love basis?
* * *

Control didn't come into play with Deb until we were settled into the A-Frame cabin we were renting in the Black Hills. Deb `n` I talked of my love of another woman at the same time as my love for Deb began to grow. Deb's a Leo and lesbian to the core. She was insecure, matched against another woman on "love basis" competitive expression, she only put up with my needs because I was "the man" she'd always dreamed of.

(If I had a nickel...)

I knew I was and problems ensued. There have been a great many "bonds" throughout my life, some longer, deeper or more meaningful than others. Still others I think are over... they've probably only just begun. Who's to say? (Time is.)

Time will tell, it always does. (In it's own time it will.)

I've had many experiences happen to me that I didn't enjoy at all, but I look back and see that I couldn't be where I am today without all the stuff (good or bad) that's happened throughout my "life of Elliott". (Living in Elliott's world - party on!) Don't get me wrong, I'm not only the image I show to the world. I've been many things in this life and I plan on being many more before my life is over.

Deb `n` I got jobs pretty fast in a close minded, male dominated, alcoholic breeding, mid-western gambling town of Deadwood in S.D.; me as a short order cook and Deb as my "hash slinger" to take to the tables to be enjoyed by the creepy clientele out gambling. Creeps because they only left pennies on the dollar for the tip, and daily Deb would come home crying.

Lesbian vengeance!
* * *

I'm not sure how it began, but it did. Debra had watched my many pursuits so she had seen my many nightly companions (at the Pegasus) and knew she would be biting off a piece of heterosexual expression. I never hid behind any curtain or veil, and I felt her slipping away because she began to see that I wanted "it" more than twice a week. She received none of the emotional food I received through intimacy with me, maybe she never did. Could it be there was only one need for men in her life, and Deb needed women to give her emotional input? Well... yes. (But again I'm rushing ahead.)

There were times I felt like Deb was returning my infidelity (Tia) to me with a Leo/lesbian vengeance. I was witnessing it everyday in every way.

We'd have sex but there was no inspiration to satisfy my needs to feel: respect, devotion, attraction, lust/love, belonging, closeness, blah, blah, blah.

There are men (and many women) who'd disagree with the way I achieve those human needs but they are not me, and never do I tell them how wrong they are. I respect all women. Women are the other half of the circle most of us men are trying to form in life. A circle so complete that in making it and experiencing it, the circle of two makes three (or more).

There are too many babies in the world, because (I feel) there are too many people who happen to give up looking for the perfect other half that may never come. They think that the magick circle comes from the baby, when really the baby comes from it.

Hi Nick! (But again I'm rushing.)

Slowly but surely, while women came out of the woodwork (the owner of the restaurant and all the girls from the bank) to give me the feelings Deb wasn't (acceptance, not sex). Deb began to make me feel insecure. My answer was to become more of a woman for the queen dyke. (I was still thin and looked pretty good in a short skirt `n` heels... or so she said.)

Deb was doing me and I was doing her. Our disagreements were one thing but when she first hit me I might as well have been the girl, for I could do nothing when my love (?) had struck me in the head.

I was crushed and control commenced it's constricting onslaught. There was nothing I wouldn't have done for her, only I kept "running dry" for her failure to fill my emotional gas tank. She was not giving, she was doing.

one-of-us

If you can!
* * *

In Deadwood there was this main street of cobblestones where all the businesses were, and on that street there were a great many tourist attractions. The bar where Wild Bill Hickock was shot dead by "Crooked Nose" Jack McCall back in 1876 if I recall. I have a crooked nose, so in 1876 there was a role being written for me to play in 1993 inside "Saloon #10".

I had grown tired of working like a dog in a kitchen at the "Gold St." so I talked with an actor in the city's western re-enactment performance troupe about qualifications.

You should have seen my face when they said, "follow us." We went downstairs below the "Oyster Bar", which was a dressing room for the "Marshal" and all the "Bad Men". Puppy, (Robert) the "Marshal", threw me some pants that went with a shirt and some cowboy boots. I dressed and looked good, and then someone handed me a gun. (Oh - I felt like a god!) The only rule was... the "Marshal" never dies. Okay, a god within limits. But a god of sorts none the less. You could see it in the eyes of the tourist's daughters and their moms too.

There were real mounted police on the street for law enforcement aesthetics and many kids would gather to look at them as they sat in all their glory protecting the street. What a huge joke... on a horse which proved to be unsafe at any faster than a walk on streets that were just cruelty to the animals they forced to walk on them. On cobble stones, a horse in metal shoes is like driving a nail into it's foot on every step. (How would that feel to you?)

Then down the street all of the "bad guys" and me... the leader... (I became fastest on the draw with a gun) came out

one-of-us

of a saloon yelling, fighting, shooting. All the tourists who were admiring the mounted police came running down the street to see action, robbery, death and me (the fast gun leader guy) get away with the gold and/or women. I was a born star and I had most of my "bad" cowboy abilities born into me. (Imagine that - born with knowledge!) Did I say fifteen years of fame? (I was wrong, it's almost been thirty.)

There was a provision for any man with no federal record to possess a concealed weapon on his person for a four dollar permit filing fee, only you needed to get that permit from the man himself. (The head sheriff.)

No problem. "The Troupe" (the acting group) was city sponsored, right? Wrong.

It seems "The Troupe" was a group of social outcasts and certainly not recognized or respected by the police and especially not by the head sheriff.

The sheriff looked at my application, shook his head and said, "No Way", and walked away. It seems I drew too fast and wore a mohawk. (Oh gosh, a cop killer for sure.) At most times our guns we wore on the street were real, only they had plugs in the barrels to protect the public from escape of anything from the them. The guns used shotgun primers hand loaded into 45 caliper shell casings and that was the only way we could work in and around the public to entertain them.

There is little to nothing for kids to do in a gaming town and I had a mission to play cops 'n' robbers to pass some of their dreary day, as mom 'n' dad threw the family money away on video (poker) games that gave little entertainment. (Poor kids.) The worse thing was watching the young girls wander around lost, (until I found them) and those girls had little to occupy their minds. So I had my work cut out for me (fancy that!), like a bond I needed to satisfy.

The bottle was calling me and my individual practice was calling me also. There was no intimacy with Deb, so when the need came for $500.00 to pay rent and bills, I could not work with a breathing blow up doll (Deb) in a ritualistic/sexual way.

Over our heads!
* * *

I had other things in mind, and I needed a girl who wanted to be with me.

(Desire full tilt.)

I explained this to Deb and in her own "dragging feet" way she gave me permission to do what I needed to in order to keep a roof over our heads.

A beautiful girl named Amy (yes... another one) came walking along in her Doc Martins and she knew I was next. I went home with her and she snuck me in after her mom 'n' dad had gone to bed. I slept well that night and dreamed of what would follow on the nights to come. The very next night she came home with me and told me she was ready/prepared with the low heels and stockings on her beautiful legs (shocking shocking shocking).

Begrudgingly, Deb retired upstairs, only to watch through the crack left by not fully closing the door. There was more feeling in her head (can be taken both ways), than I'd felt in months. It hurt Deb to watch me enjoying sex once again but the check($) was on it's way. It paid our rent and Deb pulled even further away.

Like Lori, Debra didn't like how things just came to me, but instead of coming along for the ride she turned colder. If she had desire in her heart for me, Deb could have "worked" with me. Unfortunately she did not. It had become winter... both outside and in her heart.

I got a job at "Deer Mountain Ski Area" just around the corner and down the dirt road from the cabin, which was to be a job like no other.

Tale of Two Blondes
* * *

It was not what you might believe, but rather a movie I was lucky enough to participate in while working with "The Troupe," which was the western re-enactment guys. From the way I understand it, it was a movie directed by some Reed, S.D. University directional genius , although I don't recall his name. I wish I could see it, so... if anyone could assist me in that becoming a reality I would greatly appreciate it.

Write me at: po box 614, Central Lake, MI 49622 if you could assist me with a place to go or a person to call... I'd thank you proper. Or, if you saw the movie, write and tell me what you thought of the entire movie that I played a VERY small role in... if you want. Good or bad, I'd like to hear.

I do have one picture sent to me by the man who played the bank teller that I robbed.. His name is Chuck Cavenaugh, or... "The Batman!" (I am sorry to have lost all your contact info Chuck, please feel free to contact me brother!) Anyway, I give the photo credit to him, and the movie was shot at "1880's Town" in South Dakota... sometime in 1992 as I recall. When I find out his name I'll give him the credit he deserves... and he does deserve credit. I started as an extra, but by the end it was me who did the dirty deed. (tee hee hee)

one-of-us

Hit no one!
* * *

No one should hit another... and not expect to be hit back in return. She didn't care, she was searching for a reason to leave me, so Deb hit me again in the parking lot of my ski lift job. What a scene, whether or not I slipped on the ice, the punch thrown by the body building/man hating queen (you know what) took me to the ground. Some guys I worked with watched with me as Debra stormed off down the hill to go to the cabin in my car. The guys dusted me off and took me inside for some drinks.

(Yeah, that'll make me feel better.)

I did feel a little more relaxed (drunk), when I got home. It was cold and I was not prepared for the night, seeing as I was dressed for the daytime in a heated ski lift hut. My anger returned when I found myself locked out from the inside. No matter how I cried out, I was not going to be let in. So, I put my shoulder to the door. And once inside she tried to hit me again, I exploded!

I hit Deb for every time she had hit me, one for one trade. Only thing she did not anticipate was my skill at physical survival expression. Her mistake. If I picked a fight with someone who stood eight inches taller than myself by hitting them until they hit back, how could I blame anyone but myself for the damage to come? (How could she?)

I suffered for a long time, feeling bad for hitting a woman, a woman like no other. Deb explored aspects of Elliott I knew existed but because of modesty felt frightened to show anyone else except for my reflection in the mirror.

After I was done, I realized I had given Deb the reason she needed and she traveled along her merry (gay) way. She went back to Denver, which left me alone in the hills.

one-of-us

Somehow (I know how) every woman whom I had ever met in South Dakota wanted to spend time with me, seeing as I was now single. So my schedule was now full but filled with hollow love. (Deb and I were not done.)

Deb `n` I talked on the phone (she was in Denver) both with hopes of a reconciliation / fertilization, but only after I told her of how bad I felt for what I had done. I also needed to hear her say about how she now realized that physical expression of anger with me, against me, is wrong and will not be tolerated anymore in any way. It was the most important thing to me on the contract she sent me in the mail to bring each of us back to being a "We". (But once again, I'm rushing.)

Every time Deb `n` I spoke there was someone over, or someone on her way to my place. My place because Deb lived there no longer. Although, nothing had changed, I could not redecorate. Deb `n` I were not finished. We were a perfect circle who should have never ever have come together, but we did and now we had to see it through to the end. (Which was as eminently frustrating as the ill-timed phone conversations.)

I received a phone call at 3:52 a.m. from Kari, the classy high heeled head teller at my bank telling me of her loneliness and desire to come over. Let me digress to tell you of our (Kari and me's) history...

Kari
* * *

When Kari flirted with me at the bank where she was employed I knew she had a man already, but we talked on her desire to own my car. (The Thunder Chicken!) Kari `n` I went for a drive which turned to kisses and more. But we were just playing with each other, until the early morning call...

I was awake when she called and more awake when she arrived. The first time worth remembering with a red head and more. That morning was the first time smoking crystal meth, and I found all I've heard about sex on speed was true. The sun came up as she went down... for the third time.

She became near `n` dear to my heart after she modeled pairs after pairs of her stockings and heels. (The goddess smiled!) As I was shook to the core, I returned what my humble worshiping male body could do. (Good thing I was prepared!) As we became closer I closed off my enjoyment of another bank teller who worked at another branch of the same bank as Kari. Kari won, she should have, she wasn't head teller for nothing.

Deb hated her because she wore all the toys I loved seeing a woman in, like a great work of art in an appropriate frame. (Most men understand, right? - And - I know all the women do!) It's just that Deb had used those buttons on me and she felt that after I was hooked she'd not have to give it up anymore. Deb was right. She didn't have to. There was a line of women waiting to invest the emotional food I wanted/needed to **never** give up.

one-of-us

Kari `n` I went on trips to Rapid City, looking for a stripper to share our bed with us. We went down for other reasons to Denver. So my old friends would see me and tell Deb who I was with and how happy I looked (I knew my friends would).

After six months of now living in Kari's place (I was a kept man and she the happy girl) I started speaking with Deb - she had awakened to the fact that after me there could be no other bond quite like ours. Even though she was dating Russell (the owner of a brew pub in Denver) she recognized that she needed me more than she realized before. (Or, he dumped her?)

We both made concessions of sorts, putting most of it in writing (the contract) and she visited South Dakota to see the truth in my eyes. She saw it, and she chose to show me lust.(It looks like Kari and I are over). I needed that and she really knew it now. She also showed me regret for hitting me and I showed regret also (for the ever having struck back - and - falling for Kari).

We were together again and a contract in which for me to trust for happiness in a family I never had. Deb wanted a child, and me to be the dad. (What the hell, I had a contract.) Where would we live? Not a question that I wanted to answer, so I gave up control and let Deb decide. (Portland, OR)

Deb told me of her having one ovary removed during surgery, so the chances for parenthood were limited. I said... "Give it a week!" (It wasn't my ego talking, I just had a feeling.)

I think she was pregnant before we reached PDX (Portland) but that was another one of my feelings. A child was right, and I knew it before it happened. Portland was the home of a school Deb wanted to attended to become a certified gourmet chef.

What she did not say was that PDX is the lesbian capital of the USA.

We got jobs right away at a catering company, and I got fired after the first day. They did not want me but they wanted Deb... and said so after firing me. Deb didn't want to work without me (at least not there).

We were speaking with our neighbor Geoff, a gay man, (and a thief... but that too comes later) about our employment problems when he suggested the restaurant "Old Wives Tales" as a place where they accept alternative life expressions. It was an establishment owned, operated and staffed by lesbians. It may be tough on me (my security would be affected by her going off to work in a place where her work mates would rather I was dead... and out of the picture all together) but I had a contract and a loving "wife" to help me with the many difficulties which may arise. (Boy was I wrong!) Soon after she started working there, I began to recognize/realize the emotional separation which was taking place. (And I had one of my feelings.) (Feelings suck!)

In another one of our many conversations with Geoff, she spoke on her being gay, which he already knew... (Birds of a feather?) When he asked how "the job" was going, I said, "terrible" because it was affecting me adversely.

"Great, I love it there", she said.

"I knew you would" was the reply he gave. Then he asked, "Why Elliott then?" This was the first time Deb admitted to it.

"There is only one reason for men, but it's women I go to for emotion," she said.

The truth had come out, and now I understood why I had become so stressed due to rejection.

Book 3: (Daddy?)

J. Elliott Goldwyn

A cry to heaven?
* * *

"Pink yes" (pregnancy achieved) and things became very different. Deb would go to pick up a present for me for X-mas, and I worried about her safety with our child inside. So I asked, "Where are you off to and when will you return?" Her work mate from O.W.T. (Old Wives Tales) answered for Deb.

"We're going to get drunk and we're not gonna come back."

I was hurt and once again tried the drowning of my sorrows only to find that sorrows are masters of the back stroke, and more. (Drunk/foolish me!) When I came home to an empty house (not a home any longer) I cried inside because there are people out there getting intimacy from the mother of my child who had refused intimacy with me. (Intimacy is not intercourse.)

I was asked to hold on for her to return from wherever her heart was at. So I held on for dear life to the fantasy/fallacy of family. But to return to that present buying night...

When she finally came home, I felt like she either wished I was dead, not home or fast asleep. Unfortunately none of those were true, and worse... I wanted to talk. The conversation turned heated and then physical. Deb hit me again, upside the head with the book "A Cry to Heaven", by Anne Rice that she bought me for X-mas. (symbolic?)

I started to cry and didn't want the South Dakota hell to be revisited, so I called the police. Deb spent two hours (or so) in jail until her gay friends bailed her out. I had been begging her to recognize and respect me and show me emotional exchange, but Deb's answer through expression was that she only had one need for men... and that deed was already done.

Lesbians in charge!
* * *

I missed Deb so much that I went down to her work one day to look at her through the window... big mistake. (The lesbians in charge would not allow me to come in when I dropped her off or picked her up...) (Why?) She was getting a long hug from one of the kitchen workers (another lesbian) and I had to watch (didn't really have to but...) as she gave another the intimacy I had been crying out for. Deb had become a breathing blow up doll again and that being the case, even ten times a day would not be able to sustain my emotional need. I cried inside and begged Deb not to deny me for so long that I'll no longer have any desire to be rejected again. So, that I won't even try anymore.

We moved very close to her delivery date and I was becoming a real hermit. Never going outside because I know about how things come to me and I was weeks away from a family.

("So just hold on a little longer.")

About the six month birthday of Nick, between Deb `n` I nothing had changed. I'm not sure if she had no desire for the "ole in `n` out" with me or if she didn't want to give me what I got from making love. Either way, I began to meet my own need for appreciation and respect from people I shot pool with next door to where I lived "EJ's"an entertainment bar. (Titty bar) If, I can't love my "wife" and worship her "pooty" any longer, then at least I can look. Deb's control of my self achieved orgasms had also gone out of control, she destroyed every magazine I owned. I grew tired of all this wasted time in effort and energy to deny me. I needed to be shown desire *not* denial.

Saint or sinner?
* * *

I, of course, was not being a saint or a sinner. I had not sacrificed the sanctity of our subsequent parenthood, but I did look for some form of connection from people who were willing to be a friend. I feel many relationships fail due to a disagreement on the division of the responsibilities to sustain the financial, emotional and mental aspects to ensure said relationship's success.

But that was not the case, we (Deb `n` I) had a written contract in which I thought I could place some trust. Deb's #1 thing she said she would do for me was, "Thrill me", because she "could and wanted to". She forgot the disclaimer, "until I get pregnant".

There were things which I felt (my feelings... again) that rendered me incapable to enjoy the rejection I received and the pressure of living with a lover (?) who may not "sleep around" (with men... but remember the men/one purpose thing), but is no longer carrying on a sharing loving relations with me. I felt the soldier, who just laid down his life (vasectomy) for a country who spoke of loyalty and respect for it's warrior (father) only to abandon him after the war was won (pregnancy achieved). "The country" (dream of family with Deb and son) up's and leaves the warrior to suffer the after effects of having been in a war... all alone. Deb, <u>you</u> are the traitor!

My loyalty was never in question but my gullibility was, and I fell hook, line and sinker. The never-ending dream of a family (mine) which would not turn their proverbial back on me because I needed to be me. Acceptance full tilt is what I need (we all do), but I had become the object of conditional love and left to shiver in the cold of my non-belonging.

I had no home and felt like the pet who was cute 'n' cared for, for awhile; now that there was something else, I was just an unwelcome responsibility. Not replaced, but removed completely.

I did not trade my attention for a son, I traded all emotional exchange for a "pink means yes" pregnancy test. If there was nothing left for me after a day of Nick I'd understand why everything slowed down, but I don't understand why everything stopped. I was still the same guy, maybe in need of acceptance more because of all the fears / concerns which came along with expecting parenthood, but it was not I who had changed. Someone else had been doing personality reformation and I had to suffer the subsequent relationship transformations which followed.

To endure is not in my wide range of god given talents, and it is not one I'd spend a lot of (wasted) time trying to increase my ability at. Deb knew that, I had said as much.

And here I was, left to make decisions which I'd really rather not. (My choice was to remain happy... or at least try.) I was allowing Deb to assume the role of a paddle, and I her target pinball.

(I will bang needlessly no longer.)

seems perennial
* * *

Deb 'n' I are arguing on whether or not I know my own needs and how to have them met. And because of this constant disagreement, I have needs which are being ignored. Since my desires are really inconsequential, am I being told by Debra that her desires are also inconsequential? I *need* answers, not more excuses.

I realize now that Deb has no sexual drive or attraction to me and you'll forgive me for finding it hard to believe that any intimate activity will return.

I hurt because I know Deb must be going through great emotional requirement at this time in her life and I realize that she is not having any of those essentials (emotional or not) met by me. She's not even asking. Although, I guess I was shown in the past that Debra does not go to men for those needs. Rather, she goes to women for emotional gratification. Because of my non-self-imposed inability to satisfy Deb's needs, in turn, my desires viciously go disregarded. It's not my fault that I have requirements which are satisfied inside an intimacy exchange. The feelings of being desired, respected, admired, attractiveness and the deep seated awareness of not being alone in this life were missing and missed dearly too.

If a person has needs which demand to be met by a specific person who calls themselves a partner, there should only have to be a mention of said partner's desires.

Lovers should be lovers, or they are nothing of the kind. Since Debra has no needs, or at least she doesn't ask that they be met by me, what am I to think? That I'm meeting all her desires, or she's having them met somewhere else by someone else?

one-of-us

My question is this: Why was it acceptable for Debra to meet my needs; whether or not those wants were mental, emotional, physical, or any combination to any degree before the pregnancy but during the pregnancy I'm to subject myself to nothing but denial of what could be life supporting... definitely love supporting requirements while I'm to continue giving to the emotional "well" of Debra?

The pain I feel is because even the best water producing wells go dry. When you've found out you only need four cups (or four minutes) of water to live but the well now gives none, what's a man to do? I feel like the spring (my only spring) is drying up. Debra, don't you ever fear that there may be four minutes in our future where you'll want from me something which takes my time and effort with special understanding, but I refuse your request? Not because I'm physically unable to meet your request, but rather because there is something else which I'd rather be doing. (Just like you are doing, Debbie?)

I cannot help myself from being Elliott. I will not stop being a human with a penis. (No sex change of mine for you Deb.) I have no intention of forgetting the fact that I <u>do</u> have needs, and those requirements must be met for "us" to survive. I know I've never hid behind the mask of a "no sex for me" person. For me to adopt a "no sex" attitude cannot happen, although Deb knew that years before we ever dated.

For as long as I remember, I've been a "love junkie". I'm not necessarily proud of my ability but I receive many emotional and mental benefits from intimacy and there are many ways to provide me with what it is I need to "grow" in a relationship. But the "well" had gone completely dry.

175

J. Elliott Goldwyn

Please remember, I'm talking about basic necessities, not covert fancy.

If I could, I would facilitate everything that I require. Unfortunately, since the organization of our "partnership", I'm unable to give myself what it is I feel will eliminate my 2nd. nature reckless despondency. (Deb threw away all my magazines.)

I often feel like there is something I've left undone or incomplete. I'm not speaking of that "moment" a person might feel as they're locking up their home before a big trip, but I do feel sometimes as though some ingredient has been left out of a recipe we're making and the whole thing is messed up.

All of my time and all of my effort has been wasted only because I've simply overlooked the most important ingredient. I do that often. I believe that I may get in my own way and often make things difficult on myself. (Which is a purely subjective reality!)

All alone?
* * *

I remember how my whole life was planned out for me with no mistakes to be made. But I had other plans for myself and "my" life. There have always been various things which I was a part of that did not fit into their scheme (parent's scheme) of life. I was not really given goals but I had them thrust upon me so I didn't have to make choices. That may be the way some people choose to live, but I was *not* born to follow.

There are many avenues of expression to enjoy in life and I'm saying nothing against any one of them. At least any one of them that does not harm someone else directly.

Although I do say,
"I will not be another Tom, Dick or Harry. (And/or Mary, Sue or Jane!) Now, that doesn't mean I avoid all things which are trendy but I would rather not do what everyone else is doing or tag along with the crowd. Crowds are ofttimes wrong. I don't always believe in the adage "Two heads are better than one." Because if there are two people (or two thousand million) who all think the same thought, that group of people are really *no* better than the one... all alone. There are, or could be as many different viewpoints as there are ideas, but that's __not__ how it is in the real world. In reality if you think your own thoughts you're labeled an outcast. It doesn't matter how differently you think. If you do believe in yourself, and your ideas, then there *is* something "wrong" with you. "You're different" or "you're bad." I think it's sad that "difference" is a four letter world in most of society, and I don't much care for the correlation between

different and bad. This may not be true for all, but I'm not all. And my ideas today are not just my own... anymore.

It's not just where you live, but today I find myself surrounded by others whom feel as I on many topics. Although, if I had big money I'd be the next 'incast.' For those of you who don't know what 'incast' means: The opposite of outcast.

Myself!
* * *

There is a very good reason why I choose to be myself. When I get up in the morning I need to be able to go into the bathroom look in the mirror and say, "I like that guy."

I *am* different, I am Elliott *not* Joe.

(I'm not Joe surfer, Joe punk, Joe skateboarder or Joe mama!)

I look different but that is another visual tool I use to keep closed minded, judgmental and hypocritical people at arms length. The further those controlling people are kept away, the more free I feel.

There are people though, who claim to know the "right way" for me to live. I will not waste my words or pages in my work to name all of those mostly hypocritical groups of conformists.

i.e. The police were founded to serve and protect. When "we" needed them they were there to look out for the common man or woman. Now, the police are watching the people. (Scary thought!) After all, the people are greedy and my opinion is that greed is the reason for much of the crime "we" experience. It is the reason for war. "We" know that but still we continue along the same avenues which will take us eventually to the same destination.

Singular hell. A home in the 'burbs, two cars, kids, dog, cat or all that and more. "All I need is 1,000 more dollars in the bank, and then I'll think about being happy." Hearing my dad say that made me crawl back into my shell. Need this, need that, greed, greed, greed. If I had it to do over again...

"Fuck the money daddy, spend that time with me!" But that's not how it was, not hardly.

Money is love and a show of love is to give lots o' money. Money will fix it, money can make all your problems go away. (Right?) (Pardon me while I sarcastically giggle.)

I knew, way back when, that there was another answer beyond the picture that was being painted for me. Love *is not* money and for that matter spirituality *is not* religion. The church was another way to separate the people (less than/better than) and keep the commercial wheel spinning. Buy, buy, and buy even more until you owe your whole life to their system. (Who are they?)

Keeping a person in debt is just another way of keeping a person (common man) a slave. I've heard it said that America is a free country, I don't believe that, and here's why:

1) A person (consumer) is born and given a number. (Like a holocaust victim.)

2a) That number is directly responsible for it's percentage of the national debt.

2b) When this person grows he or she becomes one of a faction (people group) who needs to be better than the other groups of people. (Sometimes even their own.) Or maybe a whole country of persons just across the border.

3) A percentage of said person's (consumer's) wage goes to the government (slave driver/national debt owner).

4) If that person's employment doesn't pay taxes, government makes it a crime. Sends the person (man, women or child) to jail, to (re-)train them to shut up (those "different" crazy ideas), get in line (conform), and buy - buy - buy which means pay more taxes.

5) When the slave dies, his or her family must pay whatever bills are left behind. (Seemingly endless circle.)

I must now insert a disclaimer:

I realize there is a number of others who are not infected with this wrong headed aesthetic of greed. (I *know* I'm *not* alone.) There are "baby boomers" and others like me who are seeking alternative methods of breaking the cycle. (Like writing a book or walking the line you talk, ya know?)

I don't wish to beat the horse until it's dust, so I'll let you prove me right by asking a question:

Do you get anxious (<u>even</u> <u>a</u> <u>little</u>) when a police car is right behind you and then turns on its red lights? No? Then you must be either a cop or a some reasonable facsimile thereof..

(Have I mentioned Us/Them yet?)

I'd be anxious, and it's not because of something I've done but rather because of who I am, what it is I am wearing, the music I listen to or how I wear my hair. I know that most police-people can legally put a bullet in my head and get a two week suspension with pay. To take my life all he or she needs to do is say I moved my hand too fast or looked threatening. (And maybe put a "Saturday night special," the pig might have for just such an occasion hidden in his or her waistband, into my lifeless hand?) This is NOT true with all policepeople, but it only takes one to spoil the bunch and sometimes that is so sad.

But that is true for every group of people... it's just that those wimps wear weapons.

Which brings me to a thought I had on bigotry or prejudice. Like many people I watch T.V. talk shows, (which one doesn't matter) and I saw a show on this style of dress called "Grunge". The show had some kids dressed in clothes made for (in my humble opinion) farmers. Nothing wrong there. (Right?)

Wrong. There was something *very* maladjusted. According to the policemen (no women) on the show, there <u>was</u> something wrong. These kids, even though they were wearing clothes any person could walk into a K-MART and buy (and cheaply too!) didn't matter to the officers.

As one policeman (L.A.'s finest) said, "Those kids look like criminals and should <u>expect</u> to be treated like such."

Wow! I remember the days when I looked different (oh, I still do), but I'm no criminal and don't think anyone (but a lawbreaker) should be treated that way. Disrespect from a man (or woman?) who carries a gun. (Scary thought!)

(Although, the police <u>need</u> criminals to ensure their jobs.) But It's also like saying, "If a woman dresses for a date in a sexy little black dress, since she looks like a "whore" she should <u>expect</u> to be treated like one!" See how that saying is a carryover from the "Those kids look like criminals and should expect to be raped (in effect)... by the police?

(What have *we* become?)

If he had said that about women, I'm sure there would be outrage and subsequent damnation. There would be protests or other forms of backlash. But since they were kids (not people <u>or</u> organized), they should shut up (those crazy intimate individualized ideas), get in line (make concessions and conform), and buy-buy-buy... more expensive clothes that resemble everyone else's in line. Or, remain an outcast and be subjected to harassment by the hoards of slave drivers

/ fear mongers / storm troopers. Unless of course I'm making them money... then I'd be called 'an artist.'

I know that there is no person who is above the law. Even my dad, who is the most "fit in" kind of guy I know, if subjected to police harassment would have to go to jail.
(Or retraining... if that sounds better.)

See, it's a simple equation: Outcast = non-consumer, outcast + retraining = consumer.
(And consumers write their paychecks with the taxes they eventually pay!)

I am not here to jump through any hoop for any (police)man, woman or child. I don't want to "fit in" their world. It's more important that I fit into mine!

Elliott's world, excellent... party on!

(Your world should party too.)

Now is another time for a disclaimer: I am a good boy. I will break no rules, because I don't need to like I used to. Today I help my fellow people if I can, where I'm able. Since the Light but not without personal growth, I'm like a "champion" here to serve, and respect is all I ever request for my service.

J. Elliott Goldwyn

The future?
* * *

I just saw something on television a moment ago, on channel 8 - PDX, OR. A commercial for the news talked about how the kids of today have "hit the skids". I believe, because I've been there, the youngsters of today are "fed-up!" There's only one difference: "Hitting the skids" is only the act of, "having no reason at all to live anymore," or, "I give up."

"Hitting the skids" is a derogatory comment to incite conformity in people who have given up on compliance to the hypocritical role models, like Bill Clinton. No one would say he has hit the skids, he is a conformist and a "two faced person" if ever I saw one. On first glance I would not say that about him, but he is probably hollow. Remember my theory about H.P.'s and the "looks are deceiving" in their elemental existence equation? Mr. Bill Clinton may be a beautiful example.

Like myself, the future adult generation is trying to say by their rebellion that there is a direct action / dissatisfaction concerning the way "free citizens"(whoever they are) happen to be treated as they are trying to express said "freedom". I'm not saying the kids are all "good" or "bad" because individuality is neither of those two extremes. I *am* saying... "the scales are not exactly balanced."

This work is not dedicated to introducing a conspiracy theory to the public in any way. Although, if anybody wishes to be a "conspiracy buff" they **can** *and* **will** find too much supportive evidence out there just aching to be taken.

I cannot speak for any one but myself, and I am not trying to convert anyone, but I am trying to open eyes. I'm

one-of-us

no longer chasing after that imaginary "American (success) pie". It does not exist. Sure, anybody can be successful in the financial world, but not without a very steep price. Since just a handful of the elite rich have personalities which go beyond the "us / them" ethic, so, there isn't anybody inside their eyes to be a friend of. "All the expensive lights on in that majestic mansion... but nobody's home."

They will disagree with me, and that's just another example of their narrow-minded 'better than / worse than' mentality. Although, money is nice. I, my self alone for myself alone, have decided that there is more to life than money and the chasing thereof.

Like everything, there are always exceptions.

(You know... I just can't think of any.)

It didn't take even a decade for me to understand the scales which weigh out the amount of responsibility in relation to the amount of enjoyment one may experience. Children have more fun because they have less to be responsible for. The obverse is also true. With more money, any person will have more responsibility which <u>will</u> hinder any enjoyment hither to. I'm sure there will be many who will disagree with my observation, and it may not be true for them, because they have validated and rationalized their own... and that's okay for them.

The shoes don't, the car doesn't and the money will never make the man. Experiences <u>do</u>! The lessons contained therein that were learned <u>do</u>! The group of people who he or she calls "friends" <u>do</u>! Being real, "<u>sure does too</u>!"

I'm lucky... because I believe if I have five faithful friends during my life I'm doing great. There are always a great many who I call acquaintances. Friends are like hope.

J. Elliott Goldwyn

    I need hope to survive as I need my friends. Although I've not needed a major organ or bone marrow transplant, none the less, my friends are the reason I'm alive and able to love. And you know... those five friends are often never the same five. Both on a lifetime schedule, or a day to day basis.

one-of-us

Hypersensitive?
* * *

Other people see the miracle-ness happening inside Deb and for some reason I'm anxious.

I was trained to be something, and even though that protective nature comes easy, it's the nervous fear that's tearing me apart. I'm not sure at times that I'm ever enough for her. (Or that she's enough for me?)

(Time will tell.)

See, it's not the physical effects of the accident that slow my social interaction. Things happen that hurt me almost every day and it always happens with another person. It's not that I'm insecure only. That's a part of it, although it's not all of it. I do have my "feelings" to deal with.

I'm hypersensitive. Sometimes, various stuff that would make me laugh, makes me cry. Instead of 100% happiness, I'm fearful that Nick will be taken away.

Forms, steps, methods are all just chains which restrict the creative imagination. This I learned over and over, or rather, this I was taught by "ones" who felt the need to obstruct my imagination. <u>The</u> prime example was my photo 1 and 2 classes in college. I may have taken a great shot and developed it well, but my work was graded like it was comparable to nothing but trash. That hurt, and even though what I was doing was art, I found that even art has methods `n` steps (that *must* be followed). And it needs to fit into a form of an acceptable artistic aspect. (Which means the "art work" has to be of value to someone) The question I now ask is: would anything be art - if - the artistic world was not immersed in greed?

Between classes one day, I was lucky enough to meet the photo 3 and 4 professor. He looked over my portfolio and shook his head in disbelief... and said, "This is <u>good</u>". That was all I needed to hear... No more forms to expose, no more methods to compose.

There would be no art critics, without the "all mighty" dollar. There may be no musical critics if it were not for the money in mass media. But, there is.

There always will be. Always another customer. Always another convert (weakling) to get in line (after shutting up) and buy, buy, buy.

(Sounds familiar huh?)

All the world needs is more Tom, Dick, and Harry's. More consumers who let others choose what he or she needs. That's nothing but commercial slavery to me!

Even the 'outcasts' at school, who wear different sorts of shirts, skirts, shorts, shoes or slacks... were all bought somewhere after being made by someone. Those outcasts are just another cog in the compendium of commercialism, how programmed they are.

I was.

Dreams
* * *

When I was a child, an innocent child... I dreamed dreams. The world could be paradise. This "heaven place" could be right here, right now. Beautiful childhood dreams... but I'm awake now. No longer room for fantasy. This is real 3-D existence.

I'm no longer able to see any growth in the masses to foster the needed peoplehood to exist and cohabit in an orderly fashion on this ever shrinking world on which we live.

(Now awake *in* reality.)

I know it's because I'm a "new parent to be", but I did have the same view about the complications which come from avidity in the power = greed equation. (From the start.) Doomed from the very beginning, but we hang on to our antiquated form of government which had it's day when there were whole great territories yet left to explore. Our governing system is based on hunger for money, and that reality is passed on down to it's citizens through constant repetition of an ideal we see on television or some other form of subliminal message transference vehicle.

Today I need to survive in a world where there is no suburb with a home, a wife, two kids, car, dog, cat, pool, mortgage and <u>another</u> car in the garage for me to escape to. (Escape with?)

No "american dream" for me. Not because it's not possible, I already know that it is (or was... I believe I've pretty well fucked up my chances for that now). But, who knows? More horrific things *have* happened. Inside a capitalistic society anything can be bought, but the price is often out of reach. Some goals are reached with other's help, a basketball game for instance. While other goals are ruthless, cunning, cruel and as heartless as the big cat on the prowl for it's dinner. A not so friendly game of cat and mouse.

The more you take for you, means less in the end for me. Competition, human competition pure and simple. The market place is a ruthless, cunning, heartless and cruel (to a fault). Why is it that way? Do *you* want it that way? Why is it that no one even wants to talk about it? (About political evolution?)

I'm called crazy. My dreams and vast knowledge are ignored. I'm not saying I'm special. (But I am.) I have seen future days that could be. (Will be?) Who knows.

I believe everything has it's need to grow... to survive, but even growth has it's price.

Our price for "easy street" (success) is the loss of face from the lowering of others in order to raise one's self on the all important religious rating scale... your "social class".

What kinda car do you drive? Wow... do you have any idea how many kids in the Detroit (per ce) area went hungry because you really _needed_ that import? (Although, in some people's defense, they don't make all the vehicles you might need here in America, therefore: importation is the only answer. But far too many people still run the 'race' that the Joneses are now winning, and you need to keep up with the Joneses don't you? Why? Is it because of their obvious high religious standing which is often directly proportionate to their active line of credit? Commercialism has made a God from the dollar... and God says, "destroy the financial standing of your fellow man in your fruitless pursuit of me... your hollow god." Hollow people follow hollow gods. It's what they know and understand, period. Those people help themselves, never helping their fellow humans. Always seeming to arrive in your life "under foot". Usually foaming at the mouth with greed. Greed is the enemy "we the people" must kill to end the force fed subordination... to end the moral slavery!

"The care of human life and happiness and not their destruction, is the first and only legitimate object of good government."
(Thomas Jefferson, March 21, 1809)

As the government loses touch with the people, whole factions of our population go disregarded. Pity, some of my very good friends are members of certain forgotten percentage of our populace. Yes, they are real. The reason they don't "fit in", per-ce, is that they don't really want to fit into a system that is no longer feeding the people, but rather now feeding off the people. Something's gonna give. I predict the first shot fired in rebellion against the government (now in place) has already been spent because of our democracy's becoming... oppressive. But who notices that? People who pay attention, that's who.

Thomas Jefferson was a great man who said many great things. I do not wish to discuss or dismiss his very individual morale trueness, because he lived in a different time... and in a completely different place then we do now.

He foresaw the possibility for a government, even the one that he helped in the construction of, to become oppressive.

Mr. Jefferson felt strongly about oppression:
"...life, liberty and the pursuit of happiness...

> whenever government becomes destructive to those ends, it is the right of the people to alter or abolish it, and to institute a new government."
>
> (T.J., July 4, 1776)

Let's talk on oppression for awhile:

Our speed limits, which are posted everywhere are <u>not</u> oppressive. (Even though, on a grand scale we disregard them everyday.) Although, if a person is lying on their "death bed", that person cannot take their own life so they may be able to die with honor. Instead, (by law)... every effort must be made to keep the dying person alive.

(Although, there is such a thing as a 'living will' but not everyone has one.)

No matter what the patient says, or what the patient's family can afford. The "almighty dollar" system in charge even owns your death. You must pay the "medical community" for the short time it is able to keep your heart beating with the assistance of artificial life support... which may cost your loved ones more than they can afford.

So your family takes over the rest of your hospital bill you were unable to pay (a legacy... of sorts). The system feeds off the people, then once dead, the deceased girl or guy's family.

Which is another example of the reality in:
People die = $ equation.

At times I feel the entire actuality of the afore mentioned equality is lunacy. Therefore, if we carry the social and/or monetary mathematics to it's conclusive end...

reality = insanity.

I am disgusted with what we as a peoplehood allow to exist. Aren't you?

I, myself, wish there was another system in control in which to leave our children.

To assist in the formation of the happiness and care for their lives like T. Jefferson and I believe are government's only respectable objective.

(Maybe I should run for office?)

Anything beyond expanding our liberties is treason.

This is only one man's opinion, or maybe more?

(I hope so.)

If "we the people" stand tall and vote, things will change.

(End of story.)

But not the end of my explicative. Our elected officials have become greedy (hoggish) because we allowed them to have the power needed to facilitate such total disregard of our welfare, and those political puppets continue to line their pockets. We need to take the power back! And never again accept such total social disrespect from our leaders, whether or not they hold an office in the administration or a law-enforcement organization or the IRS offices. Maybe we should not vote in candidates, but rather, vote in policies.

J. Elliott Goldwyn

Writing/Talking?
* * *

Sometimes when I'm writing I have a point to examine with words. While other times I ramble aimlessly, wondering with carefree abandon, examining every aspect while posing continuous questions. Questions to open windows of understanding where the doors are all shut and bolted in the house of possible specific information on a street of collective knowledge on a planet called, "all knowledge". Where most brilliant minds live. (Analytically speaking.)

What I'm trying to say is:

Either I examine one subject, or I ramble. I'm not sure why I ramble, I have ideas though:

1. I have shown signs of A.D.D. by not being able to stay on one topic for very long at all. I get frustrated by ignorance and closed minds. My weak memory does not help matters much.

2. My mind travels freely between light\deep, concrete\fluid, subconscious\conscious, and realistic\abstract (just to name a few) levels of concentration in mind generated thought about most everything. So many topics that my mind is bounding off on another new one while my hand is oftentimes failing to keep up. I don't have enough dexterity to type at my speed of thought.

Debra
* * *

It seems as though Deb's acting exactly like the description of "hollow" I've given earlier. But, I <u>must</u> believe in the promise of family. I should listen to her words and not be affected by her actions, right? The promise of long term emotional investment is better than the reality of selfish short term gain to come.

Time will tell? Yes, it will. (Read on warriors!)

Very soon after our (Deb'n'E's) (E means "me") arrival in P.D.X., we had pitched a tent in a campground not far from the city but still very rural of an area. On the first day we were in town I knew she was pregnant. (I just had a feeling.) On the second day in town, I said so. On the third, Debra got sick in the campsite. I guess I had a feeling from the very beginning, although she swore that she wasn't pregnant when we left Denver. (Hmmm...) I had even wrote about it in a song I had unsuccessfully begun, but she did swear, and I believe her. Although, Deb did point out on a few occasions that the pub owner in Denver she dated 'could' screw for hours. I wonder why she mouthed something so sublime?

Maybe for what happened in S.D.? (My practice with Amy?) Surly not that... for that was nothing but an exact reflection of what happened to me. Let me explain my "mirror work":

I had been slowly becoming less secure in South Dakota and I needed Deb. But "she" (whom will remain nameless... because she doesn't deserve recognition) was over at the cabin and I felt nothing but the fly on the wall in a lesbian bar.

My damn feelings again. Mostly that came from Deb wanting emotional exchange with her, and for me to disappear. So I did. I went upstairs and fell asleep. If she would have said goodbye to her friend and came to bed with me, things might be different. Or instead of creating a lie, she explained her need to do her. I understand needs, especially if they are explained. But she didn't and they're not. Whether or not she had sex really doesn't matter because the end result was the same. She had disregarded me and my needs so she might get what it is she needed from another woman before I'd even met Amy. The only difference between her experience with another downstairs and mine was... I didn't watch. But that was then.

Back to Portland:

Our daily sharing (Deb's `n` E's) turned from three or four times a day under bridges or overpasses, and bathrooms in various motels rooms while on our way to Oregon... become a chore for her twice a month in one hour's time. Yep, Deb's preggers.

I was smoking a lot of pot Deb had brought along from Denver and I now feel that was her way of trying to ensue us having (no, "her" having) a girl. Usually a man who fathers after smoking pot, fathers a girl. (But maybe that is just another old wive's tale?)

one-of-us

So, I told her she'd have a girl, look at all the signs... (I found an "It's a Girl" coffee cup), and I got this feeling.

I lied, I knew it would be a boy all along, only I did not feel safe telling Deb.

If she could hit me again, could she hit him?

But forgive my momentary pondering. I told her that the pregnancy would go well physically, I could *see* that definitely. (No lie, in my mind/eye.) And the whole pregnancy long, I joked about her "pooping the baby out". She laughed, but I knew already that it would be the truth.

I went on every prenatal appointment.

I was very curious and involved. I even wanted to come in the bathroom when she filled the cup for a pee test. (Request/denial our running theme.)

I was always full of questions, and I asked with respect worthy of a loving parent.

We decided on names before the birth:

Clara (blank) Goldwyn if a girl. (We never decided on a middle name because we didn't have to.)

Nicholas Elliott Goldwyn if a boy. (Great name for a great boy, I hope he'll enjoy it.)

Nick, after her grand-dad. Clara, after my grand-mother.

Although, we never had a sex determination ultrasound. Because that is true, Deb never had any idea (but I did!) that we were defiantly having a boy.

Circles of light!
* * *

In the fourth or fifth month in our apartment on Ankeny St. in PDX, (which would be fourth or fifth in pregnancy), Deb `n` E began to see circles of light move about on the wall and ceiling or hovering in midair. None came through a window and they were visual and obviously not coming from some light source originating somewhere else. The lights never moved in union or with any form of unison, and none were that completely solid bright in tone like an ordinary light bulb. They were rather soft colors from another dimension it seemed, when mixed together (I'm sure) on their own "light spectrum" I knew that they in combination would construct a light so white no living person could see... and see (at all) again. How could I know? Because Nick was _my_ son, and besides... I had this feeling. The lights on the wall would enter Nick in their own time, this I felt, but what were they? His soul?

From the very beginning of the pregnancy I had slowly grown accepting of the fact that this (baby thing) may never happen again. ("Hold on longer Elliott" - might be forever.) So to every appointment I bought along a tape recorder to document everything I could. (Some do, some don't... this dad did.)

Everything went smoothly enough physically (not emotionally for me) right up to her being in false labor once, the clock had moved all the way around for nine months and I knew it was just a matter of Deb being mentally ready to give up the child to live on his own now. (It _was_ time.)

I had started my political tee-shirt co., (loud 'n' clear). A company name with no capital letters, because (loud 'n' clear) "your true voice"... is not capitalistic.

(The reason I mentioned my business is because...)

While I was painting shirts one night I watched Deb sleeping and remembered how the moon looked that night, and I knew the time was right (my feeling/correct). The colors on the walls looked complete, and now I needed to do just what I did.

(This gets graphic...)

While looking at Deb's beautiful body in full expression of womanhood with the physical construction of a miracle occurring inside, which is as close as we (the human race) can come to the creative power of a god or goddess (I'm not sexually biased with entities, either) I began to practice (ritualistically).

As I looked upon her femininity, I performed. When I finished (release of energy) I called my son to me, because it was Nick's time to come... together. (There in my own words... *is* a ritual.)

As I cleaned up, Deb started shaking. She rolled over to face me, opened her eyes and said, "you would not believe the dream I just had."

"Oh yes, I do know", I breathed... "But tell me."

"Someone was trying to take the baby forcefully, like with a gun or something," was her dream in a nutshell. "Do you understand... Elliott?" (I hope you, the reader, do.)

"Yes, I understand", and I felt my work was done, so I fell fast asleep to dream of success and Deb "pooping the baby out". (I slept soundly!)

one-of-us

While I slept, (four hours or so later) Deb nudged me with a cramp or something.

Like clockwork... she had two more before calling to me.

"It's time," she said.

"I know." As I began to pull on my clothes and gathered her over-night bags, Deb had another clock-work contraction. She knew what "they" were now, her cramp-like pains, and she needed to empty her bowels, NOW!

She ran to the bathroom and I heard her piss a little, then poop, then throw up in the sink. Then... I heard clear as a waterfall's roar -- Nick's protective water sack break. "Wooosh..." (It *was* time!)

Deb panicked, and I became more serene. We were always the pair, (loud 'n' clear). When Deb became "loud-headed" I became "clear".

We arrived at the hospital without fail, and that's when the fun began. It was 4:58 a.m. when we walked in. The place was empty. Deb said fearful words, only I don't remember any of them. But I do remember what I said, "Oh, were at the main entrance, we need the emergency gate." In that door which was barely around the corner was a woman who just looked at us knowingly and said, "second floor", while pointing at the elevators.

Calmly and easily I got us upstairs and put my "wife" in the hands of qualified medical personnel. (Qualified... because I had one of those feelings.) I took a deep breath at that time, and looked at my watch (5:00 a.m.), and I thought about how all I'd been working for was coming true and coming to us.

The nurses had her on a table, so I set down her one important bag. The medical ladies reassured both Deb and myself (the proud parents to be) that there was nothing to fear...

Deb was only 1.5 centimeters dilated.

I started to speak with another nurse about how long we've got before the "big moment".

"Oh awhile yet," was the reply. So I took the gown I was offered, but as I was putting it on there was much confusion in the room. Not chaos, more like professional people doing busy professional activities, so I asked someone else if everything was alright. (nervous/concern)

"Sure," I was told. (Very business like, very professional!)

(Did I say "qualified," yet?)

Then I thought of the Rebel (my car, "Barney Rebel"), I had bought off my neighbor in S. Dakota, but I digressed (excuse me). Barney was in the "super emergency" zone right at the front door. I thought I'd better move him and grab more stuff we would need after the birth. I even went as far as to tell someone in the room when Deb said...

"I'm feeling a real big urge to push!" It was like the magic words, the whole room changed. Everyone but me showed just how qualified they were, as Deb was quickly lifted onto the examination table and checked for dilation.

"You're ten centimeters now, the next time you get the urge to push, Debra...
GO WITH IT !"

"Go with it," was the last thing I remember, because it all happened so fast. Deb floated, (they carried her) to the large delivery table and put her legs in the air. They gave me her right leg... she pushed twice, and I could see my child's head. (The most beautiful hair ever!)

I touched my baby's head first (happy happy joy joy) and momentarily daydreamed of all the first's to come in our future. In what only seemed like a heartbeat later our child's head was clear (outside Deb), and I began to see those "Lights" I had grown used to seeing. But now they were only in my peripheral view circling our baby and they were changing colors like light refracted through crystal.

Our baby's shoulders were cleared and then, for lack of a better expression/explanation, Deb... "pooped the baby out!"

At that instant the "Light show" really began. All around my vision of our beautiful baby <u>BOY</u> (hi Nick!) turned into grey nothingness. Nick was the only thing in the room I could focus on. (Typical?) (Maybe.)

All the lights were still there, but they were changing (description is difficult because words are so... incomplete) into crystal like shapes, crystal wands shaped like precious cut gems with light refracting (producing?) angles to magnify and... separate. Always they're changing shape, or turning... like a crystal hanging on a string. Only every side showed a separate individual magnification. Refraction of that great Light I had visited once. (My interpretation.) It was like frame work in Light for our son.

Nick's body was "life-full", but not yet able to sustain it with oxygen he would draw in with his own breath. (His cord was still attached.) The nurses were cleaning/clearing out the large amount of fluid in his lungs and nasal cavity... when his body began to shake as it got ready for that "all important" first breath...

The "crystals"(?) began to become more solid (they'd been fading in `n` out till then), and it was clear that at any one time all the colors combined in each and every circle of crystal would make a light so white and so bright to look on it would make you blind. Which is to be knowledge like knowing that to look upon the face of God will make you forever sightless. I don't remember if anyone or anything said such... it's just generally known. (Maybe the Lights on the wall *is* the face of God?) As Nick's body shook so did the crystals, they were all around him now, changing shapes and colors too.

(Faster and faster, I watched them move.)

As Nick exhaled for his first time, he cleared the last of the liquid from his lungs... the Circles of Light around him also breathed out. Like an arm cocked back to throw a blow. (In effect - remember it's often hard to describe something you've never seen before.)

As Nick breathed in (his first), all the crystals around him just slipped... and yet slammed into his body. (It's very hard to explain.)

Slipped in because of their silence. Slammed in because of the speed they took.

Nick was still the only thing I could see in the room, a whole six man emergency delivery team and all of their equipment came rushing in because Nick was born so fast. There can be some problems with being born too quickly, but neither Deb or I had seen the team enter. (There was something more important going on in the room with the light show and all.) Now Nick <u>was</u> the Light, and you could *feel* it too. (He lit up the room.) I felt the delivery room

one-of-us

had special effects built in, and for days I was embarrassed to mention my (head injured?) hallucinations for fear of a laughing public.

Although about a week later, Deb or I said something to each other about what we saw in the delivery room being so beautiful... and then it all came out. Deb had seen everything I did, right down to each and every crystal. Now what? What does this mean?

Nicholas Elliott Goldwyn was born from Deb at 5:46 a.m. on April 24th, 1994, and on that day at that time my life became real. Things were happening so fast I barely had time to breath myself. I was blessed with a family, and I tried to do my best with the responsibility life had given me.
I did well, or as well as I thought could be for me.

Worry too much?
* * *

I was awaiting an important decision to come from S.S. administration concerning my head injury and whether or not it was severe enough for me to receive some assistance.

I thought about how I'd been paying into the insurance policy called social security for years for just such a mishap, and how the S.S. people were making it very difficult for me to ask for help, let alone receive any.

Now I found that I had to get a lawyer to get "my" money back, but things were moving along smoothly enough so I didn't worry... too much.

I was getting a monthly check from S.S.I. to help support me while the S.S.A. worked out some numbers on my red tape inside their "great" tape player. When I realized Nick was now four months old. I had grown very tired of Deb's, "Hold on a little longer"game. Although, now she wanted me to get sterile through a vasectomy. "I'll feel better about sex with you if I don't have to worry about another pregnancy," was her new request.

So, I set the appointment, feeling (hopeful) that now I could do something to increase our intimacy level. While on the way to the hospital I looked at Nick and asked him, "What should I do?" His answer was to look at me like I was crazy, and his eyes said, "I want brothers and sisters, Dad!"

I stopped the car, I told Deb, but Deb gave me just what I needed to hear (in effect) to cut my balls off. (More of the same effect)

"More sex, more sex, more sex", and the promise of love was better then nothing.

(Or so I thought.)

one-of-us

I was to be sterile, looking for intimacy from Deb but only finding my hand.

(jerk, jerk, jerk)

Deb `n` I moved again (really... I moved us) upstairs to another apartment in the same building, a new place but still the same ole home of denial.

I became more frustrated than a man in jail. I was sleeping next to a beautiful woman (that I loved), but there was this invisible immoveable impassible wall up between us.

Looking at a beautiful woman who was the mother of my son, who I could touch but could no longer touch me (in return).

I wish I could have heard, "men only have one purpose," before I had satisfied that purpose. Because then I'd have seen all the cards in the deck Deb was playing with, and I'd have a more informed position from which I could choose the option of parenthood with her (or not). In her defense, I must say that Deb's first words (that were not asking me what I would like off the menu) were, "I'm a dyke."

Maybe I should have paid attention then, but the pushing of buttons (sex and stuff) by Deb was far too pleasurable for me to believe she was what she had said she was. My family was slipping away, but I had foreseen everything that was taking place. I had allowed Deb's expression of love (my interpretation not her's), with the pushing of my sexual buttons to hook me, and now there was no one to push my buttons anymore. Debra, the lesbian, was about the best lover till that time and I wanted no other above her.

That is one reason; and I needed to perform (sexual practice ritualistically) to bring "my" S.S.D. money to me, but I can't work with a girl who does not want to be with me, and that was the other reason I was so despondent. This was a feeling I had, and it's quickly becoming "Do or Die".

At the club next door (E.J`s titty bar) I was getting friendship, pats on the back and respect from people who went there (some people who worked there also) so my tanks (emotional ones) were being filled somewhat, but still not the important ones... especially not at home. (It's like I was living alone.)

I spent more and more time next door, not to avoid parenthood because Deb was a doting mother, but just because I did not feel anything but rejection at home.. Although, if a situation should arise where I was needed, I was there. I had a job next door at the club, which was admittedly a man's playground. (Big screen sports T.V., beer, pool, and girls - girls - girls!)The job I worked at was an illegal one, I sold pot there. I had to, Deb had quit her job (got fired for her own error) and to keep food on the table and a roof over my family's heads. I couldn't hold a job, but I could sell pot. (I'm not trying to gain your acceptance, but I need you to know that I would do <u>anything</u> for my child, and I'm sure you would for your's too!)

My logic was to not work out of the house for fear that selling pot would put the parents in jail and the child would be taken away. If anyone would go to jail, it would be me. (Just me!) The club next door had the darkness I needed and a pay phone, plus I knew everyone who worked there and went there as a patron so the very undercover policeman stood out like a very big sore thumb. I felt safe enough to be

one-of-us

welcome there, and I also felt safe at the home of the guys I shot pool with, especially Dan's crib.

I was over at Dan's (jeweler friend), who was one of the "pool guys", when Keesha (stage name) came over after working as a dancer babe at E.J.'s all day. This was the first time we had seen each other outside the club, her shields were down and my eyes were open. She sat down, looked at me, our eyes met and she reached out her hand, seemingly to say hello, when...

She took my arm, bent her knee to the floor, then lightly pressed her lips to my hand. All while our eyes were reaching inside each other. Like a princess, she kissed my hand. The most "touching" of experience I've had in about a year, and I had to draw back and collect my thoughts because my heart wanted to run away with her, and she knew it too. (witchy woman thing!)
<u>My</u> <u>brain</u> said, "go." No... screamed "GO!!!" (loud `n` clear). The goddess (Keesha) was offering me solace and sanctuary from the emptiness I was in, but <u>my</u> <u>heart</u> was putting on the brakes. Not saying, "no", but softly whispering, "not yet". So, it was just a matter of time, huh? Well, I got more time than money.

One night soon after I offered her a ride home. (Like Deb in Denver.) I'm not sure why, but it just came out of my mouth. When she said, "sure," I knew why. Part of me was with her, unfortunately I couldn't give her 100% because part of my heart was really still buried in the hopes of a family. Which is admittedly my fantasy/fallacy.

Deb had been consistently pushing my emotions away, but I now had one night of being harbored in a bay of expression/emotion. So I may continue to live, I "ate" all night.

Ida (her real name) knew very little of me, so love wasn't there but the desire I deserved was. So I used that to bring me the money in what my attorney says was very "red tape break neck speed." I got a letter the next week that said I was finally approved, completely. Now it was just a matter of time for the check to come in the mail.

Along with the news came more news, Nick would get a monthly check also from S.S.A. Unfortunately, Deb now had no reason to stay with me. Sex, (if any) was not to stay. It was a reason to leave. I had seen my error* with Ida, and that night became a one night layover.

As a matter of fact, the night was spent talking like two very old friends, who had not seen each other in a very long time. Lifetimes? (If I had a nickel...) To catch up on each other was more important than sex. It was like the "sex thing" (desire) was assured, we were lovers before this life. Only I think she was the man, and I a woman last time. (Appears to be a completion of a circle... to me.)

Deb pulled further away, and I (the mirror) now realized what had been happening for me must be happening for Deb also. Keesha was not the only woman drawn to me. Just the only one I let in. Of this I'm assured, so I felt no guilt. I'm a mirror, remember? (Appears to be another circle's completion.)

I had requested intimacy expression from Debra to grease the SSI's red tape wheel, it's just that it came from someone

---

* Mistake may be *too* strong of a word.

else. Unfortunately the "someone else" routine was a reality I'd rather avoid. It's not that it was un-fulfilling, but rather the avoidance is due to my frustration that I could not give 100%... because until that time my love was with someone else. (Debra)

Bright eye!
* * *

About that time I'd noticed this pair of legs while sitting on my smoking alcove which was a common law balcony for the whole building in which Debra and I lived.. (Deb `n` I did not smoke around Nick.)

Even from above I could easily see she was taller than I... by an inch or so, and her legs were maybe one whole foot longer than mine. She had eyes that made me smile. I guess I wanted to see her again (to see more of her?) and look into those eyes. Maybe she'll move into "my" building. (I ran the place, sort of.) She did go into the manager's office, so there's hope, but I don't remember seeing her again for awhile.

A couple of days later I got one of my nagging feelings. "Go somewhere, there is something waiting for you." The problem with my thoughts is they don't draw a map for me to follow so there is this fear that I'll go to the wrong place, maybe. It's not happened yet, but that *is* a fear that's very hard to escape. So, next door we go. (Maybe there?)

As I went inside, the feelings that goes along with the right place/right time were enveloping me in the comfort that goes along with hearing "job well done, Elliott."

Like an all important pat on the back which came from a source both internal and external but the origin was both everywhere and nowhere at the same time. (Another one of my feelings, does anyone else have these?) I felt like the fireman who has rushed into this "burning social hell" (titty bar) to find someone who was there, maybe in danger. Who... I needed to rescue.

Titties are not bad, on display at a bar is not bad either (for some!), but there are others who should not be working

one-of-us

in those establishments. It could be because of age (legal reason), mental condition (another reason) and/or emotional stability (which is a big one) or spiritual placement (the biggest of all!). What I feel must be done is for a prospective dancer (from goddess to scag) should understand that their mental, emotional, spiritual and certainly her age will be different after working inside a male dominated playground... very different.

I've seen good girls become evil women, but not because of growth - there is little growth in a typical dancer's fast paced life. Some do! Please don't get me wrong, there are women out there who have asked all the right questions and have kept what's important to them (themselves, their children) the most important above all else.
EJ.'s was the best club (that I knew of) both for quality of management/owner (a woman) and the entertainers (all very beautiful in their own way). The dancers did not perform with an "in your face" attitude... except for Keesha. Most men like that (right guys?), but I'm *not* most.
I've spent most of my life following my heart (soul?) to the extent of being an outcast when I grew able to *really* say, "No, I don't wanna play your stupid (go nowhere) social games!"

I became a loner (hierophant or hermit to a Crowley Tarot card lover) who's job was to observe and grow wiser. I guess I've spent more time in reflection today than ever. Very soon after the conception of my son I became ready, willing and able to place into words with which to explain / describe my life... so in case I cannot be there, Nick could still learn from and about my experiences.

Why did I think such thoughts? Was I going to die? Or, was my fear (that was growing) that Deb would have the baby and leave me really going to happen? I saw it coming, I tried to set up "warning signs" (by talking about my fears), but even though Deb had not bought a plane ticket I was all alone in what used to be our home.

Nick would take naps (three daily). Both Deb `n` I would be at home, but there was just no love left to make.

But back to my story:

I had just come into E.J.'s looking for something for me (a customer? a friend?), and to my surprise (I'm *never* surprised) up walked this new dancer to say, "Hi." Gosh, she was tall, 6'6" in heels. "My name is Selene, what's yours?"

"Elliott, Hi." (Duh... some slick line right? Mr. Smooth, yep that's me!) She had beautiful bone structure, and nice eyes hidden behind her false eyelashes and big "foofed up" hair.

one-of-us

I loved <u>her</u> hair, it was like wind blown and not all "hair sprayed". We talked a little, you know, "small talk". She was new to dancing because I could see into her eyes. (She had not learned to hide her inner-self yet - maybe she'd never be able? That meant she'd be in trouble soon!) Like I said, E.J.'s is a pretty good place for a dancer to start, but it was also a jump off point into working at a big money club.

(Or, an "in your face" place.)

I knew that would kill the little girl from "Michigan". This was not a life for her (my feelings again)... but she is in charge of what she does with her body (not me). Although, there was a bond I could see (hoped for?) in her eyes, and I needed to become her friend before I could help.

We talked off 'n' on. I went to go shoot pool - not more often - but always when Selene was working. She had grown comfortable with the fact I was not a leering man (like another customer for her), and Selene began to show me more 'n' more respect.

Now I knew she was getting off early one night (or was it 2:00 a.m.?) and like the "big brother" local kinda guy I am, I asked if I could give her a ride.

"Oh, I don't need a ride," she breathed (Great, she's got a limo or some millionaire to pick her up) followed by, "you see, I live next door. You may walk me home, if you like." (I liked very much!)

"Sure," says I. (duh again)

"Let me go gather my things, alright?"

"Sure." I spent the next few minutes knocking balls around on the table. For some reason I couldn't make even one. With one eye on the girl's room door (no wonder), and my mind and heart racing simultaneously (in competition?) on thoughts and feelings her eyes had inspired in me.

(Love sick puppy?)

Inner reflections:

(All of the above was seen by me before it happened, through my fears "that really were gonna happen" no matter how I warned... Well, you can't stop destiny. The fears came from dreams, and also the "video tape" I had seen while at home in "The Light". What I had seen was both Deb showing her true colors after the pregnancy <u>and</u> her replacement finally coming into my life.)

Debra's needs -or- Desire too!
* * *

Now Deb needed to find a reason to leave where it would be me playing the role of the proverbial "bad boy" or "deadbeat dad". She was convinced I was sleeping around. In a way she was right, I <u>was</u> coming home with a smile on my face. Only she was wrong, my daily smiles came from me getting my mental, emotional *and* spiritual food from people without having intercourse.

Deb became madder because I was telling her how it <u>was</u> possible to share needed intimacy (and fill up) without having to perform sex with me. (Lesbo goddess forbid!)

She did the bad deed with hell bound fury until she got pregnant then the 'no more' line was drawn in the proverbial sand, and now there were others (one in particular) who were willing to feed me with their friendship and respect. (Desire too?) (Maybe... a little.)

(Time will tell.)

Sara!
* * *

Back to waiting at E.J.'s to walk Selene home (happy happy joy joy):

When the bathroom door opened a light streamed out to guide "the princess" and she slid over to my side. She had changed into a goddess with her hair pulled back so her face was fully visible and no lashes to hide her eyes. Selene was sexy on stage but dressed for the street with all the "flash" off her face she was the most beautiful woman (innocent girl) I'd ever fantasized about.

Selene, which was not her real name, <u>was</u> that pair of legs with deep sweet eyes I had seen outside weeks earlier. We went to her place where I felt more innocence than street smarts, but more desire than innocence from her room filling vibration, aura, blah blah.

We talked a little, light "deep" talk of Magick, respect, astrology, love and other aspects of our seemingly unrelated lives which seemed to be tied together with a "red thread". (A very real bond!) Where do we go now? (I asked myself.)

"Into patience, my young friend," was what my heart said.

Sara, (her real name) was seeing another man. (Jeff) He seemed nice enough but it was obvious to me the first time we shook hands that we were to be competing "Madges". There's no such thing as a warlock. Unless, it's on "Bewitched" or in a movie, maybe... but not in real life. At the time I didn't know how we would battle, but now I can see more clearly. (Hindsight) Sara was the prize, and I knew how precious she was.

one-of-us

Jeff didn't or it was not in his repertoire of ability to show it. Sure he could fuck, but almost everyone can. He had a problem with punctuality, which equates to disrespect for most. Sara was above that, so I told her, or the big brother in me did. I had not even the desire to kiss her yet, (you believe me... right?) we were too busy becoming friends. Like clockwork (or so my clock said) Jeff started coming around less `n` less, until less became not at all. I still had no desire to kiss her, if I did I would have, but it just wasn't time yet.

We both had irons in the fire, but minc(?), if I could call her that, had a child.

Climb so high?
* * *

Deb needed to step down from the pedestal I had built for her, which was not as big as the one she put herself on. The Leo dyke man-hater who is "always right" had her ego build an unstable platform for herself was so tall I could never build one so extravagant.

I could not allow myself to climb so high on a faulty foundation for safeties sake.

I will not make my own pedestal because the "ego" makes an poor contractor.

I choose to allow my significant other to be my mirror in building my box (pedestal) to compliment the one I'm making for her. Is that not what a "partnership" is all about? "Doing for your partner," not denial?

Oh but I have forgotten, Deb only needed men for one reason. Women were her emotional, mental and spiritual contractor for pedestal construction. (Silly me!) So, really I had no more reason to suffer with a sexual dead horse. It wasn't gonna build anything in me but a lack of desire to deliver my daily denial.

I was no longer banging on Deb's door for the food that I wasn't gonna get.

It's a matter of trust
***

About that time I'd still been selling pot but I had more in the house than the federal charge of "distributing" would allow. I needed a safe house in which to store a 1/4 lb. Deb suggested her pal Geoff. "He's pretty set in his ways," she said, "and I trust him."

"Okay", so I dialed his number. "Say Geoff, would you come over?" He did and we discussed all the responsibility.

(Or so I thought.)

"Don't you fuck me Geoff", were my last words. Geoff didn't have a lover so he was pretty reliable.

(Or so I thought.)

I told him so he'd know, "we owe money for what you have, so don't put my family in a financial hole, or I'll put you in the funeral home."

"Okay, Elliott, I won't", were his words. Soon though, Geoff got a lover and things became different.

My job a E.J.'s (selling pot) was just like Deb's job at the restaurant O.W.T. I feel, for it does not matter how the money comes into the house, it's going to be spent on the same things either way you go. (But that is not the only similarity.)

When, along time ago Deb started working there (O.W.T.) and, my security was adversely affected, I had requested her finding another place to work. My feelings fell on ears unable to hear, so I knew that I'd have to arrange something. (Turn it around... so to speak.)

Sometimes, I have to place the other person (Deb) into a situation where they can see how something they are doing affects me in a derogatory fashion. I don't like hurting others, but I also need to have my feelings recognized <u>and</u> respected.

Sometimes, I *need* to be a mirror.

My work (sell/pot) was at a male (heterosexual male's) playground, while her job was at <u>the</u> lesbian playground where she "fit in" (unlike home). When she quit her job and the responsibility was placed onto my "head injured" shoulders to be the sole bread winner I scrambled around not knowing what to do. Even though she was officially fired by her manager (or so she said), it was because she did not perform the duties she had already agreed to do (or got caught with her lover while on the clock in the 'private bathroom'.

I felt force-fed but did the best I could do to keep things as comfortable for her and my yet unborn child as I could.

I could not hold a job any longer than a couple of days, or until my damaged brain ran into abilities which the job demanded and I was unable to perform.

I started to sell pot because it was the only way I could satisfy the financial obligations. What I had said to Deb about me someday working at a "playground" like she had found for herself (trying to put the shoe on the other foot with words) she had laughed. But now it was moving into it's realization, and she grew very scared. Did the reversal frighten her?

Mirrors can be very unflattering!

one-of-us

Can I trust him?
* * *

Geoff's new beau seemed alright but... can I trust him?

He came from across the river in Washington state. He was gay, and he had Aids. I grew scared for my child. Geoff's guy was a dead man who, I'm sure had no respect for anyone including Geoff. (My pot?) He had spoken on taking, with my permission, the 1/4 lb. bag up to Washington to sell. He'd then pay me and keep the profit in pot, so I told him how much the whole bag was, and he said he'd think about it. (There was never any more talk about it, so I assumed my bag was still at Geoff's.)

To make a long story short: Later that week I called Geoff to bring over my bag. "Sorry, got important stuff to do," then he said, "tomorrow alright?"

"Sure, don't forget."

He forgot. I started to get angry, he only lived four blocks away. So, I called again and insisted he get over here (my place), "<u>NOW</u>!" He came over with about 3/4's of an ounce of shake and stem.

"What's going on!"

"Didn't my lover (he doesn't deserve recognition) tell you, he took the rest to Washington."

"We had discussed it", I slammed, "but I gave <u>no</u> approval!" I saw people coming after me for the money I owed and grew even more scared. I thought to myself... I'm head injured and now I'm living in the responsibility and under the stress that I thought even a normal man might crumble. (I'm not normal.)

All the pressure of being the sole bread winner and coming home after a day of work to frigid unloving lesbian heart was beginning to kill me.

J. Elliott Goldwyn

I will not die. I've been close, but there is always more for me to do. I need to fill my empty heart, and I realized *I* needed to do that. Unfortunately, not in my own home.

Sara, had been letting me walk her home for a couple of weeks. We'd get to her place, she'd kick off her shoes and play with her toes. (I knew there was a reason I'd been buying ladies' shoes that fit my foot.) I could easily see she wore the exact same size shoe as me, and when I recognized this fact my heart began to beat differently inside the circle which was being drawn around us. (Soul-mates? Wow, if I had a nickel!) Sole-mates assuredly.

I was feeling the sexual tension in her place so I excused myself to take care of stuff... (really nothing at all). But I could not breathe because my sexual desire was growing too strong to allow me to catch my breath that had been taken away. I told her that I'd come back later. (I meant it.) (Always will.)

I went home to Deb who now wanted me to end my friendship with that dancer / neighbor who is kind, respectful, considerate and endearing. (The <u>one</u> person who is making me feel real... once more.)

"Sure," I sighed. (I lied.) I did not want to remove the smile from my face. It had been so long. (Too long.) I was going to go over there later, and I'd probably "in the end" concede the control of my life to Deb. Later in the night, I walked over to Sara's door and knocked...

"Come - on - in", she purred. (She's a Leo too!)

I was not prepared for what my eyes saw.

one-of-us

Selene was often dressed for her customers next door (E.J.'s), but Sara stood there dressed to the teeth - for me! (She said with her eyes - "I'm ready.") Only Deb had not given me permission yet. (A feeling I knew would come eventually.)

Maybe the toughest thing I'd deny myself, but I really did try to be a "stand up guy". In my own way I thanked her but came home to Deb.

It was my day I guess, Deb was also dressed to the teeth. Unfortunately, it was too little too late. She said she was sorry, but she's back now... (where were you?)

Deb looked sexy (inviting), only there was no desire. So the invitation was not there at all. I had seen sexy before (minutes before) and Deb could be sexy, but I had felt desire before (minutes before) and Deb couldn't fake that.

Deb had a saying that fits very well:

"If you lead a horse to a watering hole, but after you tie him up you hit him hard with a 2 X 4 when he tries to drink eventually he'll go to other holes (no pun) to get his fill of life sustaining fluid." (Thanks Deb, your saying fits very well)

Permission finally?
* * *

I realized after I was done - that I'd been "done". I also recognized the fact behind the feeling that there never would be desire or respect to any extent from Debra. I certainly did not wish to ever revisit our last night's love fest which left the taste in my mouth like I'd just raped a dead salmon fresh out of the frigid foam. Should I have stayed by Sara's side? No. Because...

Somewhere in the middle of the next day Deb asked me if I could spent the night at a friend's. "Sure" was my answer.

(Mr. Smooth again) So I spent the night at Sara's.

Deb had given me permission - finally.

(Symbolically speaking, or so I thought.)

Sara `n` I had a wonderful night - finally... (our first!) In the morning I awoke feeling horny (nothing new there) but so was my new partner, Sara. (Already I was loving her, and it was not even 9:00 a.m. yet!) (happy happy joy joy) It had been so long since I had felt emotion, and receiving it before I got out of bed to pee delighted me.

I had finished with a strong craving for tobacco but I had none with me. So up I go to where my tobacco is... my place.

Put the key in the lock and turned it, but the door was not opening. The door had been locked from the inside. (Does this sound familiar?) No problem, shoulder time.

Deb screamed... I caught her in the middle of something (of some girl?) but I didn't care - I had my tanks totally filled. So I could really care less who or what was filling hers. (Even trade, right?)

one-of-us

Nope, not yet. I didn't look around for her companion(s). What did I care, with a girl waiting for me on the other side of the building with her heart afire with desire for me.

(I didn't care at all.) But after I returned to Sara's ("my sanctuary"), two "pigettes" (two dyke police-"men") showed up with orders for me to not go home. She'll (Deb) be gone in an hour. I complied. (I hate cops, but they do have guns.) I don't have a gun, so I let them *think* they're in control. I'm neither stupid, nor a place for pistol practice.

Sara looked at me with sadness. She was trying to feel me through my eyes and mirrored my emotion. She was able to feel through me, and I knew I could feel through her and felt the bond between and around us grow. We had found each other finally, and both she `n` I needed to struggle no longer.

I knew her before, this I said. So I asked, "How do you feel about that Sara?"

"Yes, Elliott. Oh, yes." (The purr thing.)

Where have you been Sara? "Getting ready for you, Elliott." (more purring)

Why did you come now? "To give you what you deserve."

Oh gosh, when the goddess smiles occasionally "Pan" the horned god grins. (When it rains, it storms in Elliott's world!)

When the pink cloud we (Sara 'n' I) were on together does not disappear after three months, complacency could set in. But a smart man does not allow such stupidity to enter the picture.

My job was to keep our cloud afloat forever. I was getting assistance now, I was *allowed* to succeed. She permitted me to touch her, and I deserved just that. After so long, there was a lady who had desire to be with me and the desire was returned.

(I had a lot of emotional energy saved up.)

I don't want to dive into graphic description concerning our sexual expression. But suffice it to say, Sara let me bring her to the edge and allowed me thrust her over said edge. I am given reason when I can effect another so. I gave her (she let me) everything she deserved.

There was a feeling of total completeness ingrained through-out our togetherness. Is not that what we all strive to achieve? (Belonging!)

Out of touch?
* * *

A whole new topic offered for discussional (learning) purposes:

Today is November 15th, 1994 and it's time for a whole new view. Even though everything's "same old, same old", everything is so "new and improved"!
It all seems so complete... now.
It all seems so obvious... now.
But, allow me the opportunity for capsulated digression:
As clear as light I saw the storybook of "Deb `n` Elliott" come alive with a voice which is "loud `n` clear," (your true voice).
And I'm sure if Elliott would have opened both eyes (love often has the ability to blind infatuated fools) he would have seen it coming. What good would that have done?
I don't know... I really don't.)
(No vasectomy, probably.)

"Elliott, if you do, things will be different," (hint-hint) fallacy complete.

It's okay, lesser men have returned from the very gates of The Great Journey. And to follow that, I offer an analogy:
If an intelligent animal climbs an attractively deceptive tree to eat the seemingly sweet fruit, only to find them (the fruit) hornet's nests which are on the verge of an anarchistic revolt against all who dare to come close.
The animal (me) would climb another tree... if he could see.

Unfortunately, the animal I am speaking of loves challenge. Sometimes over his head. And why? Because the deeper you go, the more you enjoy the desperate first breath once you've reached the surface -AND- all the cool shit is at the bottom anyway.

But, to crystalize my ramble. I didn't need to fight the obvious lie. If she just wanted the child, she should have paid me cash. A business deal is just that. As I feel this is an accurate representation of the "ever loving" commercialistic society in which we all exist in our own way and at our own individual intensity. Watch the ball and think contact, contact and more contact. (Baseball day's instruction.)

I feel misled. I don't want you-all to believe I'm angry, only because anger will not allow me to concentrate the way a warrior needs to at all times and in all ways. Rather, my energy needs to hone a razor edge upon my true will so it may and might cut into my will's goal to separate fact from fantasy. For... "to separate _is_ to conquer".

Seeing is all important in the realm of understanding. Understanding knowledge and information is an all important aspect in the game of war, which is no game. Battle ground, chessboard, or the inclusiveness of realistic survival on earth. The biggest chessboard/battleground of all, and until we discover another planet capable of sustaining our lives...we are predestined to destroy this one.

No one will survive, but... oh what a game!

It doesn't matter what or why it is in your life, what matters is: it is in your life! Either way it should be enjoyed `n` utilized, or removed. In the days of despair sometimes salvation appears from the abyss, but sometimes not. Still

one-of-us

I stand, and I must stand tall for myself and those around me.

For the world (Elliott's world), will crumble without me to assist in the physical / emotional / spiritual reinforcement of the pillars and their respective cross supporting connectional arrangement.

All things become one in the end. (Sara, it's been too long, far too long since we've worked together on a common goal.) At this moment I have a list of selfish ends and I'd like to see to the end. Selfish because no one else can evaluate the importance of my direction without being able to see through my eyes while walking in my shoes. Selfish because many will suffer due to the imagined, or real, effects and aftereffects of me leading the life of Elliott. Hollow people will be hurt because I refuse to follow/swallow their hollow lives, and I must finish the book.

It's all a part of the great work. Everything's a part, everything's of value. No stone left unturned in the world (Elliott's world) which has been so ruthlessly shaken. In time everything's to become one. Although, patience will have it's role in discovery.

Instantaneously speaking is often the rust which corrodes my chariot. New horses subjected to my whip and a new direction has placed itself in my path with a new view just over the hill.

(I'm coming home.)

Difference is often times what is needed. Placement is the key to the prospective involved. Often it's not the event or the action, it's the view of said occurrence which is all important.

Life will play it's funny little games with you while the rules change as the world orbits around it's sun and in turn is affected by the moon which circles it. It's not fair but it *is* real. What you do may be what you'll be. Many fear change but without change there would be no growth and without some growth we would not be alive. Stagnation *is* death.

Thanks to Deb for giving me life. Nicholas, the entity of Nick, is *not* the life she gives, but rather the tearing of him away from me to satisfy her own personal direction... is.

Change was thrust upon me and in accepting this challenge I've been able to re-stake the boundaries of Elliott.

To live / to breath / to love.

Painful as it was, because how much change is needed doesn't matter, it's the fear of the unknown. I woke one morning to an empty house... Deb and my child are now in Florida... I wasn't even allowed to say goodbye. (There's more, but that'll suffice.) Never let people convince you that they "know better" than you concerning what you say or what you do. Because if they do, then I have a question:

"Who are you?" If you only follow others then you're not a "self". There is *no* "self-ness" and that's what you'll become. Fortunately, some of us have left following behind. Not all do, but that's a conversation for another day with another cup of coffee. (Or bottle of gin to quell my inner frustration!)

Now we're here with a new view, although in its coming I lost most of my reason. Thanks to Sara for her role in my re-examination of self and needed self appreciation which was gained through her acceptance of me, as me. She has seen little of who was left after this holistic wreckage, but Sara loves what she sees.

When all was finished there was only a glimmer left. Thanks to the goddess for letting a glimmer be enough.

one-of-us

Where I'd be without that saving refraction is irrelevant, for it's not the view I've had (attemptedly) forced upon me. Deb left to leave me, alone. (Sorry!)

My new view is bringing happiness to me. Why did I even try to drag my heels? My heels were not going to help matters much. The script was already written and I only needed to play the viewing audience. Foolish me, spending good money and wasting valuable time mixed in with emotion. Foolish me, refusing to see things as they were. Foolish me, selling pot and risking my freedom to make sure that there was a roof over Deb's and her baby's head. Foolish, because she was going to take my son away from me anyway.

Nick has been mercilessly removed from my life, but that may be for the best. In the end, everything whether or not it's good, bad or indifferent becomes "right." And, in it's very application, it reaches realization. Once it is history it becomes part of the greater whole, oneness. With oneness in being lies a level of complete communication with the greater whole. To accept the good... is to accept the bad. A person should not acknowledge only half of the circle involved. (More on this point later.)

In Debra leaving I have really been offered a new, even more challenging quest for me to enjoy the toil and tribulation of while I strive and stroll through its many demands upon me. So, I assemble the tools which are needed for survival along the way. Meanwhile I am looking at all the ground which must be covered to get from where I am to where I want to be. What can be avoided to make this journey with as few "life threatening" confrontations as possible? Always do needed work which will move me further forward along? In every turn, or before it, there are signs which need following or disregarding. Sometimes a symbol is encountered which demands to be worn as a shield or just another "set of wings" to assist me in flying over the worst of territory I must now travel.

Escaping the Holy Grail analogy for a moment:

There is something which I must now complete. The great picture is unfolding for me to see. It's dazzling and able to confuse and bewilder within it's brilliance. A picture is often made from smaller separate scenes which after compilation and complement within a structured environment are assembled into an unmistakable/unbelievable individual artistic work.

Goddess bless thou who gives unto the great work, often times unknowable of their valuable addition to the greater picture. There, is the definition of life worth saving from all threats, and also "love" worth returning in full.

May the goddess bless those who love in full.

All the turbulence, which has in effect placed a hellacious adventure inside my life, now makes it hard for me to see my bearings clearly enough to feel safe in the decisions I must now make. There are now before me many responsibilities from which I need to make decisions that will send off ramifications for all eternity.

I can't write, not right now (but I must write, especially now). I'm too scattered to examine one singular topic. I am looking at the bigger picture though; I've been searching for a family which I could call my own for as long as forever. (Belonging!)

At the forefront, my one and only "blood relative" Nicholas. Nick can hang on a little longer for me. He can, so he will, because he's of "good stock."

Never will there come a day when the ones I love will do without what they might need. I'll do what I can to see they get whatever their heart may desire. First on my list is the "li'l-E-man" (Nicholas <u>Elliott</u> Goldwyn), and he will probably hold the #1 position forever. (My #1 son!) (Rest assured.) Although, at this very moment Nick is in the best hands (I feel) possible... beyond my own.

Debra, who already is second guessing her decision to take my son away, is now asking questions as to why what happened, happened. (Like I know!) I can guess, though. "Because an easy answer is better than performing the very hard work that maybe you wanted to avoid at all costs, and all ways whenever possible." Her "easy answer" was to assume the attitude that I would not need any more emotional input after Nick's birth. In fact, I needed "it" more. But the more complete answer as to why what happened actually occurred is: "Because it's exactly what you wanted to happen Deb."

Now if I can see clearly, and I'm not being once again led down a (personal) control chamber, everything will work out just the way it should, once again. Everything works out in the end.

If it happened once, foolish me...if twice, hell hath never seen such fury.

"Love is the law, love under will."
(A. Crowley said it, I'm not sure when)

It's not that I have an axe to grind or believe someone needs to have a kneecap smashed, but I have never been either willing or able to cast my protective netting around those who are not logistically or emotionally close to me. Therefore I have concern for my boy because of the mileage between us. I cannot be on hand to defend him if ever the need should arise. (I pray never forever... but this world can be difficult, especially for the kids.)

Do I need to ask for assistance? No, I think not. I do believe Nick can and will protect himself until the time is right for me to be who it is I can be for him... and myself. I need Nick as he needs me. (So mote it be.)

Now I need to think about now and not the future or the past. What did happen, happened; what must happen, will.

Not anymore!
* * *

Nick, in the back of my mind, Nick in the front. No escaping him, never could be. I needed him. I was talking to his mom but she didn't *want* to actually share parenthood with me. Parenthood is a time of denial (Deb said). "I don't wanna be denied… not anymore!" (Was my reply.)

I knew that certain expressions would be slowed, but just because you have a child does <u>not</u> mean the love that brought us together should cease to exist. With no love there is no family. That "no love" reality would be very hard and confusing for my boy, Nick. (As it was on me in my childhood.)

I cannot subject him to the actual horror of living in a home of "no love". I had to grow up without my father in many different ways, he was there… but there was no affection in which to foster growth. The same is true concerning my mother.

I am a man with no father or mother to speak of. I see the incredible loss of my parents having been there, then abandonment of me took place. I see things differently now. As a man with no mother, I beg of you to… love your mother. You may not get another.

love love love
* * *

I needed to keep my head above the bankruptcy line, but I had much more responsibility than my meager pocketbook could satisfy. Rent, bills, food and the debt left after Geoff's mistake. Things became desperate for me... and then Sara said, "Can I help?" (love love love) If it were in my power to say how Sara's saving words allowed me to feel belonging like I had not felt in a long time, I would. But, in this case words would not fully encompass the explanation worthy of an emotionally written expansion. (It's at these times I feel "less than", due to the effects of my head hitting the hard pavement at 75 mph. I have problems in being able to find the correct words to describe anything at times.)

"Sure, you can help." (Smooth, real smooth.) "Would you... please?" I accepted the money (all I needed) on the condition of it being a loan to be repaid upon receipt from my first back payment check from S.S.I.

Deb started calling me. She had to, she left no destination information. (Did I say "stole my son" yet?) And she did not like the fact I had a new roommate at all. I told her it was a survival thing. The money aspect was, and so was the emotional input. (Although I didn't tell her that.) Why should I tell her what she already knew? I told Deb of my love for Deb, and she conceded the same for me.

I was loving two women (careful what you practice/pray for). One (Deb), for our loving past which I could not forget. The other (Sara), for her return of all it was I had been giving.

Body and soul
* * *

Sara's from Michigan. Some little town; a suburb of Detroit named Waterford. Not a bad place, but she left by the age of twelve or thirteen she thinks.

Sara could not remember everything that happened last night, but it doesn't matter at all anymore. Of course it matters, just in a whole different way now. I'm feeling alive (now). To me that's a combination of not only being accepted but "growing" into an even greater acceptance. Because I'm really not a bad guy, and it is nice to see someone else recognize the truth. (I suppose I lived inside the Debra fib for far too long.)

My body and soul have been charmed and captivated by a very young lady. (Anyone who had seen her dance I'm sure would agree and understand.)

Let me explain what happened last night:

When I spoke with Deb last night, she still refused to accept the possibility of me having just returned/reflected what it was earlier she gave to me. Trying to save her own face, after she had ripped mine off, was royal 'n' regal in direction (motive) but ludicrous in expression. What I must never forget is the reality of it all: she is the mother of our baby Nick, and... even mothers can grow. (Or so I'm hoping, for Nick's sake.)

I'm not expecting anything beyond the respect, honour and honest communication I feel I am worthy of and therefore... deserve in return.

I've been surviving through Deb's imposed parental "Hades" and the question is now, "will she survive mine?"

Probably not. She'll have her own place to visit or stay indefinitely. I'm not in control of someone else's spiritual catastrophe. Although, I've been a singular walking expression of karma for as long as I can remember. (Forever?)

Now what? Do I disassemble even more of my selfness or do I refuse to turn my back on the very fact that the ducks are lining up quite nicely. (kiss kiss, bang bang)

All the above
* * *

Deb wants to return to Portland. I will not ask Sara to leave, but my son screams to be realized. Why is Deb playing the "poor me" routine? Why does she dangle Nick like bait?

"If you don't let me return to run your life, you'll never see your son again." Not quickly, but followed by, "I already have new S.S.#'s and we will disappear into society...if you do not comply."

For me to say, "You controlling cunt!" (Or more truth...) "You fucking child thief," would be far too kind, so I said neither.

I detest manipulation. Deb doesn't realize that I *will* become the alternative father because of the distance in miles she's put between Nick and myself. If Deb wants my son to have a father and she wants that man to be me, she shouldn't have taken him away. By her leaving she was saying that I have been removed from the "people who are responsible for Nick list." I am a "non-parent". I was a donor. (An unpaid one.)

I don't like being "removed". I've never been removed before. I will <u>not</u> be removed now. Deb started her walk away from me when she doubted my value as a person, as a partner and as a parent.

All of the above and everything which takes place in my brain (thoughts, dreams, nightmares - in effect) go on at such a high rate of speed; therefore, are impossible to write down because by the time it takes me to write the first one down, I'm thinking about the 200th.

My brain doesn't like "not knowing" anymore than yours. But it's my brain I gotta listen to twenty-four (seems like more) hours a day. Other people (the big unknown) are always trying to control something or some part of my life or my body that I'd rather have complete control of.

"Why?"

Is there something I don't know? Maybe someone? (Hmmm...) Maybe I just need to realize that this planet is covered by animals (that I must cohabit with) which have an inner drive to control others (me)... when in fact they can't control themselves. At times, all of "those others" seem to be playing in some game, where control is the goal. Not only don't I have a "rule book" but I don't know the "grand prize". (But then again, maybe I do!)

Everyone wants to be a leader. Everyone would like to be the goddess (or god, if you still play with those stupid gender based semantic importance tactics). What better way than to become the devil. (Lucifer to someone else?) Ruin the other's life while trying to build their own. The more people work on hurting me means nothing more than more people to be hurt by me.

How can I say that? When something happens to me by the actions of another so there is change in my life, but the change is in direct conflict with my own true will, it seems as though that energy is returned to them. Positive intentions are returned positively. The more naughty of intentions are returned also, to the power of three.

Back to the point: I will let no man be my ruling god.

Everyone wants to be a god; let's explore that "want" for a moment:

To be like the Christian God (bible one) or some other entity which is at the top of whichever organized religion's

one-of-us

food chain (Buddha, Allah, Jehovah, Mohammed, blah, blah) is just about an impossibility. Our bodies don't allow it and if they did permit such perfection society will either not believe it -or-disallow it all together. (So what's left?)

Satan. They're everywhere... satanists. Living next door, maybe crawling the walls (reality *is* perception). Or maybe not. Maybe it's all paranoia. Maybe it's fear.

My fears are only that, fears. When they come true, that's when fears become reality. That may be why I have them, they do prepare me for the inevitable. Things could be different, but they rarely are. So when people try to control me, it is my duty to control them... I am not my bother's keeper, but after seeing how much their own actions hurt themselves in my karmatic reflection... maybe I could be their teacher?

(I'll pause here, for the collective "hmmmmmmmmmm.")

People have a 'need' to control everything in and around their lives while avoiding the control of behavior in their own lives, or, of themselves. How can they be so bold as to try to control my life? (Or yours?) Although, it is easier to try to control someone else, when you lose or "fail" you don't have to feel their pain.

Like the heartbreak when the promise (contract/fallacy?) of a family has been completely torn asunder. That's not fair... but it *is* my reality.

The assuredness (nothing is sure) of the future which is holding Sara 'n' I together is *not* reliant upon my ability to entertain her 24 hours a day. That takes more pressure off me than I can say. (This is important...) To me, this may be the most important aspect of a successful relationship.

J. Elliott Goldwyn

That, and... her looking <u>really</u> good in a waist cinch/garter belt.

But returning to the point: It's the acceptance/belonging "as-is" (no warranty expressed or implied) that I've been looking for, and on every turn... <u>denied</u>. I've finally grown weary from my fruitless quest... as Sara walked out of the abyss.

All six foot two of her soft spokenly screamed salvation. Out from the dark, lighting the way with her eyes.

My big day?
* * *

On Jan 27th (my B-day) Deb called to ask me what it was, if anything from her, I wanted for the big day.

"Bus load of willing cheerleaders would be nice", I kidded.

"I don't know a bus load," she answered.

"Well, you're one" (and I know and dated about twenty more but I didn't say that).

"What else?"

"For you to come back, and bring Nick with you," followed by, "and for there to be no stress about Sara leaving."

"Well, you're gonna get what you want then," her words nearly knocked me off my feet. I sat back and my mind raced.

I've certainly stepped into this, or so I thought. I was drawn to both but I needed to see (feel) both Leo women together (not sexually) and to look into their eyes and to see what I see. (Really, see what I feel.)

More 'n' more conversations both at home and on the phone. Trust me when I say, "I didn't know what to do." How much pain should I feel as a father. (Any at all?) I knew things would be different, so what better way to get answers? (questions)

"Will things be different now?"

"Will I live without having my needs met?" Which I feel are honest questions deserved of honest answers, and Deb replied.

"Sure, I do what I can, but... (fuckin' but's) I can't satisfy your need for stockings and heels." (Funny, but you did at one time.) But that was before, in a galaxy far far away.

Sara understands!
* * *

No desire, no sex, no way... but I could see Nick, and that became the most important thing. Deb also had another demand, "Break up with Sara." So I did. But that did not mean Sara broke up with me.

Sara understood (she always understands me) and said, "You need Nick and Deb both in your life, in time you'll understand more. Right now you need that, in time you'll be back."

(She was right, but I'm rushing the story once more.)

one-of-us

Life's operating manual?
* * *

I'm nervous because I'm being pulled in ways which I've never even dreamed. Love kills (or so the song says) only I'm not ready to die. So, my internal battle has only just begun... it seems.

No, not just begun, all my life it's been one after another. Everyone wants to wage war, no one will say so, but everyone wants to "play". Like life in the middle east or wherever. "Is that an olive branch in the mouth of a dove,,, that is crammed into a 50mm cannon barrel?" (Well, is it?)

Is Nick a bargaining chip baby? Not in my life. But I'll do what I can do to see that never is even a thought for me. I can't control others, but then I see things being how it is I need them to be. Which is not as I want those things to be I might add. Remember need? Needs are a funny thing. To say the least... funny.

Here it is, the 29th. I'm still as anxious a mess as I was before. I'm ready for Deb to return and then again, maybe not. The problem for me is not that I'm unhappy. Rather, I fear making others not happy. (i.e. Nick)

My main difficulty is that I dearly love both Sara and Debra. The only choice which I can make is to continue to love. I'm in heaven and hell simultaneously. Heaven, because I am surrounded by love. Hell, because I'm no longer in any kind of driver's seat. In fact, I've never been more 'just along for the ride' if seems.

At no time am I able to decide who it is I'm no longer to love and all the while being subjected to being left by both Deb and/or Sara. This would be so much easier if they weren't both Leos.

Sometimes I wish I had Life's "operating manual", something from which I could draw upon to facilitate making the correct choices upon life's various "choices to be made" experiences. Two Leo women under one roof, what have I gotten myself into? (I'm in love, that's what!)

The age is dark
* * *

I see a correlation of the situation I'm in with Sara and Deb, and the love affair between Lancelot, Lady Guinevere and King Arthur. (Only this time I'm not the lady.)

Lady G. (me) was in love with the King only to be left by the "way side". (Somehow in someway, the details do not matter for the connective correlation's completeness.) Deb was playing the role of Arthur and I the Lady. (This time?) Along comes Lance in the guise of Sara, to save me from the hell of being in a relation with no intimacy real or imagined... expressed or implied. Lancelot (Sara) is here to save me from an experience of being left again by whatever "side". There was no more desire coming from the King (Deb), but Lancelot never allows the emotional river to slow. (In fact, Sara's river grows as it flows.)

What's a Lady to do?

This time I'll not be left behind from the scene which unfolds before our eyes. I've served my impregnation duties, and now I go where I'm more value than money.

The King receives a monthly child support check, but after all Deb told me concerning love, I now see that was all she ever wanted from Lady G.

Two cats in my crib?
* * *

Valentines Day `95, was the day for Deb's flight to come in. (How dramatic, just like a Leo - gotta love `em!) The stress I was feeling about the soon to be reality of two Leo women under one roof was clouding my introspection. I needed insight, but I could see no answers in the fog inside my head. I was dreaming of my quest for something.
(Life, love, happiness, family... or the Holy Grail?)
I was looking for something in this beautiful reoccurring nightmare fantasy. Nightmare, because I never found what was calling me - and the call was becoming more desperate `n` urgent, and the subsequent anxiousness flooded my very being.

The night before Deb was to arrive I had a dream, and this is how it went:

I was lost, on a journey far from home. The time period was somewhere in the dark ages. I was often in dark cold clammy castles, looking for something I couldn't name, but... I could see it (feel it) all the same.
Sometimes it's just that way. The quest is often the purpose. What's along the way means more than the object (?) you're searching for.
Now that Sara has entered my life, the dream became more welcoming. I no longer had the overview of despair. I had found a new direction and a magickal horse assisted me in my dream. Magick, because this horse was a master (mistress?) at being what it was I needed it to be. When I grew tired from a day full of travel, we (me `n` the horse) made camp with a fire to keep warm.

one-of-us

I pulled the covers over me when from outside my tent the horse began to snort and whinny. The snorts turned to soft breaths and whinnies turned into giggles. By the glow of the firelight coming in through the flaps of my tent, I saw a hoof come through the opening. As it crossed the threshold it trans-formed into a soft, slender foot. The animal was a woman also... and I was no longer alone.

Which gave me the symbolism needed to decipher the questions I was asking. (Searching for answers?)

Life is full of quests. Maybe the greatest one of all is concerning our "purpose" here upon this world. Had I now found my purpose? My companion (horse) was all I really wanted to compliment my ever constant crusade, or was this horse (Sara) what I have been looking for? More questions means more explorations. Symbolism is there and I try to recognize it when it rears it's beautiful head and stares at me with brilliant eyes. But...

I did not expect this one. I had just woken from the dream (same ole dark ages story line) (which is a reoccurring theme for me) when Sara suggested a shower. Fine, I love water. (The Aquarian in me.)

Sara reached into a bag of hers and drew out a bottle of **<u>Horse Shampoo</u>**. (My symbolism transverses into reality?) (YES!) After our shower, I built or constructed bondage equipment, and I found my riding crop. (Now I knew why I bought it - way back when!) She just giggled, and Sara smiled when I told her she's going to wear a collar I'll make. She shivered, like a woman in orgasm. (I began to shake.)

J. Elliott Goldwyn

Lying eyes
* * *

Deb's gonna be flying-in in a few days, and my anxiousness was settling in, for I was accepting of the possible outcome. I did not have long to prepare for her arrival, let alone find Sara an apartment of her own. I would not throw her out on the street. We had split up the day before, and she was going to move out eventually. But, there was going to be no stress coming from me. I could do nothing but promise Deb, "things *will* be different." But she didn't want things to "really" be different. Deb wanted things to be the same as the day she left. (How could they be?) If I was to survive, things needed to be changed.

I knew inside that I'll know not what it is I need until I see (feel inside) her eyes.

(Deb's voice can lie, but not her eyes.)

Heaven -or- Hell
* * *

I had received my money. And after sending a check for $2,500 to my mom, I gave $400 to Sara girl. She smiled because (even though I didn't appear to be one) I <u>was</u> a stand up guy. With money, I'm better getting rid of it fast so it doesn't cause problems.

I bought a video camera, shotgun, and outfits for my girl, also.

"Heaven, I'm in Heaven... " I sing.
"All of me, why don't you take all of me... " is Sara's.
Sara was falling too. My guilt paramount, "What I have done?" I couldn't help myself, I was going down. I've had a footing before which was unsure and now I had to do my best to dance upon it. I had no choice in the matter. It <u>was</u> going occur, and I had to watch every step I took. You see, I'm not allowed to make any mistakes (like other people can). No, not me.

I'm not allowed. The being of human is not allowed (for me) because I'm special, I'm the one. That was impressed upon me by mom `n` dad as it was ingrained in my soul which has become my "act" of reaching out to those who need assistance of some sort.

At those times, I'm in "no control". I never am. I am nothing but a tree and I'm not responsible for other trees, even though "life" says that I am. How tall or how strong other trees grow cannot, is not... my concern. (I don't live their life, do I?)

I don't run their show, I just play a role. A good role. An important one, maybe, but still just a role.

J. Elliott Goldwyn

The world of hollow people gives me the responsibility of reaching above not only what I'm offered but what it is I can dream. Because life on earth is also life in the land of the H.P.'s, and they don't give anything away. (They are greedy.) Hard reality but not sad, because I give myself the finishes (goals reached) that go far beyond enjoyment. And you know, I wish you were there too.

The completion of my soul has become the only goal worth reaching or attempting to accomplish in my life.

one-of-us

All the rest become pale when it's seen that they have a hollowness inside. To make the bond that transcends time is what we try to find. The sad reality is that people try to make it. It cannot be made, it is... or it is not. (end of story)

But we've gone over that before, haven't we? But going over it again and again doesn't matter when the people who could be assisted have no intention of listening. They have other plans and they don't need to be educated on a greater dream of reality. Once the rats run the maze they don't knock down walls to make it easier to run, they are like dogs. Dogs who don't care if there is food floating around in their drinking water, either way the water satisfies. (Chunks or no chunks.)

I'm sick of swallowing the chunks (hassles) in my drinking water (living life). I wish I could tell the dogs of life to stay away, but if I were to do that, wouldn't I be removing the thrill behind my eminent survival? That's another reason why were here, to experience a "lifetime" (per-ce).

To be living in eternity becomes a race with no finish line. We're subjected to no time limit in which to draw completion or conclusions of any kind.

We are here to stand up for our beliefs while we condemn no other's. (But we do.) We all play god. We do that every time we tell another he or she that they are wrong. (We don't really know what's wrong for the other... unless it's harming someone else.) But we like to play god... don't we? It might be more than I can process, but for #1 person to say that person #2 is wrong... is that like calling the #2 person "**SATAN?**"

People are never wrong, their actions might be but not the people themselves.

J. Elliott Goldwyn

Afterthought disclaimer:
I know there are others who believe as I do, and I respect them all. Even though I do not know them, I don't need to. Although, I'm always open to making new friends.

Let things slip
* * *

Let me return to the story at hand: I'm not able to explain my feelings which were paramount on Valentines Day in `95 when I awoke next to Sara. It seemed as though I'd be asked to perform in ways which I'd never been able to accomplish before. I wanted not to let things slip through my fingers. Not this time.

I did tell Deb, "that things must be different!" But Deb didn't want anything different, even though she said she did. I didn't know what to believe, but I know what I felt.

Deb wanted parenthood union with me, and she knew all of what I expected for a loving return of my fatherhood actions. (A sense of belonging.) I will always be the boy's dad, but (fuckin' but's) Deb only wanted me to be the father and not an emotional partner to share her life with. Which is not what she said, but everyone knows the "words lie / actions do not" equation... right?

Deb was to fly in to Portland at 6:00 p.m. which turned into 8:00 p.m. because of delays. (Typical) With each moment, I saw my life needing and calling for recognition. My son and his mom will be returning, to what? I was not sure.

I guess a lot depends on her so I'll wait and see what's to come in a few hours.

Deb asked for me to make the house baby proof but I was not sure how much Nick had grown and how I needed to arrange everything. I tried, but like earlier (always!)

I failed. Deb let me know this right away. On the other hand, Sara applauded what it was I <u>had</u> done.

See how my dilemma became real? One lady wanted me as I was. While the other wanted me to change into someone else. Sex change? (I don't believe that would have helped any.)

Whether or not I was a man or woman, the object was control of me. Boy or girl didn't matter. She had no desire for Elliott or Bambi. (My pseudonym, when I wore heels for Deb.)

As Deb became the man, I became a girl. Two years ago I rode a Harley, now I shave my legs. (What have I become?)

A chameleon! I'm able to provide anything to the one I love. I've been many things to find the love - to ensure the love from the other. Deb was the first I'd completely been a failure with and the question was not my ability. It went deeper than that. I *was* a man.

If I became a girl, I'd still be an inferior one because of my borne gender's incompleteness.

Endless war!
* * *

The greatest battle I've ever fought was for basic unconditional love and acceptance from the mother of my son. I saw her in the airport, and I realized I may never achieve acceptance from her. She wanted nothing to do with my needs, she had said just that over the phone and now I saw it in her eyes. I really didn't want to believe her, and I hoped like hell it wasn't true. Of course it was, but love can blind. (Can't it?)

My first observation when Deb `n` I actually met eyes in the Portland airport, was the look that a prostitute gives the trick who short changed her. "I'm only giving you the shit you pay for, boy!"

I already felt despair for I did not have the currency (or pussy) she honoured. I'm not saying, in any way, that I find alternative methods of emotional interaction wrong.

"My body My rules" is the cliche I try to live by. Respect my rights as you wish me to respect yours. Seem simple, right?

If it were, some people would have no reason to mislead others to achieve their own personal goals. Deb had problems with my new found happiness and my unwillingness to relinquish it. Foolish me, I did not know this world demanded unhappiness.

I've lived unhappily long enough. Now is time for me to smile and no one is going to remove my smiles. That is a choice for me to make and others will not assume the role of "The Ruler" in Elliott's world.

J. Elliott Goldwyn

In the three months Deb was gone I found everything I might need was just around the proverbial corner. I suppose I should thank Deb for forcing my eyes open. If she had not I may not have seen what was right there all the time, waiting for me to reach out `n` grab it, use it, let it use me and enjoy.

Deb `n` Nick only stayed in town for about 12 hrs. and that time was not spent trying to reach a compromise. Rather, she had a list of things she wanted from me but offered nothing at all in return. I was ready to do almost anything but not in response to her evident disapproval of me and the meeting of my needs. My needs seemed to be not important to Deb and I needed to accept inherent denial contained inside our parenthood partnership. (Love *is not* denial.)

Deb called me the unaccomplished one. I've shown her nothing which was not exactly as it "should be". She grew tired of my constant tugging on the chains which were my restraints attached by her do's `n` don't's. In those three months she was gone, I managed not only to free myself from the bondage I was in inside the "Temple of Debra", but in doing so (like Samson), I had pulled out it's supporting pillars and the temple came crashing down all around me. (The dust still settles.)

Deb knows I'm probably the most powerful man she'll meet, and that <u>might</u> be the reason for her attempted control of me. Every "Delilah" (dyke) would like to take down a strong man. Only this time the hair was on my legs, and I still stand!

Although, it <u>is</u> the reason her temple lies in ruin. There was a day I worshiped there and now I go where my worship is appreciated and justly respected and returned.

"Long time coming" is what my heart was saying. Can't say I blame my heart for saying such because it was true. My heart has not yet led me astray while I've been on any of my many journeys. (Hearts don't lie, brains do.)

The line of life is very straight. There is a start and it's subsequent end. It does not matter why, how or what, but rather that you just get "there". Getting "there" is what's important, not how. We all will get there in different ways. And to reject any one of them is to say it doesn't work, for you.

They all work, don't they? How's are individualistic. How someone lives their life could be as different as religion, or as to where on the earth they live or which toothpaste they use (if any). It seems to be a control issue when some feel the need to prescribe to others their "reason for being". Because it's easy to believe in your own "reason for being", and it will have more credence if more people follow it. (Which doesn't make it "right". It just makes it organized...)

In the morning after Deb arrived, she spent the morning searching for reasons to leave. Questions were followed by more of the same. They were leading ones but were answered none the less, and I could see she had a strong desire for nothing to be changed for any growth to occur. While she was pregnant I was becoming nothing while she was becoming two, we lived together but were growing apart.

The query Deb asked of Sara was the proverbial straw. "After you (Sara) move away, do you think that you will screw Elliott?"

Sara said, "Yes, I love him", and I can see where she was telling nothing but truth. Even though we were split (Sara `n` I), Deb had a feeling, like everyone else in the room, that Elliott will put up with no denial for denial's sake (control's sake). And I'm sure she thought about Deb's promise to assist me in no way concerning my needs when they turned to intimacy. Sara knew she'd be my close friend and things would probably become more than just friendly.

Deb didn't ask me, but that matters little because I would have said the same thing in my own words. Deb was the builder of the maze she wanted me to run, and with no change made to the maze means the outcome will eventually be the same. Deb's not an alcoholic, but she follows one of the A.A. definitions of an alcoholic, which is:

"To do the same thing, but expect different results."

Days when she ultimately had control of Elliott (look at what my life had become) were very good for her, satisfying in fact for the man hating lesbian. She didn't want any different Elliott (same old - same old). I think she saw that I had regained control; I still loved her so she had some of it, but I was again being Elliott. (Unlike S.D. when I did *need* her still...) Now I was enjoying "me" because my purpose for connection with Deb was born, and his name is Nicholas.

I'm only sorry my desire to belong in a family environment with someone (especially my son) could not occur with his mom, and she took him with her. If I knew where Nick was, I would do anything in my power to be with him. Although in spirit... I am.

"Super-physical"
* * *

If God (or the Goddess) was against abortion, much like anything else, it just would not be in our knowledge or our experience. For the great entities have all power over all things. Although, forced miscarriage is inhumane and desperately requests improvement, or a complete removal from the list of human activities. I am pro choice (I was adopted). I also believe that every baby deserves not only a life, but a quality life, because quality lives make quality people. (Quality has nothing to do with wealth of fortune, or how much time if any has been spent in jail... because some of our lessons are only learned with pain.)

No person has the predominance or preeminence to name what is, or is not, acceptable to the powers which are "super-physical". Although many think they do, but it is their enormous egos eloquently speaking as to what they themselves wish to enforce upon all. Those "many" have no idea beyond their own sphere of existence. Most of the most are self proclaimed god fearing people. (With god, there is nothing to fear.) Understandably they might fear another out-break of the bloody crusades. Where "God fearing folks" ran a massacre across what was at the time the extent of the civilized world. Christians seem to forget that reality.

It was okay to kill then with a terrible blind vengeance. Countless numbers of innocent people have perished in the very name of god, and I believe it's time for that selective expression of oppression to stop. I will not be condemned to satisfy their "need" to place the "blame" on someone who is not to blame at all. I will not speak on my conversations with Jesus while we were together in the Light. For to do that would make juvenile something that should not be taken lightly. Although, we discussed how and why humans have been doing selfish gross interpretations of the messages he made an attempt to convey to us on the philosophical levels of communication. Man has taken, twisted and then preached the ideals contained in his teachings to the preacher's own self-seeking ends. There are a great many good people in religion... unfortunately not all.

The <u>ONLY</u> voice (vibration) of God is his own.

No human should allow someone else's belief to control their own. All any human can offer another is a view, or an interpretation as far as their vocabulary matched with their own skill at articulation <u>and</u> the willing listener's level of coherent understanding of the information being shared.

Every street is a two way street. As much as you become aware of teacher's knowledge being taught, the student reflects in return the teachings to the teacher on a purely individualistic level of refraction. After class, the professor/student ensemble are both walking away wiser about the same topic on separate levels. (The student through the instructor's eyes, and vice-versa.) Purely idealistic thought. But you can only accomplish what you can first dream. Which is only reliant upon consistency of progress while striving for perfection.

But I have spoken before on that level of social implementation before, haven't I?

No free rides -or- law 'n' order
* * *

In this world at this time we must all in someway make money to survive. Unless you are an inmate, but I purpose that this reality is soon to change. There should be no free rides. Even I do what I can to contribute to the society, which by association, I am guilty of being a member of. (But I'm not.) Before you can be another member you must be accepted.

Acceptance is first given by the family you are the child of, hopefully. If the parents lead a child into formation of a personality, but upon completion of the child's persona the parents notice that not only did the kid (me) pay attention to everything they said... but how to do what they do, too.

Because I've sampled most every up or down, left and right, in 'n' out of most everything, I'm able to speak on many different views from several separate viewpoints; still I only speak for myself and must say that for me the best experience that I've had until now is meeting the people along the way.

Listening to them and helping where I'm able, but only after my assistance has been requested. (Which is the important prerequisite before I even open my mouth.) That is what I'm here for, although that may not be true for you. But that is okay too, for I'm not you. You need to be true to you. I will be true to me and my individuality while living by my rules.

My life
My love
My law

I'm in charge of me. I will never come into your life unless my attendance is requested. I will make no judgement on you or your persona, and I will pick up no stone to throw.

I do not need to. I'm okay with me. I have no need to put you down to raise me up. I'm not here to belittle, I am here to assist. To speak on, or be able to, most topics with a level of understanding has been my quest. To do that I've needed to live in those various lifestyles.

Experiences <u>can</u> make the man.

In a nutshell
* * *

Maybe I should go back to the beginning to explain the how's and why's of things which are now inside my life. In a nutshell; Deb 'n' I got back together in South Dakota, she got pregnant on the drive out to Oregon (a wanted child), then she began to grow apart from me (and subsequently I from her). When I wanted Deb back, she wasn't ready and/or welcoming to the idea of actually being back with me. When she wanted me (much later, but it did happen) I was not ready and/or welcoming to the idea of being back with a woman (Deb) who I didn't really know at all.

Deb had become different.

The difference scared me because I couldn't understand it. We were both growing as people and as parents but we were not growing together. Deb says I wasn't there for her and I wasn't (just like she refused to be there for me). She's angry at me for doing what she did. This world's a crazy place when people expect you to act differently than they do themselves.

There have been many times when the "shoe" has been on the other "foot" in my life.

I suppose I could make some Freudian connection between that and my uncontrollable attraction to women's feet... and their shoes. But that would be flippant.

I wear as many hats as physically possible. Wouldn't you? (If you could?) I know many people are afraid of failure or success; but I am too thrilled by "feeling" a new experience and/or situation. Boy, I'd say things are about as crazy, no... crazier than they've ever been but... I've said that before. (Many times before.)

My son is in limbo without me. Nick would be a different man if I were in his life on a regular basis, don't you think? Although, where do I draw the line on being a father and being myself? Is it possible to be both?

Absolutely. I *am* both. Can't be avoided. I tried.(sort of) I shaved my legs, dressed in skirts, wore women's shoes and stockings too. And tried to otherwise become a more perfect man/woman for my Leo lesbian lover. (ARRGH!) Oh well.

Now I see what it was I was missing, or so I thought at the time, Sara. Here is a beautiful lady whom had laid down her life for me (or at least placed her neck on "the block") in our union and subsequent confrontation with Debra undoubtedly in the near future. I was too wrapped up in the pain of the moment. (Change…)

Change made from pain. Change is an aftereffect from decisions being enacted, decisions to remove the pain. All animals do it. Drop a cockroach on a hot frying pan, it doesn't think, it just does something or it dies. (Mostly, it does something.) All animals, large or small, do it without thinking. We (humans) sometimes have to stop and think about it. (Why?) Some/most of us, in our own way are secret S & M'ers. We love pain.

We have to love pain, because how much or to what degree you feel pleasure you must feel pain. (The circle theory.) Deep inside we know that. Religion tells us to feel no pleasure or you'll feel an eternity of torture. Now that's okay for some (the no pain / no pleasure game) it's just that… I need more. We're all here on this 3D tactile earth to experience and enjoy as much as we want without hurting others, but not subscribing or being force fed someone else's morales, values or regime. (Unless you want it.)

one-of-us

You're a grown boy/girl. Stand up for your own identity. Be who you are (inside), not who dad/mom want you to be. (If you don't want to, then don't. But if you do want to, so mote it be.)

The government has made individuality difficult. By writing laws that gives permission to the police (storm troopers) to teach me (the individual) a much needed conformity lesson. "Cut your hair, and we'll leave you alone." (Haircut prejudice*?)

Many people didn't fight society's (government's) ever present drive to make Tom just like Dick, who's just like Harry. That's them, that's okay for them. I don't bother them, why must they bother me? Do they have a need to control? Does misery love company? Or are they just greedy for something that is inherently out of reach? (You decide.)

Back to the moment: Deb loved me, for what I don't know, or maybe I do. Although, she had no desire to keep me, or at least none that she expressed. So I guess I'm saying that rather than Deb being a whole book, she's just a chapter... only I just keep writing.

Nicholas is another story. Maybe there's a whole series there. He'll always be number one. Unfortunately there's more involved than simply my feelings alone.

---

* another form of being an HP?

J. Elliott Goldwyn

Rape?
* * *

All I've ever wanted was to be a person and thus far I've been many. It's just that none of them were acceptable to me. That's where the running began. I needed to escape living a lie. Lies, because I was none of the hats I wore. I became confused because I wore them all so well. Do I understand them? Yes. Do I regret any of them? No. Everything which does not kill me allows me to grow stronger and more intelligent.

Every way of life is valid, although some more than others. I've seen the benefits and drawbacks of quite a few areas in life, and I'm willing and able to speak on them all... truthfully.

All I've ever wanted is to be appreciated. I've been lucky to find acceptance then and again, even though I have suffered through denial the same number of times.

When I felt love from Debra, I also felt acceptance of appreciation. Then after pregnancy achieved (2 hours after) I was made to feel as if any show of intimacy with my son's mom was... in effect (or affect) a rape.

Those frightening feelings following a sexual assault were not coming from me. While lying in bed with Deb after a physical expression of love, it appeared as though she had turned off all emotional and mental input. Like a woman (or man) does while being raped. Removal of her selfness from sex completely encouraged me to feel as though I was no longer accepted or appreciated. Deb was acting like a raped woman, and I felt a great deal of confusion and pain.

Why was intimacy okay before, but Nick is now six months old and it's still not. She just wanted my sperm and subsequent offspring. I was mislead. I was misinformed.

I was in love with a lie. <u>I was raped</u>.

And now Deb has our boy. Seems as though we entered into parenthood together. Now all we do together is:

1) A 250 dollar plus check comes to her monthly because I am Nick's dad.

2) As the mom, Deb cashes it.

Parenthood in the `90's. (Wow!)

Of course Debra does not let me speak with my boy, she is afraid because... I speak truth and she has something to hide.

Sometimes...
* * *

This work is of my very "real" life. This is not a movie. (Even though it could be.) What I've written <u>is</u> very important. (Sometimes more than others.) Although, if you pay attention almost everything is somehow transferable to almost everyone else's life. (Look for the similarities not the differences.)

The lessons I've learned are much more comparable to other people who live today than a book written a very long time ago. I do not discount any other work, written or not. I have <u>no</u> complaint with other trains of thought which are separate from my own. As a matter of fact, it's because of those different levels of spirituality that I'm able to be myself.

If it were not for an offering of various "forms" of spirituality, I'd be just like Tom who is sometimes just another Dick. But because I am eclectic, I <u>CHOOSE</u> to be myself and not another "religious lemming" on it's way to the spiritual cliffs. (Bet <u>not</u> that I might follow that catastrophe!)

I've have chosen to be self empowered.

I do not give responsibility of my actions or their subsequent moral ramifications to anyone but myself. I do not need a responsibility avoidance tool, or a savior on a cross which is on a string around my neck to save me from the predicaments that I place myself into. (I do not enjoy the idea of praying to a instrument of torture and eventual murder, that seems so sadistic.) I'm stronger than that.

"I am Elliott." (And no one else.)

You are you, and no one else too.

one-of-us

Sometimes I feel as though I'm not human, but then again... I'm nothing but. I am just like you but I'm nothing like you. I am myself and so are you. My selfness "is", *and* has nothing to do with you. My self would die if it became identical to yours. Your selfness would perish if it attempted to be me. That is why were here, to experience the joy and pain of living in a singular body rather than being only a part of the greater whole. So you could be free from the constraints of a monopoly (the Light). The Light is oneness. The Light is all. There are no shopping malls there to allow for individuality. (There *is* here on earth, just remember the really cool shit is never at the mall.) Instead of placing hurdles in the path of uniqueness we should be encouraging it. (En)Courage, because inner strength is ofttimes needed to follow your own path of expression, and should not be answered with a social application of the label "outcast".

Sometimes the title is correct, unfortunately that often makes it tough on me in the field of acceptance. (Don't look at me if you don't like what you see.) It's not my duty here on earth to judge your value as a person. Is it your's to judge mine? If I don't like what I see in you I certainly won't look at you, or force you to follow my rules for style of dress or something else which is an expression of "you-ness". Unless you are harming me in a direct or indirect way, then I'll tell you about it... and the rest is up to you.

When I was made, the "mold" I came from was mine and mine alone. It now stands on it's own pedestal never to be destroyed. I am Elliott, and that makes me special. Whoever you are means you are special too. Unless, someone or something at sometime tells you who you are. If this is true then you are no individual. Since that is why we're here, you may be failing your elemental earthbound examination.

But that is okay. This is only a dress rehearsal, not the *real* thing. To be anything you wish is possible, only step on no one else's toes while on "your way". If you do fail the test... that too is okay. (You'll get another chance next time you're here.)

You will not escape the inherent duty to live free. It is hard work... but nothing on this planet is easy.

To live free is also allowing others to do the same. That may be the hardest thing, but the rewards go beyond compare.

One word
* * *

I have so much to be grateful of, and so little paper left in this notebook I'm using.

To place all into one word (if that is possible)... <u>Sara</u>.

(Not only possible, but quite the qualified success.)

It's not that I receive gourmet meals like I had with my last roommate, it's just I now eat with a woman who not only says she *loves* me but shows it to me in ways I understand also. There is nothing wrong with how I comprehend love, or enjoy it either.

It's like a social equation. (For explanation I'll use the male\female relationship.)

If one person has a "drawing" to any other person, and that person shows the first guy that she is willing "to do" various things for him to remain attracted to her (and vice-versa). Once the union is established, one or the other (or both) exhibits another covert second personality, it is at that time that the relationship has completely disintegrated.

When Deb and I decided to live together, it was going to happen in a house that was filled with love for each other and our child. Only our house of love turned into a jail. That is the true horror of incarceration... there is very little love in jail. (It's the "no love" that kills you.) The no love in our house became hatred for me and my gender (which I'm certain was always there) only I'm sure if she would have shown it, it might have frightened me off early off.

(That is covert if ever I heard.)

Good thing I bounce back. (I love you Sara.)

(Thanks, Deb.) You became different, so I did too.

J. Elliott Goldwyn

    I must say that I rather enjoy the growth which has transformed me into a creature who now lives in a house of love. I never would have moved to Portland to meet Sara without you first bringing me here, then leaving me by the wayside after you received from me what it was you desired. You've helped me and I must now say, "thanks Debbie."

The end?
* * *

I'm not sure how to begin this paragraph, so I'll return to Deb's and my last phone call. She informed me of her planned trip to the state of Maine to spend summer with her parents in their summer place. I said, "alright... please give me a call, collect if needed, to let me know how our boy is growing."

She then told me of how she had no intention of doing that.

For months the only connection I had with my boy was an answering machine at her parents house in Florida. My mom received photos, but I did not even get a postcard.

I admit at the time that no input of how Nick was doing made me have feelings of dissatisfaction or disenchantment, and I probably made my emotion evident.

(That may have been a poor choice.)

As my weekly phone call to Mr.& Mrs. Fortin's machine was ringing I had my tape recorded message to my son already planned. So, when Dick (Deb's dad) answered I could not speak. I was at a loss for words seriously, and I told him I'd call back shortly.

I did, and Dick's first words were, "I'm going to record this phone call, do you understand me?" Sure, was my reply. I've been waiting to hear Nick maybe utter his first words, but that was not going to be close to what it was that was about to happen. There was some information as seen through Deb's eyes and filtered through Deb's information processing area she has in between her eyes coming through Dick's mouth. I knew there would be no way to convince the dad that his daughter had done *anything* wrong.

The way she told the story I played the deadbeat dad, and the society we all live in has a way of blaming the dads so the moms are never wrong. Dick then informed me of Deb leaving and leaving no forwarding address.

"Bye-bye Nick."

Afterthought reflections:
My fears, their forecasts and the subsequent formations of them, are equal to the forecasted formation of my fantasies. In a way... they *are* the same thing. (But maybe those *are* words to begin the next section of my work?)

Follow?
* * *

Some are followers, and I'm none of that. I follow no man (or Deb's) and to assume such is simple stupidity, to demand it is insanity. Some need to follow because of it being easier to follow the masses rather than blaze a trail all their own. Hard work blazing trails. But like practice magickly, no reward can compare. No one writes the rules for your body (unless you let them) but yourself. That's where I get a correlation between police (rule enforcing storm troopers) and slave owners (because "they" enforce too). <u>In no way am I saying the rules the police are upholding are incorrect,</u> it's like flying a kite on the end of a steel cable. (Overkill!) They (the police) talk on it being them against the world. The police are as much to blame for that overview as we (the people who do not wear guns) are. You get what you give, and I believe they've not been kind to me yet. (how about you?)

I, myself, go beyond that... I live free.

Free to choose what feels good to me. The moment I force my rule's (for my body) onto someone else's is the moment all I have worked for disappears or disintegrates. (Literally and figuratively) I have grown comfortable with me and what surrounds me, there is no way I will put all that in jeopardy. For I know what's important to me, not anyone else, let them run their own lives and keep their hands off mine. (Want to run another life? Then buy a hamster!)

Your own life needs all the attention you can give, as mine does for me. (Of that you can rest assured.) My words don't lie, and my actions do less. Seems like the more a person's reality is shit, the less control they have over running it. So they try (and often succeed) "running" (ruining) some other poor soul's life. Misery loves company, and I'd rather be alone. I will not feel your pain. Mine is enough for me. If I need to own a life,

I choose my own. (I like my life, do you like yours?)

I don't wanna hear how much money you make or what kind of car you drive or where it is you live, because all of that can be taken away. (It *may* soon.) But without all that material stuff, where is it your life begins (?), or would it end if all that expensive stuff were to disappear. Doesn't say much for you as a person with higher selfness, does it?

To have your identity wrapped up in what you have, or you can buy. I'm more, much more, than my bank account says. (How about you?)

If your bank tells you what you are, then I pity myself for living here with you. I'd rather go somewhere else, but there is nowhere to go. (Nowhere to go is why I'm an outcast.) I will not play the game even though it's the only one offered. Doesn't mean I'm gonna stand for it. Neither did the pilgrims, but they had a place to go... I wish I did. I understand there are people who would like me gone, but that's just their "job security" mode kicking in.

Lowly me. (Fancy that!) Their job mustn't be (that) secure.

Idea #1: A person who does something for a dollar, paycheck or cold calculating currency, etc they *would* *not* do for or to their own mother, <u>HAS</u> <u>SOLD</u> <u>THEIR</u> <u>SOUL</u>... period.

But not completely, they have not as of yet stole a buck off their mom.

So, theoretically... there's still hope.

The end of afterthought:

I'm not here to ask for something from you, I am here to give you something you didn't have before you read the last 300 or so pages. It is my hope you can see the connection between the devil (or the idea of him) <u>and</u> greed itself.

Does that mean the devil may have tempted me into a cutthroat high pay job before, but after some reflection... the loss of face was more than I could afford? Maybe.

(I only have so much good face left.)

I can't spare to loose anymore... not even the scars.

Book 4: (Questions)

J. Elliott Goldwyn

Reflections?
* * *

As I sit, think and look at the sheet of paper I'm writing on... I ponder about all the things which have entered my life. Many of those items were valuable, expensive or a complete waste of my time. In no way, and at no time was I able to discern those facts before I entered into the foregoing experiences. I have made many poor decisions during my life, but there have been the same number of correct choices. (Appears circular.)

It seems as though I have two people living inside my body. There are times I believe I have two different voices which often dictate to me directions to follow... and I do. My higher self is often in disagreement with how my brain accomplishes the survival tactics necessary to exist on the earth in our cannibalistic society. Which is a behavior that is acquired <u>NOT</u> innate.

Cannibals because of there being someone on the ladder of success above you which must be "eaten-up" on the financial level of spirituality to increase development of your soul on a purely materialistic rating scale. Destroy the upper other guy, and the person right below you has their eyes on you. (Another circle.)

It's my brain which handles (or tries to) the actions this society demands of me to perform which are considered survival skills. With my brain "on" all day long it's hard for me to turn it to the "off" position when I get home, and I find it hard to enjoy what it is I *do* have. Like most people I turned on the television which then told me about all the other items I want to complete my soul. (When want-want-want becomes need-need-need is nothing but an exhibition of greed, the original sin.)

one-of-us

Sometimes a person bends the absolute truth in order to sell a used car, a buyer usually expects that. Already the purchaser has subscribed to the "bad apple" theorem's realization. (Pity.) Before the buyer walked onto the lot, the seller was gonna lie.

It should not be that way with any business, but it is from the home based shops to corporate levels. You are buying what you're buying. The high price does not mean the automobile is better, but the lie about the used cars condition *is* a show of disrespect to another human. All to get closer to their god... which is hollow, green and has numbers printed on it.

Disclaimer:

Not all used car salesmen are bad, but the occasional bad one does ruin the bunch. Car salesmen (or women) start fighting below the water line of acceptance on levels of trust, how unfortunate for "them". Because you accept a job working with "low life's"... does not mean you have to act like one. Although I understand the need for a "soul" to experience that theater of social hell and certain subsequent deliverance of pain.

One thing?

* * *

Remember the day when oral sex was illegal? (It still is in some places.) What's wrong with our values? To make it against the law to please your partner? (Silly system we had/have.)

We only need to change one thing, we need to change it all. (Scary thought?) What will happen? Who knows? I do. We'd grow as a peoplehood and as the entire society in which we live. Most are afraid of change which is inherently contained within growth.

So, that may not happen. There are reasons for people's insistence on keeping things just as they are. "As they are," is never how things will be. Without someone to change the oil occasionally, any car (government), no matter how well made will begin it's decline. Because the road (country) will always be changing for the car (gov.) to adopt and adjust to the road conditions (state of nation) at the present moment. (Whatever those conditions "we" gave ourselves to deal with.)

To make things better for future generations is why we're here. But if that's true, why do we allow our liberties to be removed and replaced with limitations?

Limitations are the walls of the maze in which we all run. Life is a challenge in itself. To increase the difficulty is a ludicrous action, or is it a result of inaction? I am insistent upon the return of the respect I give and if I receive none in return, then none will be given in the future. This is more than a promise. I've met more males who had an inability to give any respect, or have they been conditioned by the overview that life is respect-less?

one-of-us

Even though the ability is <u>not</u> limited to female humans, it seems as though it is not an equal division at all. There are men who are able, it just may be they're tired of hitting "brick walls" unable to return anything at all. Brick walls are to be avoided as we "drive" down the "roads" in this "country" of ours. (Speaking in analogy still.) Why do we, as a people, "drive down"? Consistently we go down the "roads" when we are <u>not</u> forced to. (Or are we?)

To be something we're not is what the governmental system we're under (the thumb of) demands of us daily. We're not going to put up with this are we? (probably) And why? Because we're told "by T.V." (and other sources) that things will get better if we conform. Being the trustful sort of animals we are, we permit our keepers (law makers) to not only make our daily cage smaller and smaller, but we allow them to supply us with less and less (soulful) food with which we need purely for survival purposes.
(Here I'm using "food" to metaphorically symbolize the monetary/emotional/spiritual state of the nation and it's inhabitant's survival.)

Barrel time!
* * *

What do farmers do with rotten apples? Throw them out.

What does the rest of the world do? Throw them out.

What does America do?

Put the "bad apples" in gilded cages with all expenses paid opportunity to further their own "apple-like" existence. If they choose to respect the opportunity, fine. If an unsocial-like creature chooses to be concessive in acceptable mannerisms to facilitate the "post (prison) creature" into living socially <u>and</u> if that is desired by both the society and the individual... fantastic.

If the apple chooses to live off the unwilling "good apples" in whatever way, is nothing more than disrespect borne from greed. (A bad apple is a criminal <u>or</u> a con-man.)

For people who show disrespect for whatever reason, be it the sex of my body or the color of my skin or the class of my clothes or something my great great grampa did to your great great grampa...

It's <u>not</u> my fault! Get over it.

What I <u>am</u> responsible for is how I choose to move through life today. I'm either sand or grease in the working cogs of existence. (I choose grease.) Especially in relation to other apples, whether they be bad or brilliant. It takes many types of apples with varying levels of uniqueness to make the very best "American apple pie".

I don't believe there is so much blame to be placed on the people's unrest because of racial or class difficulties like the T.V. says there is. The police have even stated that

one-of-us

the country is on the verge of a racial/class war. They are wrong.

The "police predicted" social anarchy *is* concerning the amount of respect the common men (you `n` I) have for the government's failing economy (if it were not failing we would know ALL the facts, because it is our money... not theirs) and administration which is literally dying before our eyes. It's always someone else's fault, there is always someone you should fear... or blame. Politician means: finger pointer.

The system (T.V. and other media) tells blacks to fear the whites, mexicans to fear the blacks, and the whites should fear everyone (or something like that). And don't forget about those "Mohawk - boys", now there's a group of "real people" you should fear and never talk to... just open fire. (Excuse my dry humor.) The scary thing is that some H.P.'s actually believe that's true. (HP= hollow people)

If the "system" in place keeps "we the people" arguing within ourselves, we will not be much of a resistant force when some oppressive power comes into America and takes our freedoms away from us. Life, liberty and the simple pursuit of happiness would be impossible for most to afford if the prices keep rising in the astronomical way they are. Even the middle class cannot afford a one week vacation sometimes. Who would ever try to come in to the USA?

The system, our own system, that's who! (Commercialism.)

It's already in, greed is running the game. And greed <u>will not</u> let go easy. Thus, the opening of that infamous conspiracy theory. The big corporations own the world because the big businesses pay for that privilege. The governing force of the USA is the biggest corporate enterprise of all. Greed, the life's blood of satan.

Isn't that what capitalistic means? Everything's for sale? Everything, period. You, your life, your guilt or innocence, your ideas, your liberties, your love, your dreams and your children.

The problem begins in many ways in many different formations and directions. Looking at the grand picture... because for me to individualize the directions of the sins of man against his own fellow man (his children really) would take far too long to discuss. Rather.... I'll make an overview of my own opinion:

Disrespect. Far too many people are giving disrespect to others who have done nothing to warrant such behavior. True, a person (any person) deserves respect when they show respect... *period*. When someone shows no respect because he or she feels

no respect for whatever reason there's no respect built up, is a purely relative thing. Respect is not given blindly by all.

Although, when I am walking down the street not bothering anyone, and someone decides (for whatever reason) to harass me because of my clothes or my haircut but no <u>real</u> reason, isn't that bigotry which is another form of disrespect... or greed?

Sin?
* * *

Prejudice, which is narrow-closed-minded behavior, can be putting yourself up by putting other people down. In effect, not rewarding but obviously destroying another's individuality.

Individuality is not a sin. Individuality is not a sin. (So good I said it twice!) Individuality is a gift which is relative to all humans. It's my life and my love that lives by my law. (Love is my law, love under will) (more about that later.) To say that I live wrong or in moral conflict with you, even if you don't know me is the very meaning of disrespect.

Still I must change to accommodate you, is that to say that I am a slave owned by you?

(Fuck You!) To say you own me... is the greatest show of disrespect, or greed by another name.

A friend of mine can offer me an opinion or knowledge to help me, to educate me <u>not</u> condemn. Any person who says they know better for me, is *not* my friend. They do not discuss the matter with me, they just tell me I'm wrong. That was a very un-wise thing for them to say... period.

My life, my law. It's a respect thing. I respect my own body, I respect anybody who shows me respect. I show honour to anyone until I know better. For the person who I pass on the street, seeing as we have no relationship to base any amount of respect upon, it's acceptable to show indifference or no respect because as of yet there is no respect built up... but there is honour! Completely different from respect and no respect, is disrespect.

Disrespect should only be shown to people, and <u>only</u> to people who are showing you disrespect. Things, animals, and most children don't even know about disrespect. (Yet.)

Children will learn about honour *if* we teach them to respect by matching our words to our actions.

(So, what are you teaching the children?)

one-of-us

The kids?
* * *

When we are old `n` grey and in "the home" our children will be in charge. If we don't teach and show respect to our children, what will they show us in return? One more simple equation which has become simply hell. When "we the people" became "me the only person (or the only one who matters)" is about the time that greed, or the very idea of greed, began to disassemble the internally reliant structure which is the supportive framework of our social culture. ("The Family")

With no family, there is usually no order instilled by the elders of the clan. (The Divorce clan, etc...) If a group of autonomous beings gathers into solving a common difficulty then the group could be called an alliance, dynasty, family group, society, fraternity/sorority, city, state or country. (etc...)

With no input which has endured the trials and tribulations of time, there may be a large amount of information missing to assist in the making of correct decisions socially.

Unfortunately there are circles of friends joining together in a quest for their god... which today is the almighty dollar. They have "hit the skids"... or "sold out" or just given up following the rules on their bloodthirsty drive to reach the most holy of places,
"easy street."

The news has named these groups of brotherhood, "gangs". The media tells us that you may die if you go to their territory. (And it wont be pretty.) You just might perish if you disrupt their viable, vicious, valuable velocity of visible business.

Who gives these gangs money? (We do.)

Why? (We buy their product.)
So, there's greed involved? (Yes!)
Who can blame them?
Not I, and here's why:

Our information devices (the media) has programmed many into believing the false "product promises" are true "fulfillment of the soul" answers to the "money is my god" religious questions.

There are buyers for the gangs product, whether it be stolen stereos or drugs. The "gang" or "lone wolf* is risking their freedom to build their pile of money bigger so as to be able to stand on it and touch the face of god.

Which is a spiritual correlation I will **not** make. So I no longer work in a marketing position where I even need to make a sales pitch. But that's me... and I've found:

Every other person became the enemy or a customer in the search `n` fight, hit `n` miss financial structure which is the very meaning of the capitalistic society... in it's truest form. In the formation of said social platform, money is paramount. In not only the relationship aspect of social endeavors, but organized communication of church and state. It can't be helped. Money *is* power. The powerful write the rules. Money is the power now writing the rules. What was once a government by the people for the people, is now becoming (and has for awhile) a tyranny by the almighty dollar... for the almighty dollar.

We the people have allowed commercialism to replace the divine, the goddess of love, with something divine which bites back.

*lone wolf, is a gang of one

My goodness! We are self defeating people, aren't we? And we call ourselves intelligent *and* civilized.

But, we weren't done. We need to replace the bible as task master because we were getting even more greedy, so someone went and invented "purity of soul." (holy on sale!) Some of the people were even getting curious and started asking questions that the "all powerful" (at that time) preacher man couldn't answer without talking in riddles... rather than just saying, "I don't know." But it all comes down to this: I need to change... somehow. I <u>need</u> to become *more* holy. Which means more wealthy in the land of the H.P.'s. (I do not go to them, they'll come to me.) When the Jehovah's Witness people knock on my door, it's like being force fed a really bad comedy routine.

There are other divisions of people, but few are more important then what we've become. A nation under "God", that has become a nation under the dollar. In this social system of capitalism you are holy if rich... and if that's so, what are you if poor? Not holy? Not gonna go to heaven? Nope! Can't afford it here, can't afford it "there" either.

If you pray to the dollar, you're not above crushing others in your path. It's a lack of respect born from a system (a maze) we've built for ourselves to live under (or in). Why under, and not with? Because that <u>is</u> "the solution" to our maze. As we humans run the maze, real people (not rats) help other people to finish; where as unreal people (the rats), don't care about the others in the maze. (How many rats do you know?)

If we remove or replace the maze then we also remove the race that the rats run. Can't blame the rats (hollow people) for running, we only have one maze (right now).

J. Elliott Goldwyn

The bummer is that not everyone is a rat, and that's bad. Wrong, in fact. Which means whether or not we want to... we <u>must</u> run (or be an outcast). I want another choice. America has become exactly the monarchy we rebelled against. There is nowhere else to go. Surely there are great minds around to lead us into something better than this downward spiral. We (as a people), threw our arms up (guns up) against a governmental system (the king) who we found to be incorrect in their judgement and implications of justice. (I won't even mention taxation = no representation.) I'm sick of living (surviving) in this, I want more... I cry out for freedom. And, real freedom <u>is</u> <u>not</u> a tax break.

Which incites another morale placement question:

If another person tells me my own soul is in jeopardy of being sent to hell for an eternity, not because *I* sinned mind you, but purely because of "non-union" with said other person's preservation payment plan. Whether or not the $'s in question are time spent at church on Sat. or Sun. morning or... "the almighty" deposited in the collection plate. The church owns people's minds, souls, time, money and the children they have inside their Sunday schools?

(Yes.) Just like the armed forces owns their soldiers? (No.) The government also owns their lives. (Gasp!) Now comes the time for fear.

The church as your grandma or your great grandma knew it... is dying. A punishing god is <u>not</u> an *all* loving god. An eternity in hell is <u>not</u> the punishment of <u>my</u> goddess. Today is the day when I follow my heart in deciding what I should believe in. I mean why not? I should aspire to greatness (divinity), not lowness (vindictivity*). Many of the

---

* I think I used this word first!

believers who follow blindly are judgmental hypocritical Christians (or some other title) and should be thrown to the lions so to instigate a visit to the Light to have conversations with Jesus himself (or some other godhead) about his teachings. More importantly, about the message of love and respect for other men (or women) contained therein, not the pigeonhole path of persona persecution and destruction they are on.

There are many godheads, there is only one real message: "There **should** be more love."

J. Elliott Goldwyn

Bullshit?
* * *

The organized religion god is too human for me. Too angry and non-forgiving... or is that how they, "the greedy preachers" kept us in line to donate more money to their god. So, to keep their god from getting upset again. (Bullshit!) God wants your money to help the poor, down-trodden, sick and hungry - not to buy fancy things to decorate his house of worship and especially not for the men entrusted to speak on his behalf. And when the men or women speak to me on his behalf and tell me of my imminent damnation to hell...

I must laugh.

I've been to heaven because there is no hell, if anyone can and should have gone to hell - it's me. So with knowledge of my not having hell in my future, I giggle... for I see my purpose clearly now. I know better, I've been there. I know what's there <u>for me</u>, I know how to communicate with what's left over inside from being there. Now I ask you Mr. Preacher man (or neighbor who informs me of his being 'holier than thou') how can you say that?

<u>All</u> you know, Mr. Preacher man or neighbor*, is what you've been told. I've seen the Light, my Light! You... have not. I am <u>not</u> your son, or a member of your empty minded flock that pray to your vindictive god and unfortunately follow you blindly on a spiritual treasure hunt... when you yourself do not hold the map.

No one holds the map, but unlike you I've seen it. (Other near-deather's may have too!)

* If you live on earth, you are my neighbor.

one-of-us

If preacher men truly believed, they would know it's time for a great change in the "fear developing organized religions of the bible twisters." (Or, at least accept <u>new</u> forms of answers to the same old questions. Everything grows, especially perception.)

"Follow your dreams, not the machine!"

There is no dream too extreme to follow, as long as the conquest is kept to yourself while harming no other. The action of loving yourself and all around you is "the law" that should rule the land. (More later.)

Are you?

* * *

Let me make one important point right now: I've met people from every walk of life or possible combination thereof, and you don't have to be anything to be real, nothing can be done to make you real, not a religion, or a social class, it goes deeper than that...

You either are, or are not.

You'll see, afterwards, and you'll also see (as I) that too much time was spent on/in opposition of others finding their true will (purpose) and not being real (as a person) and really there as the friend of others (that you say you are)... and acting that way too.

(Your words might lie, your actions do not.)

More?
* * *

If a person is molesting my child or any child, and I find out - I'd probably kill. (To rid the world... and all that.) I know you probably feel differently whether a little or a lot, but that is how I feel. (It's a respect thing. Hurt my child, I'll hurt you.) If that person showed no respect for my child's life, then maybe that person should not have theirs!(?) There could not be a soul inside that person, so theoretically the world's population would not change. No person with a soul could do that. (Talk about hollow!) Some of us are born with a basic morale list, and that's one of them. "Hurt no one", said the Goddess. If a person can do such evil, it's simple, there is no soul inside that animal (like a snake, or a slug)... "it" is a common pest. With no soul inside, it would be like exterminating vermin. (But, "No... ")

We've been far too lazy, and now the pests are a real threat. What should we do? Well, change everything. Condition the habitat so the pests can't survive. Destroy the breeding/feeding ground, and you'll kill the monster. (Where does it all begin?) Maybe with disrespect which is greed? For a long time we've been (grand scale, collectively) following a guilt based, fear inspired, disrespect breeding, organized religion game plan. ("turn the other cheek") Throughout the years "they" have gone by the Bible, which is a religious rule book, but if you pay attention you'd notice the Bible and churches keep changing to accept more of the fringe of society. (Open the gates to let more cattle in.)

Like the "don't ask, don't tell" routine concerning service for some (homosexuals) in the Armed Forces. Land of the free? Home of the "don't ask, don't tell"... routine? All men may be created equal, but... it's not happening in America, and that's all I know.

Everyone wants "one-up-man-ship", but no one wants what they may give to be returned to them. (Everyone hates mirrors.) When Deb started hitting me, for effect and not jest, we were living in South Dakota. I pleaded with her on tear-stained bent knee, to never hit me again. I felt like the girl being hit by her father. "I know I've not been perfect, but your striking me... destroys me." (But since I have a cock I cannot hit back.)

Deb played that, cock/no hit back, to the hilt six or seven times she hit the one she said she loved. And all I did was cry and fall into our beautiful (kinky) sex relationship between me "the sensitive man" and her... the queen dyke. <---(her words)

My submissiveness was abused. She was/is a man hater, only I wasn't a man (per-ce). But upon inspection you can see Deb was performing exactly what she hated men for. The man hater acting just like a man. (Why do some lesbians do that?) Or, is it just primal "cockless predudice?"

I'm not a lesbian (in a woman's body) but while I contemplate that reality... I would think that acting like "a man" would be the greatest sin to be enacted socially by a lesbian.

A part?
* * *

You either live in society respectfully or you don't. It's completely up to you, you will show how you feel about that with your social behaviors everyday. You are either a part, or you have no part in the society... and should leave. Would you like another choice? Well... I dream of "Elliott's world" where there will be other places where certain basic behaviors are allowed (even applauded) so everyone has a place they belong. If we take the time to design a whole city where drugs are legal, there would be no junkie effect crime anymore... at least not in your area, because when an addict or occasional user can go to a city where it's okay, they will go. If business men and women live where you do who choose not to do drugs, so drugs could be outlawed there, *if* the majority rules. If someone complains, all that must be done is a relocation of their home, so they may live with other occasional users.

Not junkies though, there are towns for them. Prostitutes and gaming halls may be able to share the streets. Nothing is wrong, it's just where you do "it". I don't care what you do, just do it somewhere else if it is against the local majority. Somewhere it's not a crime, far away from my kids. "Because I love my family." (my family car, freedom, knowledge, home or lifestyle... etc.) That's what is important to me, what it is that's important for you is not allowed here. So, let us help you move to where you can express yourself freely. You don't bother me, and I will not bother you.

(That's respect.)

I will let any person live however they want, as long as I can live the way I choose, and no person steps into my life causing harm or pain (in any way) to me or my loved ones due to the disrespect shown to me by their rules for their body affecting mine. No matter your choices upon your way of life, there will either be a special city to go to, or you'll build your own (we might even help). Everyone has a place to belong. As long as they keep their symptoms to themselves. (To themselves, NEVER to someone else!)

"Build it, and people will come." Famous words that are still true today. If we were to build whole cities of "ill-repute" (which is a term that is totally subjective), the scum of society (also subjective) will move there. That would be nice, but if the majority (in the city, county...) vote in a legalization of something you cannot live with, or near, then it is <u>you</u> that should move. It's only fair, the few should not govern the majority in a free country.

In a free country, no one should govern anyone else.

But they do, money is a singular thing - in many denominations and currency forms worldwide - and it (money) writes all the rules we humans follow in this way (and many others): Money buys time, time of your life in repetition. Repetition forces familiarity which breeds comprehension, and it becomes (slowly) a second nature reflex in the voting booth for one example. "I don't know his record, but I've heard the name so much he or she must be the right choice" or "if I vote for him or her I'll get more free money (food stamps or tax cut), are the very (greedy) words which are bringing the country (slowly) to it's knees.

Money is taking away our liberties, by allowing us to feel guilty. We have these weapons that kill people (for instance) and out of the millions and millions of people who

one-of-us

live in America, one "snaps" (actions = insanity) and uses said weapon in a horrible way. The people we pay with our taxes to guard us from such (you know who), and we pay them well... and they can't stop one out of a thousand. Maybe we should rethink our system, into removing what it is that drives our brothers (and sisters) to the breaking point. Stress? (Maybe) Greed for power? (Is there any doubt?)

    If we were to work toward perfection, then we would reach to those people and save ourselves from certain cannibalistic catastrophes. Everybody jumps in (sort of) to help the victims of a tragedy (whether man-made or not).
    Why don't we invest a little effort for to cease the tragedy before it even becomes a thought? Helping one another rather than competing with them. (Poor li'l pinballs need to work with one another, not kill each other for the game.) I'm sure any person who felt loss from what has happened in Oklahoma City in 1995 to a loved or respected other person's life would gladly have chosen to have that person back, in trade for what could be an hours' or more worth of listening to the potential murderer (the man or woman who "could" do the crime) and show understanding to remove all, or at least some, of the potential criminal's reason to commit the crime. (Or maybe it was not a person at all?)
    The time my soul (effusive energy existence) spent in the Light was consumed by learning. I had access to many trains of thought, many of those trains were like great existence's of yesteryear. I must affirm one point; I am not saying I have all the answers, but I might have the questions we should be asking... or at least some points we should ponder.
    Unfortunately I don't remember the exact points of "survival or coexistence" that were shown to me in the Light

in the way I'd like, like a vivid memory of a conversation I can recall at will. The feeling I get is to follow my heart and let my pencil write. There was a reason I was born, to be adopted by the Goldwyn family and have lived a life full of various enterprises so I may be able to show various lessons learned that channeled me into who I am today. (Which *is* the message I need to communicate.) As I write this I'm unsure of how to capsulize it into one sentence, although I do paint t-shirts with the "respect" exclamation of:

    My Life My Love My Law
       (loud 'n' clear)

I suppose if that were to become fact we would begin to see some great amount of change. (The "c"- word, argh!) That is where growth usually stops. People are so very afraid of change. Something needs to happen though, I have seen the terrible things which might occur.

As I watched my "video tape" of my life (which at the time was just an option?) I saw what could happen to me if things became insane in our society (or, if I let them?). When I say let (I am no god, no one is), what I mean is this: I do have something important to state and maybe someday someone would read it (my son?) and carry what dream I could convey to it's further growth (as a dream) and to it's subsequent recognition in reality.

Many men and women have had dreams which they have followed in the past, and the only difference is... I'm from the present. I follow my dream because it will happen, it must - or - we might continue on this social existence downward spiral containing no love than by just name alone. Everyone needs the room to breathe and feel welcome by the people he or she shares the air with.

Help?
* * *

We grow the food (because we can!) and we could send some to Africa, with the training to accept a god their society does not comprehend. They get fed, get well, get educated and get with the "program," or so it is the church does say. So the people with the food extort actions from the starving masses into adopting a 'new' God. The people with the food are holding a possible starvation (sword to the neck) of the masses until the masses do exactly what the food suppliers demand. Which to me is nothing more than a modern day Christian crusade! (Or, greed in the name of God?) If 'missionaries' would like to do good for other people, then feed them for free and help build ways for them to feed themselves.

We can't make money or the idea of it go away, so we remove the food which feeds the monster called "greed". Greed would no longer be possible, if there was a minimum wage (with benefits) there would also be a maximum wage. Which is not "my" idea, but it does make sense. It would be high, because some jobs take more out of you, doctor, paramedic, teacher or some other person who is working to help other people - <u>the true heros</u>! We remove the food for the monster that says, "It's okay to totally shaft a consumer, who is just another pinball, so I could get (maybe?) that bonus sales trip to Maui." We pay money to the machine so it could take care of the responsibilities it assumed, and our country underpays <u>some</u> of the most important "employees" and their enterprises. (schools, fire-fighters, teachers, or elder care nurses...) And there is so much more, I know, please don't hate me because you were not listed. (You are in my thoughts.)

We fight with the system (the machine/game) to do what it says it will (only does not); teach our children, teach the adults, reach for perfection and stand for nothing less than progress!

Oh wait... "<u>it</u>" doesn't say that, I do. (I hope you do too.)

We let them?
* * *

It's not that I complain, but rather "squeak" like mad. (I want grease.) Why can't I have a difference of opinion and (what an important key word, "and" is!) live in it. I have the right to free speech... as long as I don't actually try to use it. I shouldn't because then I'd be subjected to others including themselves (in my life) with their daily shows of disrespect. (Harassment!) Well, I've never been scared before, and now is no different.

Why do they disrespect so? (Why do we let them!) Because... we are lazy -and- we have been taught(?) to survive in society built on the very idea of endurement. When "it" happens and you let it, you've left the proverbial window open for "it" to happen again. You now have the firepower of experience to inflict said social horrors upon the world, and you'll most likely feel justified doing it too.

By letting "it" into your life... you are letting the (karma) wheel's spin to continue. While a person who demands that he communicates (give/receive) only on a level of respect would be successfully applying the proverbial brakes to future shows of said detrimental disrespect. It takes a big man or woman to work the brakes. (It's suicide to ride a train without them.)

There should be no suicide from stress. There is no excuse, but when we live in competition with one another the stress is assured, if we helped one another there would be someone there or available to help the other with whatever the difficulty may be. People who are in a medical position which is non-curable may make their own decision as to the "worth of their life" in comparison to the pain he or she may be feeling at that moment and/or the huge medical bill they will leave in their diseased wake is a conclusion for them alone to make.

I follow with my feeling about suicide: "It's your body..." and... "Please don't leave a mess." (Please don't harm your organs which might assist someone else.) But ultimately, it's all your choice. Not to be made by the machine! But, that's not the way it is now, and with some peoples' need to control or hinder other people's growth is so all consuming powerful it may never be that way in the future.

Without struggle and strife introduced by those with nothing to gain (H.P.'s), life might lose some of it's inherence of being worthwhile. Therefore, it is our duty and privilege to endure. If not, then the afterlife might loose some of it's accepted appeal. The only time life should be a struggle is when you make it that way... not due to someone else

Unfortunately, they cannot sell a ticket to a place in advertisements seen on T.V. The same is true in life, most are trying to achieve and sustain fantasy life. Most of most will fail while a few succeed... the same number of "few" (coincidentally) will fall so far into debt that they might ruin the family name forever more. The law of the land is:

"Kill or be killed." (Commercialism full tilt!) Why we (intelligent) people continue to live under the constraints of such a system is beyond me. (Love should be the law!)

Individuality VS Capitalism... (who will win?)

(Right VS Wrong?)

(Light VS Dark?)

The devil?
* * *

Commercialism can be the devil. If a person is shown the way "to be" (T.V.'s "to be") and he can do it, if he sells drugs. One of many easy money equations. Who can blame him? Why not take the easy way out? It is the American way, is it not?

The system we live under directs how it will, and when it will, cram an unrealistic reality for us to duplicate. And when we're not able, we feel less than, and maybe ready to do what it takes to satisfy the drive the T.V. (or any other media source) has for us. Commercialism sits back and laughs as we "the pinballs" rip ourselves up to be a success in the world where no one really is.

"Attack, attack, and attack again", is how are lives are led so we may destroy the other man. Your brother, who would stop to pull you out of your car, if it was burning... <u>unless</u> you were a worker for his company. As you are a great big cog in the machine who may makes decisions about hire/fire, promote/layoff, give a raise/deduct pay, just might mean that so he may win... you may die! That's the game we all endure; unfortunately, more are enduring now that the government may have more weight behind their new request, that we give up more of our "we the people rights" so that (*this time*) everything will get better.

It was that liberty they are taking away which was stopping us before, but "Now" it'll get better. (Promise!)

Promises, promises, campaign work, no truth...

J. Elliott Goldwyn

A third choice?
* * *

The rats are guarding the cheese when we let "them" count all the good important events in their own favor. I see when the time comes to take some responsibility for a poor decision which was reached, all I hear from our elected officials is the sound of finger pointing extended at the "*real*" guilty party member... never themselves. We let them count everything, including the votes we cast. You would be surprised what you can buy for a dollar (or so), "in the land of the chained and the home of the beaten 'n' bruised."

Certainly there are success stories, but they do not forgive the countless crimes to humanity which are impressed upon the common men and women who do not have the "magickal key". No key means no $ with which to compete. So it's a tough world, right?

(Yes, sort of.)

Well, I think "we the people" should look at our options. We do not have any choice beyond the political parties candidate. I feel we should have more on the list from which to choose. There are great minds (and hearts) alive today, and I think we should put them together to see what they collectively come up with. To assist "us" in making the world a better place for you, I and the children!

Maybe that could be the "Third Choice" in the ballot box. One year, to discuss all the options. (That I know are there!)

After the year is over, come back with their findings and collective conclusions, and put them (the ideas) onto the ballot to run against the presidential choices. (Democracy is

one-of-us

good in formation, but it grows stronger with competition.) Republican or Democrat should not be your only choice. Sure, I know there are other choices. Although, choices by name only... to vote in a new name here or there WILL NOT STOP THE MACHINE!

One guy, or the other - or - a whole new plan made from respect borne from the love that is life. (Love is the law!) A plan built on growth towards perfection, while settling for nothing less than progress. Rather than paying more taxes to "the machine" so "the power in charge" can finally make good on promises it made so many years ago. "The game" (is forever ravenous... a monster machine) which is in charge at this moment is growing scared of us (the people).

The machine is also growing more paranoid and is now grabbing at every piece of control it can sink it's fangs into.

All I'm proposing is an end to the monopoly now in control. Cut all the strings we the people (puppets) swing by. It does not matter what the candidate promises. Because all a new president gives us is some "new group" of people turned outcasts to call this country's enemy and blame "them" for all the problems. (What's next, Concentration camps?)

We've been doing finger pointing for far too long to call ourselves the intelligent race.

We were all placed here to enjoy being an individual, if you so choose. You are your own "ship's captain," only you should decide where it is you should sail. It's just as acceptable to stay safely in the protective harbor, as it is to brave the wild seas on your own. (Seeing as that's the kinda adventurous girl or guy you are!) I see too much of some ships telling other ships, not only where they should sail, but even what sort of sails they should fly. (Don't forget the matching tie!)

If you ask me, that's control run rampant. There are some new souls who grow so excited about controlling a human body, (or any form whatsoever) a new soul becomes greedy and tries to control yours.

It's one thing to exist by the motto:
    "Live 'n' let God."
        (responsibility avoidance)
It's a far greater thing to survive by the motto:
    "Live 'n' let live."
        (acceptance of coexistence)
It's an accomplishment beyond compare, to live by the law:
    "Live 'n' let love."
        (acceptance of respectful coexistence)

With the two divisions, right or leftwing, red or bluestate, all of us are getting lost in the middle.

Stand and state?
* * *

I need to talk to educate, so we as an intelligent race can move (change 'n' grow), into where it is we need government to be in our future, as we successfully cohabit with respect. We do not need an overlord "big brother". We need is small town governing group (per-ce) who will create and facilitate open lines of communication, with <u>all</u>.

(All areas around the world, if needed.) We should no longer trust someone (something) else to communicate in our place. Because somewhere in the red tape, "we the people" (tax paying little men) get lost in the shuffle of corporations paper push. I, myself, am sick and tired of being lost... I'd like to be found.

So I stand up and state what I've learned and show my life so that others may benefit from my errors and successes to choose the correct answer as to which decision should be enacted. (There are no mistakes, only poor decisions.) Throughout my life I've made poor decisions, and I hope someone benefits from my subsequent punishments and revelations...besides myself.

Afterthought:
Inside my body (the higher one), I have capsules of knowledge which I obtained elsewhere that are on a time release schedule I'm in no control of. So, on I write for fear that I'll have a revelation the day after it (my work) is released.

My train?

* * *

It is <u>not</u> procrastination, it is an all consuming responsibility to not brake the train of thought too soon. If I were to stop too soon, I might miss important people along the way by not showing the most correctly appropriate example of an experience which resulted in an expression of my humble message. (Which <u>is</u> my greater purpose... period!)

In the Light I was shown to love (which <u>is</u> the law) everything with a shower of respect. We (everyone) will not have any justifiable reason to show anything less than perfection in the Light. We will all be one. I can explain that fact in this way so many will be able to understand: The Light was my home, this I knew because of the way it felt surrounding me. It was like my conscience was so at home my skull opened, as if I had a form for comprehension, and my "tape" (for lack of another word) touched other tapes. Communication of knowledge was free and easy with respect for each other (other tapes, other souls), and the knowledge contained therein.

People don't have worries worth warring over, governments do. Governmental words lie, people's actions do not. If the people would take back their country (caring about other people and society) many negative aspects would cease to exist. (If you cut off the monster's food supply, you kill the beast.) Simple equation, if we return to the polls, we will see growth. Your voice (vote) will cut off it's food supply, your voice ringing in it's ear will kill the game. With no game, the pinball would not die by abuse of survival in the brutal machine.

one-of-us

No machine means no machine imposed stress initiating unfulfilled life and heart attack death, blah blah. Many of the realities I speak of could come about without violence,

I'd rather give everyone a home or an area to feel at home in. A person who chooses to not live in respect of others in a society (any one of them) might have no society to be a part of. Simple equation, no respect means no privilege. If you show disrespect for a reason, that's what court is for. (gasp!) Yes, I said court. Not court like we know it today, but one blind to the amount of $'s spent to prove innocence (which is a paid for reality in this day and age... let us together turn the page!).

Everything in a commercial society is for sale, guilt on you (or someone else) is just a matter of how much money you (or whomever) is willing to spend. Remember that the next time the government points a finger at someone (or thing) that really is (this time) the reason things have been going down hill for such a long time. (Too long for free people!)

Today we need to stand tall as a people and demand respect from the government (by voting) instead of watching and slowly shaking your head in despair, disappointment and disbelief. It's not gonna get better on it's own, we've been watching it crumble under it's own tremendous weight of responsibility which it assumed. (Or did we vote for it?)

Yes, we did... sort of. By not voting, or saying what we really want... we allowed the machine to take full control.

Complacency will teach painful lessons, we'll see. If... we refuse to reintroduce and respect the responsibility of running our country, things <u>will</u> get worse!

It's like riding on a bus with a driver who is fast asleep. We (the passengers) try to avoid the accidents, that are almost sure to happen on our band-aid repaired roads, by leaning one way (extreme way or the other) as to miss a cavernous pot-hole.

(Argh! Poor li'l pinballs are we!)

Life is very easy for us, if people of the past could see (they can!) they would say, "Enough of laziness, today is the day for respect to be shown as you live in truth for ever and ever. In today, like tomorrow, a person should live with honor for all eternity."

But, that is "the dream" isn't it? It might never ever begin to happen. It's that way with dreams, destined for failure. Especially if you never try!

one-of-us

Limited society?
* * *

As you know (or do now), I'm an advocate for David G. (1995ish), who is a functional mentally retarded man. People in his working daily life (budget manager - case worker - etc.) talk about how he uses his asthma inhaler and/or the medical facilities too much and/or too often. He does, and it's not because he's an alcoholic/drug addict and/or hypochondriac. It is because he knows no better. Doesn't know differently because no one ever taught him differently.

Society (his limited society) told him if you are ever anxious or are having a hard time catching your breath... "Use the inhaler. If you are feeling bad... find help."

When he's not feeling well, David doesn't want to be alone. So, he visits the emergency room often. You would if you were him too.

So he turns to others who are the more intelligent ones (or think they are) to help him only for the fact he's been taught no other way.

I correlate directly David's "lesson" he was taught to the people today doing what the world has taught them. (No more / no less!) There are people disrespecting other's lives, and I wonder why it is hard for them to understand when others disrespect theirs in return. It is what they've been taught also! (The get/give thing or, Karma/circle theory.)

Unfortunately, respect is not the law of the land, (pity) for where I'm going all could come along. I'll make no judgement concerning your worthiness, I'll leave that up to you.

In so many ways on so many days, you do it to yourself. Actions do speak louder than words do. People should be judged (in public) by what they do in their lives, not what they say. Too often solace is given because of some situation they experienced earlier on in their lives. Excuses, and they (the excuses) matter little to the injured party or their family and loved ones. Once the damage, no matter how performed, initiated or sustained has been inflicted... the circle will be left damaged also. (I know, I've damaged a few.)

To repair the circle takes not only time, but the conscience constant behavioral manipulation resulting in, from, or because of spiritual growth of the 'selves' involved.

Growth of spirit is difficult (hard work) on your own let alone doing it in togetherness. Not only have you left yourself vulnerable to the others actions (or inactions) but also any weakness they've inflicted (consciously or unconsciously) to the circle in question.

Magick is a scary practice (literally `n` illiterately) because of the constantness of it. The great magickal circle is always spinning, taking in all and leaving nothing at all. You are always under it's watchful eye which sees all.

Most say it's too much pressure, and I say magick is not for most. The same "most" really on the saying, "To be human is to be imperfect." It may be, but that's purely a matter of choice. (The easy way out.) And where does the lazy way take you? (rhetorical)

Growing?
* * *

I have grown up to take what life has dealt me, and through my practice change the reality to fit accordingly. The conflicts arise not from me, but my ability to be a mirror and reflect exactly. So many have left me, because in me they didn't like what they'd see. What they are, is what I'll be.

I can be no more than people allow, that is why I allow not just any person to reach me, and in such I <u>can</u> be more. I don't have to reach inside you, unless I allow you to reach me. This happens, and with that I grow stronger. What has not ended my life, makes me stronger <u>and</u> smarter. (As it is with you?)

Sometimes I go through hurtful times not aware of the "stage" being set for me to perform. Not aware, because at the time of the pain it's the anguish which envelopes my very being. If I could see the future while I'm going through the hurtful lesson I would most assuredly "drag my feet" less.

If I had seen Sara (Miss MacGregor) in my future, I'd have been more willing to allow Deb to separate from me. But, the time when she began to pull away I had thought that she really desired a passionate parental partnership with me involved, not just present and accounted for.

Being with me is different than me just being there.

one-of-us

Perform magick?
* * *

All of living your life is... even doing laundry is magick. Magick <u>is</u> <u>not</u> "hocus pocus." The steps to preform it may look majestic, but Magick <u>is</u> as mere as making something happen, anything happen, not just another card trick.... but making it happen because you wanted it to. You do not have to be a genius, but if you have control of your mind to the degree of being able to cause a change to occur, that is all you need. For instance, changing lanes on the freeway so you'll miss the dog on the road (good driving!) is: because...

<u>That is what you wanted to happen</u>. (Powerful words!)

Let me use the example of doing laundry to fully expand on my correlation between causing change to occur with the example of "doing the wash," and magick:

First you need your magickal tools which would be; the dirty clothes, the detergent, the quarters and some machines with water. The time to perform the "washing ritual" is when the laundry-mat is open and there are machines free. You go through the steps that are necessary with magickal tools needed (your great-great grandma would be frightened to screams by an electric washing machine or a microwave... that we take for granted) and in an hour or two, you have clean clothes. The 'ritual' itself contains the bodily movement of moving the laundry from machine to dryer and the addition of soap, quarters, or drying softener sheets at the appropriate times. I know that is a basic example, but it does explain fully "magick" you perform daily. (ie. causing change in accordance with your true will.)

There are so many things we do today that many powerful people in history would be amazed to tears, calling all of us "The devil's children". We <u>are</u> powerful magicians. Because we do things today, which people from the past hadn't even dreamed of yet. Everyday our perception skills become stronger.

We are going places today (the moon), and just 500 years ago (on the whole) people thought the world was flat. Today we (on the whole) think (believe in) many things which are showing their true colors everyday in so many different ways. We're just afraid to say, "We were wrong." (Important words!)

Afterthought:

I cannot turn lead into gold, but I can grease the wheels a little to accomplish the goal that was the reason for the ritual in the first place... <u>IF</u> the outcome I am assisting is naturally attainable. There is great power in the human brain, <u>and</u> there are gre at powers which are not a part of the human brain at all. That is a topic for other word-works, because what works for me, works for me... not you. I had to work hard in finding a spiritual system I could believe in. (Maybe you should too?) Everything I know came from somewhere else, all contained inside reading / writing / conversing / reflecting and practice which was all done with an eclectically open mind. Although, I have seen many things beyond belief, but those experiences may have opened my eyes... which were shut by closed by preachers with a pair of spiritual blinders who have made a complete blasphemy of the Holy Bible.

I have been painfully honest. Anyone whom has been offended by my truth probably needs to read the book again. (But this time with an open mind.) For the truth will set you free. If... you let it. I know that it did for me, and it will for you too.

Doubt?
* * *

An acquaintance who I've just met refused to believe in anything he had been listening to concerning my life. I trust I'll need to alight on the topic of, "being skeptical".

Let me explore someone's need to doubt my experiences of which I have no physical evidence (other than pictures and a complete collection of the hospital and police reports).

Firstly, what has happened has happened and that I cannot deny. My only reason to share what it was I was shown is to further our level of comprehension. This leads to the making of decisions increasing our level concerning copacetic cohabitation on this seemingly ever shrinking globe called earth.

The only reason for a need to doubt what has happened to me, is fear. Fear that I'm right, or wrong. Fear that I'm another false prophet. Fear that I, a T.H.I. victim, have always had answers to so many of the problems which continue to plague us. Fear that I'm different in the brilliant way of Mickey Mouse. Fear... that not _all_ scribes come from scriptures.

who's responsible?
* * *

Some people spend their time writing the books you have, while most folks just read them. (I've lived mine, and you might be living yours.)

The responsibility of the future was given to me, now that I've told what I can... the responsibility is now your's (also). It's not that I may, or may not, feel any more reason for direct involvement in the world's evolution. It's just now that you've been informed... I'm no longer alone.

I do have a message. (Not warnings.) As in the past, only a few will listen.

One of us

Book five, answers -or- the beginning of the end

J. Elliott Goldwyn

Forward

Okay, now is the time to take our time. This fifth book is going to be on and about the following of what it is I feel I am here on this planet to do in this life. That is why all of us are here. There are certain lessons we are to complete (by hook or crook) in each of our "human" lifetimes. Our lifetimes, both as separate and unique as they may be, only adds to their interesting individual importance in the proof that will become pudding. We were born into an equation where the only answer is assured but the factors are confounding constantly, and conversely curious at best. I've said many times, "<u>WOW</u>, I like the knowledge I've obtained, I just don't like the way I had to get it." But, as I've already stated, we are not in charge of the "lesson"(true will) but we are in charge (free will) of the color of socks we're wearing when we welcome wisdom with words of wonder by labeling it...

"Just another one of life's lessons."

Also, I notice the knowledge encased within the social, mental, physical, and/or a spiritual lessons (no doubt painful... as we should, we remember those best!) and after those years spent in some form of introspection I've come to find the knowledge is something I can not live without.

Whether or not the moralistic exercise was large or small is purely subjective. i.e. Some humans are shown that the taking of a life is incorrect when they kill their first house mouse, while other's need to experience years of (dis)organized bloody conflict in the middle east... or anywhere else for that matter. There are many grey areas in between and I've not the patience to explore them all but I do know they exist.

Now we are going to explore the scriptures of my life... the only life I can truly discuss.

The only life I have.

Las Vegas here I come!
* * *

It was the best of times, it was the worst of times. Here I was, smack dab in the middle of PDX Oregon.(PDX means Portland) With not one friend (save Sara) in sight. Alone, yet loved by the masses seemingly (except for my lazy lunatic litigation landlord) that for me to say would be pure braggery (is that a word?).

But to encapsulate:

One day: with family of blood relations and a woman I was daily selling my soul for.

The next day: without my son, but with a woman who would die for me.

One day: dreaming of happiness, yet floundering in rejection reality.

The next: living in happiness, yet drowning in the dream of the rejections to come.

(Didn't someone say, "Life's a circle?")

My family noticed when they came to visit soon after our son was born. I was guarding they said. Dad, was not sure of what... just I was scared of something. Deb, Nick's mom was sleeping in my bed therefore everything should be relaxed and secure but I acted as if I were anticipating an ambush about to occur.

I was, dad was correct, I was afraid of what it would be (who it might be) that will take all of this away from me. It was too much for me. Deb was already gone, mostly. She

one-of-us

still showered and slept there, but unlike before, there was really no need for me to even be there any longer. She showed symptoms of separateness in every turn. Her use of my male machine was over. Deb had her emotions eagerly exercised by her workmates at the self proclaimed lesbian restaurant, where do I fit in?

I don't.

At least not here I don't. But, I didn't have to leave. She already had. As I write this, it's been about seven years later. Funny thing is, it still hurts... just differently now. I am in a much better place. A place to begin to stretch out legally and see if I cannot arrange a way to become a part of Nick's life for I never agreed to be a sperm donor. It's very important it's legal. <u>If</u> she could punch me in the face... it's a very small step to planting some cocaine on me and calling the cops.

But,

I love Sara dearly, had been hurt by her dearly too... but believe her innocence (in theory). Sara is so beautiful... I cannot live this "charmed" of a life, can I? Will this all go away too?

I am here to state: as I write this, Sara and myself's seven year seven month seven day (777) anniversary will be in a few days on the summer solstice in the year 2002. The reason I waited so long to write, is... well, I was SO busy. (Read on warriors!)

Living in PDX was fun, but life with Sara is not to be just fun I felt. So, we moved to Las Vegas. Ha! Sin city USA!

Another one of my famous last moment ideas. Well, mom ***does*** live there, and so does Sandi, so I will have family nearby. The trip was as eventful as one could desire to see in an action movie with wrong side drunken drivers as one could endure yet remain unscathed... physically speaking. It seems that some drivers have a real difficulty staying in their lane when I'm around... (more soon!)

When we arrived, it was nice to see mom with her "I'm so happy to see you uh... Elliott...uh... (she never got used to the name evolution) but, you'll be leaving soon... right?" I'm famous for visiting with dirty laundry and the police hot on my tail, so no one really wanted me around for too long. But, this time things will be different. (Sort of)

Sara and I came to gamble town U.S.A. in the rebel (I bought in south Dakota) with a trailer behind, and a truck that we rented from U Haul. We decided to store our stuff in a monthly rental storage space. Some place where we might spend the night if need be (wink wink). I found such a place in just one phone call, actually Sara chose that phone number, but I won't know till I get there and meet the manager... ya know?

Bill, seemed nice enough. Kind of knew what I had in mind. Good in fact, but I left him out of the "knowing" responsibility by pitching around the batter, as it were.

"See Bill, we are artists and we might need to work all night on a project... ya know?" He did.

Then he said, "Just don't use the ally as a bathroom, morning noon or midnight just knock on my door... ya know?" We did.

Some days I'd stop and talk with Bill, some will know what I mean when I say, "he had a light in his eyes" (whether real or imagined) inspired me to ask if there might be something I need to learn from him. All he said he knew, was Karate. Wow! Stepped into one more "lesson" didn't I?
(Oh... like you have no idea.)

I need structure in my life, maybe no better way to find it than punching and kicking stuff... right? But, there was a way that I did not prepare for in the acquisition of said martial art. My immense ego's walls to it's protected spirit must be destroyed.

Life is lessons, or I was soon to find out. Small tasks, day in day out. Passing tests I am told. Then, given permission to know what was happening: I was not to be just a guy to punch and kick, but a teacher of men how to punch and kick and so much more... the spiritual side of the art will be explained and delivered to me. And I was informed who would be my instructor for the early belts. (White thru lower green) His name is Sensei O'Bannon. Out of respect, a Jukyu (any student who is not a black belt) may not use a Sensei's (teacher's) first name without insulting him... so I don't.

I drove to his house three times a week for hours at a time, he taught and I learned. I learned what it was to be a teacher of men. The dream of teaching was coming true for me at last. The dream of teaching was not something I knew I had... until now.

There was more,
there always is...
* * *

Bill, the manager of A-1 Personal Storage will be teaching me when my lower belts are achieved. He had books in his large apartment, connected to one wing of the storage unit building, titles I respected. Titles I have read, or soon will. Books about Magick, Hinduism, and Christianity.

I was thrilled to take lessons from a master instructor. Bill's rank was Godan or fifth degree black. When a Sensei is fifth degree or above, that teacher becomes a master instructor. Bill just knew stuff that I hoped to someday. He had an intelligent way about him, refined, unobtrusive, yet explosive in a moment's notice. He was everything I wanted to be. He even said one time, "When the student is ready, the teacher will come." To say I flew through those first three belts, would be an underestimation certainly. Although no belt test yet, the lessons with Master Tooman (Bill) began immediately. I no longer needed to live in a storage unit box with Sara, and we promptly moved in to his four bedroom apartment with him. Ahhhhh, relax in bliss.

Some responsibilities were directed by Master Tooman, like: because this is my home I will keep it clean both inside and out. Sara will do all the cooking and the dishes. From daybreak, I get up and turn on the coffee pot. Then I make coffee, some days two pots. Turn on his computer and clean his desk area. Go outside at 5:30 am and push sweep the entire storage yard. Unless there was a huge mess I finished by 7 or 7:30ish. Then pulled out my training mat I made onto the asphalt drive of the storage unit establishment I just swept, and run up to 500 kata each and every morning rain or shine or snow... it did snow in Las Vegas that year! I would train till noon most days. Not a bad schedule, my teacher was asleep for most of it. Although around noonish on the asphalt in summer it was about 169 degrees Celsius. (Or so it seemed!)

I used to love that ole fat guy Bill. Now, I just feared him. He'd watch me through the window and if he'd see something wrong he'd come out barking real vulgar commands degrading my ego and destroying my "boyfriend" ability. I was becoming or being made into, a soldier, a warrior... a king. Those things are not a "boyfriend" whatsoever, so that ability was no longer needed.

J. Elliott Goldwyn

My Sensei Tooman was in the Marines, most every member of the Universal Shotokan Martial Arts Family was, in some way associated with military or intelligence. Tooman Sensei's teacher was one of the biggest baddest names in the martial arts world... the true teacher of our art.

O'Sensei Nichols. As the name implies, he "wrote" the art. (O'Sensei means The Great Teacher) The beginner, the start. The man who while growing up in the orient, took classes with Gitchen Funicoshi, met and had his first black belt given to him by Emperor Hirohito. O'Sensei was also a member of the Navy Seals. The O'Sensei of many great people, like: Princess Diana. He was no ordinary man, he was royalty. Mr. Nichols is a prince of Austria, but since they outlawed royalty, a prince by name only. He has worked for NATO and that's where his international problems arise from.

He had to engineer some political moves that someone in a VERY high position was not happy with the unsuccessful mission's results.

All of Mr. Nichols' valuables were seized under the Rico Act, he said.. They trumped up something about a tax fraud of some sort. All they were able to make stick after a lengthy court trial was another charge built upon an accident at one of his Karate Dojo's (school's) summer outings. I was told they were rock climbing and a boy fell to earth from a ten foot height, and O'Sensei Nichols was checking his tail bone for fractures like a good medical professional should do... did I tell you that Mr. Nichols was a certified medical nurse in Europe yet? The CIA and FBI both engineered a forced admittance from the boy's mother, who was there the entire time, that he had in fact touched the teenager where and how he shouldn't during the examination. Because all O'Sensei's finances were tied up with the Rico fiasco, he could no longer afford his defense... he pleaded out.

Not a good choice, but one I understood. I had pled on a case I played no role in. So, I was still going to let him prove himself on his own merits or demerits... but the entire group I was now surrounded with was in utter awe of him and his abilities. Through osmosis and an innate need to believe in people, over time I did too. Everyone I spoke to concerning him had nothing to say but good about him. Other prisoners lives changed because of their association with O'Sensei. All things have a purpose I'd say over and over. He agreed. All things have an end too. He'll be out soon enough.

J. Elliott Goldwyn

1ˢᵗ beginning
* * *

Somewhere in all the hub bub of the operational scheme of things at the storage unit there were many juggling balls in the air. Part time thieves, part time beggars, and full time every possible persuasion prostitutes. Seems when broken down to the basics, all employees are wonderfully wholesome whores. In fact, as you move up the "food chain" the blatancy just increases.

"Sucky fucky five (million) dollar" (say hello to Enron!) (But I digress.)

There was always another scheme to replace the last. Just that this time, it's better than that ole makeshift crazy idea... which is fine for most people to see through as being a "sham - con" just not Bill. He'd try to get me to sign up, but I'd like to think I knew better. I did not except for a lottery ticket or two. I saw that he was wasting his energies upon financial one night stands, but a good student does not comment upon the errors of his teachers. No, not hardly... not unless he wants to do 500 pushups. (In one hour)

A very good friend of Master Tooman, Sensei Sheen, was coming to visit soon. A real Kumite (hand to hand) champion. Another Master instructor in his own right. We'd hang out and train together: Good man, good stories, and a good two (or three) black eyes. (Can't say I didn't ask for them.)

Shiners or not, the information I received while sparring with him could NOT be bought .

So, I made out on that deal.

one-of-us

I was on my way to the destiny I thought befitting. There were people calling me Sir and those same people called Sara, Lady Sara. Sara was right there by my side through all of this training training training daily morning noon and night. I'll never be able to repay her. Thank goodness she's never asked to be reimbursed. Our money was not the best. Being a student in the martial arts does not pay well enough yet to support us. But... picking up pallets and returning them to the pallet yard does pay okay. We'd take our earnings on the one night out we'd get a week and go play penny slots at the Plaza hotel and casino... and drink the free drinks of course.

My family was impressed I stayed with something so long (6 months so far), I (literally) was in the army... in effect. A martial art family... in reality. On the days where I'd have no karate to study, I'd go to my mom's house and wash windows or help Jerry with some repairs... I was becoming the son my mom always wanted. Honest, reliable, consistent, respectful and honorable too. I told this to Sensei Tooman, he saw their delight also.

And since Sara's parents were coming to town from Michigan and so was my dad from California, he arranged a formal belt test that they all could attend. (Cool!) Me on stage (with the starring role) and the whole family as my audience. Even though I'd not yet met Sara's parents, I just knew I'd like them to watch.

Sara's parents flew in two nights later, Tom and Lois! What grand parents! (Sara and I *should* have kids!) Within hours, I'd asked her dad, for her hand in marriage. Turning right on his heel he refused completely any answerable authority. He said turning over instead the conversational reins to his wife Lois... "It's her you should ask." (I shrunk two feet timidly)

Then I said, as I recall... "So mom... what do *you* think?"

What she said I don't remember verbatim, but Lois made me feel like I already was part of the family. (I "WANTED" to be part of this family!)

My karate lessons increased in their intensity, morning till sleep time I trained. I really was becoming proficient. Although, my fear of "the test" was doubling every day. I could do it, but could I do it in front of my entire family and family to be? Well, I soon found out.

The big day
* * *

When I got up in the morning, 5ish am... I was ready to go outside and prepare the testing area. The test is taking place on the self storage yard parking lot and it was my responsibility to assemble the seating area along with the refreshment table and the testing mat. I needed to put together my covered audience canopy and find chairs for a total of 15 people. It turned out that not only was my mother coming with Jerry and my dad with Rosa but also my sister Sandy and five or six (I don't recall) other chairs for the guys who would assist my Sensei Tooman and Sensei O'Bannon with the test. It would be a private examination, so there were two or three people to guard the gate to the storage unit grounds and I needed to accommodate them also.

The Jukyu (yellow belt) test started promptly at ten am when it was only 95 degrees in the shade. To make a very long story short, the test lasted two hours. They ran me through everything I had ever learned except for running a Kata (a set of moves that run in a pattern) that I'd done maybe about 10,000 times, only this time... blindfolded. I was told (a faint whisper in my ear) that if I was not able to run this set of moves perfectly... I would fail. The Kata was one where the place on the mat where you begin, is where you should end also... then as I stood there blind to the world, Sensei O'Bannon returned to his seat at the judges table to laugh at me (he later said) as I fell completely apart. I started, the moves were all correct and then I finished. I heard laughter, but it was not Sensei O'Bannon... I started to shake from fear... I had failed and am now an embarrassment to my entire family. Mom, Jerry, Dad, Rosa and Sara's family were murmuring softly. Probably silent words of despair... except I heard excitement from them through the blindfold's layers of insulation. Sensei O'Bannon came over to me, stood in front of me and asked me how I thought I did. "Sensei, I am not sure."

"Well... " he said as he undid my blindfold, "what do you think now?" Sensei had placed a piece of duct tape on the mat where my toes were before I started, and when the blindfold was removed I saw immediately that I finished EXACTLY where I began. It's a whole different world when you are in the dark... (I now had an faint glimmer of what a blind person must go through every minute of every day and a whole new level of respect was born.) Gruffy ole Master Tooman was the one who was laughing earlier, laughing because he bet Sensei O'Bannon that I **would** be able to finish perfectly (this he later informed me). I was still concerned since I had no idea how I did on the rest of the responsibilities (although I thought I did okay) now came the awarding (or not) of the yellow belt part of the test.

Master Sensei Tooman said, "You came here today to test for your yellow belt?" Hi, said I. "You even invited all of your important family members to attend, correct?" Hi again, Renshi. "Well then, with no further ado, it is my duty to inform you that I will not reward you with what it was you tested today for..." (I melted into a puddle of emotion in the 115 degree sunlight)

"I am... going to give you this yellow belt with a black stripe signifying your advancement in the black belt program!" (The puddle, gained form... the tears poured from my eyes)

"Domo Arigato Sensei!" Then both Sensei Tooman, Sensei O'Bannon and I tied our belts while facing each other. That, I was told early off, is something that happens only when you achieve promotion status that one time... otherwise it's disrespectful to observe a Sensei tie his Obi (belt) unless you too are of Dan (black belt) rank.

In fact, that is one of the reasons I continued so long in martial arts... the respect given and received. In fact, eventually I was bestowed with the rank of Yondan. (4th degree black, but once again I rush the story.)

The video tape
* * *

Tom, Sara's dad, had been so gracious to man the video camera so a tape could be made. That tape was forwarded to my O'Sensei in prison. When he wrote back, he expressed his approval. In his own words, "You, Seitosan* Elliott, have completed the examination for a high green belt." As it turns out, I had learned not only the yellow belt responsibilities, but so much more. He was VERY impressed with my innate ability, let alone what I acquired though the lessons for the last four months studying 24/7. O'Sensei Nichols said that only about 15 to 20 % of martial arts in Universal Shotokan (the art he devised, wrote and practiced) is actually punching and kicking, the rest was spirituality. And the spiritual side was simply something that I had already formed through my life's laborious lessons thus far. How could he know? Well, I did send him a copy of what I had written thus far... the finished first four books of it anyway. O'Sensei said that I had passed every "test" and now I was offered the position of "Secretariat General" of the Universal Shotokan Martial Art Family. I was officially a member and not just a student!

I was noticed by a man who was a literal god in the martial arts world. I was informed by my Sensei Tooman that O'Sensei was a four time world champion in the hand to hand combat aspect of various karate tournaments. This was just too good to be true! And I, respected it as such.

* Seitosan means: honorable student, in Japanese

I was promoted in duties for the family, and some time passed with me taking on more and more in responsibility. I wrote to as many as ten or fifteen businesses or enterprises that the whole family could use as a temple and professional training facility. I wrote to quite a few of our martial art's family members and some men in jail to further their rearrangement of misbehavior so as to live in society with honor. O'Sensei changes lives for the better every where he goes it seems.

I saw my dream of peaceful existence on earth taking form.

The first end
* * *

On the other hand, I thought that my Sensei Tooman had grown jealous. I had been told by my O'Sensei Nichols that I will be included in the international training of troops (military folk) in the deadly aspects of Universal Shotokan. I will travel the world in style! Sensei Tooman had to this moment thought it would only be him included in just such a 'sing-a-song,' in stereo, now the tune would play with three. Shortly thereafter some things were said to Sara, via Sensei Tooman, that I felt were not of a very respectful nature.

If someone disrespects Sara, they disrespect me. No, that is not correct. It's more like they disrespect my life, in effect. That is the most abhorable sin, to disrespect someone else's very being.

So, in concurrence with what I've said many times before... I packed our bags and moved us out.

My parents were sad, both mom and dad. Dad because I was ending the only positive progressive path since the head injury, and my mom because... I would not be around to wash her windows! (I jest!) Really she felt I was finally growing into the boy she could respect, and my mom might miss me. Me, the boy who before she quivered in anticipation of my problematic visits in the past... now actually <u>wanted</u> me nearby! As far as I know, that's every mother's wish for her child.

But, I was going to Michigan. (By Sara's hook, or was it her crook?)

Michigan
* * *

My god, why did it take me so long? I love it here! The people, the views and those seasons too!

Okay, they got deer up here that will jump in your path while driving down the highway...

NOT FUN! It was not long, with my dad and my dad's mother's (Ann's) help, before I was driving in a 4x4 chevy full size pickup truck. (Very used, very big!) I had many jobs to pass the time. Most everybody I had met treated me with a level of respect (that they treated most everybody with) that made me momentarily feel welcome. Momentarily was used because once you get past the (holding of the door for you, or allowing you to pull into traffic without a struggle or a motor vehicle miracle) standard gracious behaviors consistent with mid western living, the greedy behaviors of the "big city" make an authoritative appearance. I had a job working with wood for a while. I loved the ability to learn from a master carpenter. I did learn many things about life laboring on that level of employment... but nothing about wood or working with it. I learned that I CANNOT work with two bosses who don't agree with each other. One boss wants detail, the other want's it done now. Well, maybe both... *if* I had 15 years experience. I did not, they knew that. Let me explain:

My first interview was with the owner, a real detail man... or so he said. Although, on the job site there was a different boss. It was his son. (I'm not using names because I still live here, besides their lack of excellence will kill their own business... they don't need my help.) When I finished my interview, my enthusiasm was ten fold what the dream of being a carpenter was the day before. My heart was into it 150 percent... but day after day of me not going fast enough finally took it's toll. The big boss wants detail. The little boss wants to move onto something else. Maybe I should not tell people the details of my disability, it just seems that they sometimes use what I've told them against me. Not on purpose of course, no one does anything cruel on purpose in this life. (And if they do, I don't wanna think about it right now.)

One day our grunt worker (trash boy) crashed his truck. The big boss told us sadly, and I saw a way I could help. "I'll move trash for a few days while you find someone else boss," I said. He accepted. Amazing how quickly a few days can turn into a couple of weeks. No problem, work is work is work is work. That is something I remember my dad said to me as I was growing into the son everyone feared then into the son everyone fawned and back again... ad nauseam. Any job is respectful... no matter what you do, it has value. He is right, he is wrong. My dad had not even thought about the reversal of direction on his "employment-ability." I did... I had to.

I had not even thought about the career containing the conveyance of, or the capacity to conduct classes in, the art of Karate I had grown to appreciate titled Universal Shotokan. I had not talked to O'Sensei for quite some time, and I felt apprehensive to write him in fear of his scolding of my own failure to follow the (painful) lessons of Master Sensei Tooman. I fear being told, and it's agreeability with my own second thoughts, that, "Everything Master Tooman does, has it's own social or spiritual importance for you Seito Elliott."

That would be painful, I had to think long and hard as to what my action would be about the leaving of Las Vegas, concerning conversations with my O'Sensei.

Other than Master Tooman's smart mouth, I had no reason to leave. I had students I was already teaching in the parking lot of the storage unit yard. I thought I had fallen into social heaven. The only time I did receive disrespect was from my teacher in martial arts (Sensei Tooman). I was being pulled apart at the seams. Most people I know would struggle on with some amount of sorrow that I may or may not have mentioned somewhere in this novel so far... but I cannot handle belittling of someone I love's person. I thought long and hard. I made a list of the positives and the negatives. I could not come to a definitive conclusion. I stopped thinking.

My heart said "Go."

So I did. Sara came too. Good thing, after all... I ***was*** going to Michigan.

Anyway, back to the carpenter job fiasco:
So, they never got another worker of any sort, so I just worked light labors with a hammer and cleaned up after people. It was not 'bad' for a job, but then they tried to lower my wage.
Wow, I'll let you guess what I did.

A letter
* * *

I wrote to O'Sensei one day when I felt the world closing in on my lack of social adeptness. There were other jobs besides the carpentry job, but all seemingly lead to the same end. Somewhere along the line drawn in the sand on a level of respect given and received by the employer and employee is where the problem, if there is one, usually rears it's ugly head. There seemed to be differences in the minute details concerning respect of said employee's "human-ship." I did not feel a member of a family, I was kept at a distance... I was just a number. My bosses did not care about me, they only cared about how they could pay me less while getting more of my time and energy. They did this slowly, to arouse as few objections as possible.

I noticed.

I said so.

I started looking for a new job.

Then I thought back to the "job" of respect and honor. That's when I wrote, I needed his guidance. O'Sensei is a great man of great knowledge gained through the teachings of even greater men. I was foolish to not use his teachings... if, he'd even write back. My mom's man, Jerry, warned me that O'Sensei Nichols and Master Tooman go very far back. They might have a friendship that I would play no role in. Things were not left in an angry sense in Vegas, I just left. I told O'Sensei a little about what had occurred in sin city before I left and that I'd like not to discuss it in the future.

He knew.

We talked very little of it in the future. But we were talking now about my growth since I left. I told him all the details of my "life's lessons" and he understood. To make a long and beautiful story sweetly shorter: because of all the letters with and to him and all the communications with his children (students) in different parts of the world... he bestowed upon me the gift of his assistance with the opening of a 'real' martial arts Dojo in Michigan as soon as he could. I was definitely deliriously delighted! All the work I had been doing for O'Sensei will now pay off.

He also told me of his needed assistance with various contracts he need to complete for NATO and how I would be one of his trusted instructors in international endeavors. O'Sensei informed me of Master Tooman's involvement with a not too reputable business man's schemes financially speaking. O' Sensei did not wish to be involved. Soon after I read the letter that told me about Master Tooman's error in judgement, O'Sensei called and asked if I could pick him up at the train station in about two months or so. I was in heaven. "It would be my pleasure!"

About nine or ten weeks later I did. He was everything I had dreamed he'd be. I was in awe. Why is this happening to me?

I was soon to find out.

In the eye
* * *

One month before O'Sensei arrived, I started shooting pool in a pool hall and became a member of a team in a league. One of my teammates asked me what I did for a living, he was a postman who at one time was in the navy... just like my O'Sensei Nichols. So, I told him of my desire to start teaching Karate. Jim (my teammate's name) said, "Fantastic, who is your Sensei?"

I told Jim that I do not say his first name out of respect, and he understood. Although, I did say, "His name is O'Sensei Nichols."

Jim turned on his heels and said, "You mean Mark Nichols?"

Ever heard the sound of your jaw hitting the floor in front of you?

And the words just floated out of my mouth, "Yes Jim." I asked, "Do you know him?" Jim said something to the effect of: I've never met him, but I know he's a real heavy hitter with the Seals. (Holly cow!) Nothing could have given me more awe/fear in a man who I'd not even shaken hands with yet.

Five weeks later I was waiting for his train to arrive. When it did, I felt like a child who had just heard the soft patter of flying reindeer on the roof on Christmas eve.

one-of-us

I looked my O'Sensei in the eye and asked, "Is everything okay with you concerning your legal responsibilities down south?" He said they were, and now he's here to assist me. He said he had talked with some people in the military, changed his name legally and had the id to prove it.

Wow, this man is a real mover and shaker! I'd be taught martial arts by the man who owned every title for years in the martial art world. He was the best, or so I heard from people who had nothing to gain either way. Now that he was here, I saw it too.

Within six months
* * *

Everyone loved him. My neighbors and all my friends thought he was brilliant. He stayed with Sara and myself for about three days then my neighbors (Malcolm and Florence) invited him to sleep in their spare bedroom. Within a two week period of time, he had befriended everyone he met in my town.

With his esteem support he gave me and the training we did on the side, I had within six months two Dojo's in full operation. I was proud beyond words. I was of benefit to our society. I helped children with the many trials and tribulations they experienced... but the list does not stop there. There were some parents who needed my humble guidance even more.

i.e. There was one grown female student whom I spent some special time with. She was very kind and I saw a need for her to have knowledge beyond what I was teaching the children in her class. To make a super sweet story even more surreal: Her 'boyfriend' tried to hit her harmfully on one drunken night... She stopped the sloppy swing and put her foot into his chest. What could have been a real wife beating, turned into a moment of avoidance. She needed that, and so did I. It's good to hear about the positive aspects of your personal teachings.

There were kids in class who had no respect for anything, and just like myself they were learning to respect every place, person and thing. I'd like to think I had some part in their persona choices also.

It was just about one year to the day when looking down at my student roster, lesson plans and the locations I was now teaching in, I realized that I had five Dojos in various schools' auditoriums. I was also now able to pay rent at a location of my own. A place of MY OWN! Riding a cloud… as it were. I even started to teach a class in a city about 45 minutes away for the 4H as a donation to our Michigan community completely complimentary. In that one class, I had about 150 students. Oh dear Lord, what have I gotten myself into? Success comes to mind. So does responsibility!

I did it all. (With Sara's help!) For no money. (With Sara's help) Because of Sara, I was able to. The amount of respect was ever so important, and I got it all. NO ONE said or did anything to insult me. They knew better. It was about this time I received my Yondan promotion (4th black). To say I honored and respected my O' Sensei is a complete underestimation that I can only hope you understand.

J. Elliott Goldwyn

Jeff's Parade
* * *

My O'Sensei had befriended many people around town by this time. One of those people was the director of the fourth of July parade in our home town. I was placed on a cloud when he asked me if I'd be willing to be in the parade with my Seitos (students) from the Dojo in my home town. Wow, my students and me in the independence day celebration activities. I was as proud as I could possibly believe. This all seemed too good to be true.

There we were walking down the street with many people watching... but the best part was Jeff. Jeff was my first student in my town. He worked at the local library when I first met him. Jeff is the most determined Seito ever... if you ask me. He had more hurdles to overcome than most any other Seito. Jeff was chained to his wheelchair due to a closed head injury he had while he was attending the local highschool. He is a go getter. The brain damage he sustained did not stop him from being all he could be. Jeff should be poster boy for anyone who even thinks they have it tough. I saw a lot of me (after the accident in '85) in Jeff. So, I understood a lot of the pain he felt. Jeff rode his chair with us in the parade. I will never forget that day.

one-of-us

We did not win "best in show" but I feel Jeff should have, let me explain:

I had a total of about 45 students in my home town. Not all at once, but when I'd loose a student or two... I'd get a student here or there. It seemed that many of the kids I'd teach had a real problem with the difficulty of martial arts. There are many moves that take practice, concentration and dedication. Many would quit when they realized that they could not be a 'Bruce Lee' or a 'Jackie Chan' or even one of the 'mutant ninja turtles' on their first day. Karate is hard work, and most kids want the easy way out nowadays... but not Jeff. He tried, he **really** tried and in the end he succeeded. Within two months of training at his house, Jeff was out of his chair running Kata. (With assistance.) At times he made me feel less than because I was lucky, I had recovered so much. Jeff also made me feel more honored than any other student because of the gift to work with him.

Soon after he had earned his lower green belt, Jeff passed away. The whole town came to the services, and I do mean the whole town.

I'd like to think I made a difference in his life, he made a difference in mine.

Thank you Jeff.

Clouds do disappear
* * *

Seems like that no matter how comfortable with the circumstances you might feel, or how hard you try to keep the ball rolling, nothing could begin to explain how I was feeling that almost everything was just coming together. I had a location in P-town (Petoskey, Michigan) of my own. Right on the main drag, across from the Hospital. Perfect corner, perfect town. I had most everything I needed... almost. My family of Seitos came from teaching classes at the gym in town and I no longer worked there, so I worried that they would just stay at the gym. But, all of my students came with me when I made the location change. In fact, the P-town Dojo just grew stronger.

Classes were growing everywhere. I could just barely keep up. My birthday was just around the corner, and I devised a way to celebrate justly... a Karate tournament for all my students from every school of mine on my birthday. Contestants drove from as much as an hour and one half away.

I had so much fun. I hoped that all the participating students did too. After the competition ended the party began. One of my student's mother (Becky) has sisters in a orchestra type swing band and the night had a beautiful ending. I danced with everyone! God, I had the night I could not even dream of... all because of my O'Sensei.

O'Sensei was now living at Deb and Stan's and begun to spread himself out pretty thin, but I still tried to see him and train with him whenever I could. He opened a Dojo in the town of Alba, and I went there every chance I got. When he told me of his desire to go to Washington with a mother of one of his students to discuss military involvement with a military general (of some sort) I was excited for the both of us. He went and returned with good news, the details of which I did not know... but he'd never been wrong so far, so trust him I did. He informed me of his desire to move to Flint, which is downstate about four hours away to be close to a man who could keep him informed of his possible contracts with the military. That made me sad, but clouds do disappear sometimes. Clouds disappearing is not a tremendously terrible thing, but it is when you are riding upon one with not a safety net whatsoever to speak of.

J. Elliott Goldwyn

Lightning strikes twice
* * *

My O'Sensei was gone, and miss him dearly I did... but he was doing well in Flint and things were moving along with the military involvement. Those 'contracts' were to be happening sometime very soon. He need to go on another responsibility outing to someplace down south he said... and would I be so kind as to go down to Flint and remove his stuff from the trailer he bought up in my part of the state?

"Think nothing of it," was my reply.

I had never been to his trailer in Flint, so I did not have any expectations about the place. What I saw when we arrived (Becky drove me down in her van) did not shock me whatsoever, as a matter of fact I was almost prepared for it. It was a pretty nicely cared for trailer park, nice yards and well cared for mobile homes too. Then from seemingly out of nowhere came 20 or 30 kids from everywhere to see Renshi ("Master" in Japanese) Fileds. (Ed Fileds was the identification that the military people had given him before he came out to Michigan to see me.)

I was impressed to see that my O'Sensei's soon to be Dojo was having such a following so far. There probably was not a child in the entire trailer park who did not want to study with him... and I was in that group of people. No wonder, he was a great man who demanded respect from people who had probably never given any. It is my belief that even though someone has not given respect or honor to anyone probably just does not know how.

one-of-us

Almost everyone I know personally wants to live a life of honor, but when you've never been shown how to walk a tight rope... you probably will never get to the other side. It's not that people who show blatant disrespect are all of a genre destined to live an entire existence encompassing evil. Rather, they have never been shown how to operate in society with a decorum of respect to other "operators." Maybe their parent(s) did not have the ability themselves. Maybe their parent(s), or lack of even one, didn't have the "quality" time to devote to such an important structural education. Or maybe, just maybe... they thought it was someone else's job. (That, along with all the other ways a parent DOES NOT show very important lessons to their VERY OWN children makes me MORE MAD than anything I can possibly imagine.) Cannot people understand that by not teaching your own kids to act with decorum is the surest way to build a human time bomb?

I know that all those parents who feel that someone or something else will teach them (their own offspring) the important lessons concerning sex (per ce) many times has children sitting in jail for the punishment of rape or some other heinous endeavor. Let me conclude this diatribe with a closing statement, I also understand that some of the world's most brilliant minds and sprits have built themselves up without the assistance of a parent whatsoever. Some of those extraordinary people have built themselves upon the destruction battlefields prevalent in our murderous society's daily roller coaster ride's nightmare... only to become our Nelson Mandela of the time. Although, ofttimes instead of learning from their hellbent existence, they perpetrate it across their own lifetime... and that behavior is pure puerile perversion! A child who gets raped by a parent, should KNOW that to do it again is SO WRONG that there can be no excuse... NONE!

"My parents did it to me." Would be no defense in my court room.

I would remark from my seat behind the bench, "Then you REALLY should have known better. As a matter of fact, just for saying that... you now get 20 more years."

(My book, my dream.)

(The above passage about my beliefs is over, now back to my story:)

The key my O'Sensei sent me to open his trailer did not seem to work. So, after I excused myself from the crowd of adoring kids I walked over to the manager's office to inquire about him possibly having another key. He did! So I walked back over to the trailer and tried the new key... magically (and I kid you not!) my hands seemed to have a life of their own! They glided behind my back, and then I floated over to the patrol car silently parked behind me and was slammed forcefully, face first, onto the hood. All the while being assaulted with vicious words condemning me to hell for what I had done.

"What the hell did I do!" I stated.

"We have 13 counts of CSC charges against you!"

"What the fuck does CSC mean?"

Criminal Sexual Conduct
* * *

God-damn* it! Who did I act that horrible way toward? Or, who said I did? Shit*, my life is now hell! With in moments my whole reality became crushed. The crime they said I did is something I have spent my whole life trying to avoid. Teaching people that rape or sexual assault is something that can and should be avoided at all cost. My mind raced. I cannot be guilty of such a completely horrendous thing. True, there have been times since my head injury that I do not remember as well as I'd like... but never did I do such a thing.

They checked my id, and it came back clean... I was not the guy they were looking for. It *was* a case of mistaken identity. ("Whew!") Although, it was my O' Sensei Nichols who they said they were looking for! I did not want to believe this hell was happening. I could see Becky through the patrol car's backseat window, and her look of utter disbelief was exactly how I felt inside. Seems they were waiting for him to come back to his trailer and they though I was him. It does not matter that he stands about six to eight inches shorter than I and weighs about 150 pounds more... they thought I was "the guy" nonetheless.

Fuck fuck fuck*! (I did not know what to think.)

I knew my O'Sensei had been framed before, so maybe they (the political masterminds) found him, maybe the changing of his name did not stop them and now they were doing it again. I really did not know what to think, but

---

* please excuse my language, but it was how I felt at the time. Besides, it's just a prayer for God to damn the feelings I'm having or the pain I'm feeling... certainly not taking his mighty name in vain.

I did begin to wonder with a little bit of doubt concerning everyone involved. Doubt for the police, doubt for the system... and doubt for my teacher that everyone seemed to love and respect (including myself).

They let me out of the police car, and I dusted myself off. By the time I got my senses back, they were all gone. No questions, no apologies. Just as silently as they appeared, they left.

I spent the next four hours in a daze. Becky and I did empty his trailer and I did not even notice it was raining out pretty hard. My mind raced through many topics. The number one question I went over an over was this, "My god, did you see all those children that came from seemingly out of nowhere to see my O'Sensei? Oh dear Lord, if this is true, just think of the potential for the hell that he (my teacher) could have perpetrated!" That and more went over and over through my head.

We drove home in silence.

The Confrontation
* * *

It was about two days later, and I almost wanted to forget. I was watching a television show about the Titanic and was thinking how sad that the under class passengers died due to the first class cruelty to them. Those passengers had to deal with a hell that was imposed upon them by others... and then it happened. A knock on my front door. It was Deb and Stan. She was shaking, due to anger seemingly to me.

Then the harsh words started, and I knew I would never forget.
"How could you let this happen!"

Not a question really, then followed by the shaking of a frightened mother who felt (to me) like a mother lion protecting her cubs. It turns out, after the anger subsided, that she was the one who found out what had been told to me by the police, had actually occurred.

And that story goes like this:

Deb was looking for a 3.5" disk one day of photos she took with her digital camera... the same camera that O'Sensei had used quite regularly. Her camera uses those disks to store photos on, and she was not able to find the birthday party disk right off the bat, so Deb started looking at all the disks in the camera bag. There were some Karate shots of a couple of boys on one disk. Then on the next disk there was a cute picture of one of her boy's butt, not a small snap shot but rather a full screen picture with lots of detail.

"Ah, cute butt" she thought as any proud mother would, but the next photo on the disk was one with Mark's (O'Sensei's) hand on her boy's butt.

It just got worse... picture after picture.

Her obvious anger, and Stan's "I've seen it too" knowing looks told me that he (my ex-teacher) (who from now on I'll refer to as 'that asshole' or mark, because he deserves no respect from me) had done everything I've ever imagined in the most horrible dream that a restless night's sleep can provide. Why is this happening? (Which were my thoughts.) Oh dear God, all of this was **not** a dream! I was crushed inside and out.

"I have no idea," I stated. Really I had no idea, have no idea and will never have any idea how someone could impose such a social hell as this upon a family that treated 'the asshole*' with so much Christian love and respect. I will never have any idea how anyone could do such a violent example of 'animal behavior' (animal, cuz it sure ain't human!) upon any non-consenting man woman or child is completely beyond me.

---

* I do not apologize for the curse word that fits so properly.

As if there could be a good part
* * *

Years ago I had sent my story, or what I'd written thus far, to mark even before I met him. He knew how I felt about crimes against children. That ASSHOLE! What does that tell me? There is **no** curing a man who can do such a thing. When Deb and Stan finished telling me what had really happened, all I could envision was putting a bullet in his head. Unfortunately, that could not happen. He was gone. My head was full of terrible thoughts of torturing him... the man that 48 hours before I'd have gone to war with.

I though mark and I could trust one another, but I could see that no longer.

It took a while, but the detective (Mr. Simpson) finally called me into his office to discuss the crime in detail. I was more than willing, but I also knew that by living in a small town anyone who associated with mark was guilty by just such an association... I was right. I was lead with Sara into a room reserved for interrogation of perps. (Criminals) As the discussion ensued, I felt like Mr. Simpson was prying for information... I stopped him in his tracks. "I have no idea why this happened, both before and after the fact... although... The asshole did mention something before he left the area which might be of assistance." I said, "He said he was going down south to 'take care of a responsibility' of sorts." I went on, "That might be a military engagement." Simpson said that the asshole had no real military involvement. (Jesus, did he lie about everything?) "Okay, then maybe he went down south to take care of an arrest warrant. (If he lied about military, he probably lied about leaving Arizona legally also!) I remember telling the detective that I though he might be in jail in Arizona, serving time for a probation violation under a different name until the intense part of the man hunt for him here was over.

J. Elliott Goldwyn

In my head, I WAS loading the gun with words...

Detective Simpson said, "That would explain why we are not able to find him anywhere."
They could not find him while looking for him under the name Ed Fields, and I hoped
(and prayed and prayed and prayed) that my remembrance of mark's off handed comment might bring him to justice. To make a long sad story sharply steer sweeter... **IT DID!!!!** They found him, and he is returning! Boy o' boy, I'd like to have been a fly on the wall when the guard of his 'safe haven hotel' told him he's getting out in a few days... because they will be extraditing him back to Michigan! So in a way, that is THE honorable ending to a horrible story... or good part if you will. There are still bad parts though, because of his ability to use martial arts to hurt (or protect) people in prison... there might be people who will hurt me for him. Well, to encapsulate my thoughts on that matter; "If I stopped just one of those kids I saw in Flint (or anywhere else) from being hurt, but I die due directly to discussions with detective Simpson... I will have died an honorable death." Honor, something that 'the asshole' may never understand, yet preach (just like an evangelist* preaches Christianity) till he is blue in the face.
Remember I began this 'greater lesson' with the line: "I need structure in my life..."(Well, do you?) It's in the chapter titled, "Las Vegas, here I come! Maybe, in a weird way, I needed to teach some too.

---

* The perfidious prophet who purchases premium prostitutes with your profound penance pittance.How can a man like that take you anywhere but to hell? (Rhetorical)

Just one night
* * *

All this, in just one night:

Days before my birth forty years before 2003, something started to rear it's ugly head shadowing my very being. Unescapable, haunting and unavoidable in any way, like a revelation which seems to make total sense to me. But, before I continue I need to stipulate that you should please apply what I'm about to say to the minutest degree of interaction to the greatest, which is the taking of another's very life.

People in America are said to be crass and disrespectful to others. And we are. We don't know it either... we just do it. (I cant be more sad about this fact, for I feel much of the surrender to it's truth will not occur. Americans cannot be "wrong" at all. I know, I am an American.) Look at this through a nonjudgmental eyeball, please allow me to draw my conclusions before making any critical judgement.

Let me explain by showing you a night, a nice night... but very much a ride upon our society's harsh roller coaster of interaction. A college class in typical social differences between individual types of person, which we all are: "human." (Pure and simple, we are all just human.) Not Anglo-Saxon Americans like I am, European Americans like some people are, African Americans like some people are, Asian American which I hear some people who are from that general Asian area don't mind at all that label... some like Japanese American, others Chinese American or Swedish American or Mexican American or Whatever American's (there's just as many American's as there are

American's that want one... dig?) The common factor, is we are all human. With an ever growing population we (all humans) must band together to solve the world's problems for if we don't there'll be powers that be who will let us, the common American... die. So they might eat their 'cake' and in 2003 it looks like the blue ribbon prize winning cake of the year is going to be oil. Black gold, Iraqi tea.

Oh dear lord, I am so not impressed by what we have allowed our government to become! That's right, in the home of the brave there are people who do not even vote. (They say it's cuz it ain't gonna do no good no how, and it may not for a reason... #1! They might be all the same, no sure fire winner of a candidate so you'd just vote for the better of two losers.)

Ever wonder who picks these 'winners' of moral standing so they may rise to the position of being up for an election to a governmental level of office? Then be able to vote the laws with which to further enslave a country founded upon freedom? Probably people who will never lift a weapon in any armed conflict whatsoever. Although, JFK slipped in under their watch... so they had him uh... un-inaugurated. (Oops, I solved a crime that will never see an arrest... at least not in my lifetime which might be short now... see, another RK got close too, same solution. Only that time they got smart, and used a fall guy.) Kinda like they did with the Oklahoma city bombing and the 9/11 bombing or should I call that the most horrific device ever used to spur us into war to get something totally not based on our freedom but a product. But we could not do that years ago when we first had trouble with just about everyone this country puts into power in some large or small way. It's like we set up

one-of-us

political fall guys, then when we want to have something, those leaders just burp just a little to loudly and our iron fist comes crashing down. And I got news for you, no one but "them" knows what is really happening in an occupied country before we leave to allow the new "set up" political leader to take over... to be 'erased' on some unknown later date.

Although, now at war I am an unflappable American who stands behind his voted in leaders show of their diplomatic wherewithal to wage war. How I feel about the war is not a question now that we are in one. I see the reasons, and I can respect the decisions needed to accomplish the throwing of the safety net this country is famous for... the very idea of democracy.

Whew, that was a real diatribe... sorry, now back to my night:

Sara and I had gotten a 'two on the town' membership discount card for ½ off price one time, understandably, to introduce us as potential customers to their restaurant or their business whether it be new or just in the mood for a larger client base.
(Sometimes good sometimes ok and sometimes perfect, as you are about to read.)

When we arrived... I was met with smiles from the customers exiting the sleigh that was riding upon the falling snow... did I say there were many Kodak moments this year's birthday eve's eve. Children playing with the snow by the hansom horses hitched to the harness of a simple and sturdy sledge. One more photo to go! Kids petting the horses, and I think I might have seen the flash of a carrot... or two. Uh... Midwestern Norman Rockwell come to life. The sled had stopped in front of a bed and breakfast and I was told that we were going on the sleigh ride... and having dinner! Excellent!

We walked inside and I found out from the helpful and sincere manager (I knew she was by her proud posture even before she uttered a word, she liked her job... it showed) that we could buy tickets for the sledge ride and dinner together for 'so much' but they are also having a "mystery theater dinner!"

"Dueling detectives?" I blurted out.

"Yes it is." came the young lady leading the night's challenge. But I rush the eve's events, excuse me.

We bought tickets for the triple showing! Oh, I couldn't wait. I'd never done the mystery theater thing ever before... beautiful night this was going to be for me. (Sometimes birthdays are nice.)

It was a cold night, snow falling ever so lightly, but the light wind cut through you like a razor. I was that way when we left for the eve, so Sara had the truck packed already with two pair of snow boots and two blankets too.

When we walked into the establishment for the second time, for the sled filled with families full to the brim and we watched wonder filled windows to the soul of children start their sleigh ride. "It's okay," I said, "there will be another trip in forty five minutes." There was this employee just inside the door, and she said, "You should have brought a blanket, I'll bet they will loan you one if you ask."

Wow! Such disrespect. I've never been so insulted. She really said that to Sara, so I stood back and asked her, "So Sara, is this another person who feels she knows better for us than ourselves? Well young lady, thank you for your condescending remark, but we brought two blankets." Most people would not have even noticed she was being disrespectful by assuming we were so stupid to not have brought proper weather shields. I promptly spoke with the manager.

"This has been thus far and will continue to be I'm sure the most delightful evening ever!"
I continued, "There has been a problem though, and seeing as you are the manager I thought you'd like to know so you may continue to improve your patronage satisfaction.... correct?"

"Yes", she answered, "I would."

"First then, let me to implore you not to chastize me for I'm just the messenger and not to attach employee demerits for an action your subordinate performed, for she knows not what she has done."
It has grown to be the accepted norm to place others at fault so you may excuse yourself from acquiring blame in this life. There is no one around to pat you on the back, so pat yourself I say. Although, if patting yourself consists of finding others whom are not of your caliber to compare

yourself with, and then finding fault with them, then you are complimenting no one... especially not yourself. Now if you tried to help those of a lesser understanding, not just belittle, then you are complementing not only yourself, but everyone else also. We should help one another, not just laugh.

Sorry, back to the evening:

She said, "Sure."
So, I explained: When Sara and I walked into the establishment, the first thing out of an employee's mouth was a question, "Are you going on the sleigh ride?" Sara said yes. Then the employee said, "Wow, you are too tough!" with a tone like a disgruntled 5 foot tall plump woman might use to show disdain to a gorgeous 6 foot 2 inch tall model for drawing all the light away from anything else in the room. Oh, her skirt is too short, or, her hair looks terrible... as said by other catty girls sharpening their 'I'm jealous of your good looks' claws. "It's cold outside, don't you know you should have brought a blanket?" Followed quickly by, "I'll bet they'll loan you one, if you ask."

Fuck you! I thought. Right from the start, negative feelings. Happens all the time? Pity, but yes. In America it happens too often. I say America, because I live there. Who knows, it may happen all over this planet.

What I feel should have been said, or some reasonable facsimile thereof:
"Sure got cold out there real fast! Could I get you a blanket for your sleigh ride comfort?"

After telling the manager how I felt, she understood my dismay. She also understood that this small error had a greater effect than she might have ever imagined. A night starts happy, then it goes downhill from there sometimes. That and more is the reason there are places like Denny's, and places like Tapawingo. She noticed the employee's unknown application of discourtesy, and she forced upon Sara a coupon for another night's meal and macabre mystery. Forced because I did not wish to accept it, but Sara did finally after the manager's insistence.

So, our reply to her gift was to book a room for the night a month away for our anniversary. We'll probably use the coupon someday... just not now. The room, was my way of wording, "thanks."

J. Elliott Goldwyn

The present day
* * *

Now we are near the present day in my writing. I will now expand upon my life's teachings. I've had a few up's and down's this time around, and I've learned a few things along the way. Now I'm going to mention them, some of them are going to sound real obvious, while others will look like something out of a textbook of life. Although, some of them are taken out of a deep seated desire for honor, respect and freedom, or love, if you will, while searching for more Light in my life. To me, my educatee and almost anyone who will listen, love is just honor and respect. Nothing more or less.

Still more of the 'lessons' taught me some things you'd never expect.

I'll start at the beginning:

Children
* * *

Kids are why we're here. Although, procreation is penance for some, mostly those children born into a family that desired not offspring. Pregnancy, is pure pleasure for those who truly desire a child. It takes more than money to be a child's parent, it takes love... and love is everything to me. (i.e. "I am Sam") Two people who accept the responsibility of having a child should be very aware that children never go away. Some, not all, of the young men who wish to welcome a child of their own DNA do not really want a child, they just wish to spread their seed... as it were. The only correlation I'm able to make there has some animal or insect sex story involved

Most youngsters are not ready to be parents nowadays because they have very little life experience from which to guide their offspring. Don't get me wrong, there are many teens who try their best to raise the child that has blessed their life... but they in no way could do it alone. That does not mean that they should not try, it does mean they should not get the girl pregnant... then run away or leave the bundle of responsibility in someone else's lap.

I know too many one parent families. (And it's not always the 'boys' fault.)

I also know girls who got pregnant due to a one night stand when they used a rubber, were on the pill (or said they were) and expect the guy to 'step up to the plate' and take responsibility. It may be sexist of me but I feel that if a woman could kill the child without the 'partner' giving approval then the woman MUST take responsibility of her own body. Taking responsibility for her body is an important step... that means she is truly responsible, and not him. But I also feel that the man should have a say as to what happens, and if he does wish a say then he must do whatever he can to avoid said pregnancy... which means there should be no more "I don't wanna wear a rubber" if <u>either</u> of them does not desire parenthood at that time. Per ce.

After all, it does take two (of like mind) to do the horizontal boogie. Marriage in my own eye is not imperative, an honest choice to parent a child in tandem is. I have a child, a beautiful child... just not from an honest relationship. (Poor Nick)

I'd like to talk about rape, but there are many types of forced intercourse... and nothing good could come from any of them... but the children. Although I'll wait on that topic till later.

If a woman has a desire to lie down with a man, she has the power to say 'no child' and should be respected... conversely if a man says 'no child' that should also be respected. Sometimes both say 'no child' but it still happens, and there are many reasons why that occurs (even with a rain coat and 'no baby pills' too) but because that 'God given lesson' has many implications for me to discuss even one will mean I will be sure to miss a million more. So, I will not open that can of worms. Suffice it to say I know it happens, and unless I'm there and aware... I could only do injustice in examining verbally the topic.

I also feel that if a man lies with a woman he should ask about the application of 'baby proofing' himself if needed...

it's only right. If the woman is willing, then she should protect herself justly also if requested... that is also the correct thing to do. Sounds good, right? But it's not what happens in the 'real world' you say? I ask... Why not?

Did you make it that way? I didn't either, but we both did. We let it become that way, and that is wrong. I am doing what I can to make amends for my error, I'm writing this book. I started to make errors soon after my dad left the house... see my equation? Sure, there were others at fault for my fall from grace... but none as guilty as I. I watched it play out on my screen of daily life, and I just followed along... foolish me. Now I'm nearly forty, following foolishly no longer!

Nope, not gonna do that. Now I have something to say about how I lead my own life, you have the responsibility of your's.

My body
My rules
(Your body has your's)

Now that does not mean I can go (or you can go) willy nilly, but it does state that if I choose to live a life as a martial artist (per ce) and I harm no other man woman or child of any persuasion... then that is how I choose to live my life. That is one of my rules for my body.

Now let us say you choose to not be a martial artist, very well. That would be one of your rules you have given your body in this lifetime. Who knows, maybe you will next time.

But, if you are doing something that damages another man, woman, child or animal of any sort, then you are committing the most supreme spiritual sin. Greed. A drunk driver who puts everyone at risk on the road is nothing but a greedy bastard. A drunk driver who kills someone else should be subjected to the same hell he or she imposed upon the other sober driver... death by vehicle. And guess what? Drunk driving statistics would go **way** down... FAST!

As I recall, all through my childhood there were 'very nice' people who exhibited the desire to inform me of how wrong I was and how incorrect my actions were no matter what it was I did. Whomever had all the 'correct' choices... everyone was more 'correct' than I. Sometimes they were right, most times they were wrong. How I wore my hair, or the music I chose to listen to, or the food I filled my face with is nothing but my choice... and that does not make it wrong. Early off I learned that their misery loves company, early off I learned how it felt to be an outcast. Well that's okay, I did not like their choices anyway. I tried many of them and they did not work for me or my life, but they did work for them; so, I let them be them as long as they let me be me.

Sounds simple huh? Well it is, but it's been the fight of my life. So, I guess it isn't simple at all.

Oh, the doorbell. I gotta run for a few minutes to the door and hear from the Jahova Witness people how I'm going to hell. Hopefully then they'll listen to me inform them that it is I who knows our father. Knows what he looks like and what he wants from me. I am here to make others realize that they are being shown 'god' by readers of very old books. I am here to state that I have sat on the Lap of Loving Light, and what I teach is what It saw fit to teach me. Not what I've read somewhere at sometime, in an albeit very good book, and how I feel it relates to myself... nope, this is from experience. I can only speak for myself, because, no one has the Light given right to speak for me.

Just like, no one has the right to speak for you. i.c. "This is how I interpret what I've read for you and it say's you are going to spend eternity in hell because..." (ha!) Doesn't it matter what or how your own self interprets it?

There's just one important rule, "harm no other."

J. Elliott Goldwyn

Church
* * *

Church is the place where you're supposed to learn about the reality of a higher power. It does not matter what name you place upon such a power, the fact of it being true is what church is all about. Or, that is what it's supposed to be about anyway. But it is <u>not</u> that way, not hardly. What is church? The 'original spiritual street gang' comes to mind.

"We are right, and you are wrong!" "If you refuse to believe our way, we will torture and eventually kill you!" Okay, those days are mostly gone, but... "We own your life, your money, and your children too!"

Children in this way: We do not train our children about moral standings, because what we say is <u>not</u> what we do all day long. So, we allow the church to educate the ethical elbow room that is people proper because we cannot. It all starts very early for most, as it did for me.

Money in this way: Let's say you are a member in good standing in my church (if I had one) you would not go hungry if there is any money at all in the church's bank account. Or, if there is some labor to do within the community in trade for a meal. That is not what many organized religious foundations are doing. The Catholic church has sooooo much money that starving Catholics in Africa could eat like real people for years to come and not quiver like the huddled masses they've become.

Men and women from America, and elsewhere, will die this year in the name of a God somewhere on this planet. Not the name I've given God, some name somewhere some church gave god. i.e. suicide bombers make the ultimate donation.

God is love, the church is hate. They play a real good 'spiritual shell scam' con game and we just continue to believe. Can't get into heaven without them or their false moralistic lifestyle. They take your donations, preach to you 'ideals'... and rape your children. Okay, not all priests do, and that is true... but **<u>one</u> <u>is</u> <u>far</u> <u>too</u> <u>many</u>** for 'spiritual guides.' Catholicism is not the only one guilty of such horrors but I don't wanna get into a fist fight with words, so I'll leave it at that.

The only church a man or woman needs is in their heart. Your heart does not lie, your heart does not need money, your heart does not rape... your heart is the place where you become 'one of us.'

One of the whole, where we are all from... and all to return someday. We were at one time, not long ago in the true scheme of things, just another ray of color connectedly combined to create the Light of white. No one needs to tell you the way of God, you already know. Just ask yourself in meditation* what God means and 'It' will tell you. Only problem might arise when you realize that God does not care about your car, job, money market account, or your home. God cares about Love.

So, you might be crushed to find out that all that struggling to 'get ahead' was a mere misappropriation of time, although... it *is* a nice house. Don't get me wrong, a

---

* sometimes meditation means, 'just being quiet.'

nice home, car or whatever is not wrong; although the way you came about it might be, but that is between you and your higher power.

We, as a peoplehood have grown used to the ungodly ways of our swollen social and spiritual excuses we call religion. We have allowed priests to rape our children and we hand deliver the pardon. The world kills in the name of god without the shedding a drop of blood daily.

"They couldn't help it, we've kept them as eunuchs for far too long. They were bound to explode. They were born men, and we demanded they become something else. Maybe it was the 'church' who made the mistake in the first place," it has been said by defenders of the priests' innocence. No, it was not the church who made the error in the first place! But for the church not to burn them at the stake (like they did the 'witches' of the recent past) is.

They should be made to suffer at the hands of the ones they made suffer, and if suffragette doesn't want to do anything, then it is up to 'us' to let them know we won't tolerate that behavior any longer. Period, it's over. "We are Americans, we are good people, and we don't act like that... but if you push us we will fuck your entire world."

There are unfortunately people walking the streets whom have no right to. What do we do? We put them in the zoo (jail, not Detroit) so they may learn (most times) how to commit more crime but visit jail less. We will let them into our community with un-welcoming (side)arms because we cannot stop 'them' from returning. We cannot in most cases arm ourselves for basic protection. Sometimes we do not need any extra anything, but until it is proved to me (or you?) that the valuable lessons were learned so there can be a level of honor among neighbors... I'll keep a watchful eye. The law will let them live on my street, the law will not let me protect myself where I'm most vulnerable... on the street. I am not saying that all criminals are due to re-exhibit downward spiral behaviors, but it don't look good for the home team. The cards are not stacked in their favor concerning past behaviors, so it's a uphill struggle from the release date.

And, if you're a jailbird who is angry about anything I just said, then **prove me wrong** I say! Become an upstanding citizen in a our society. Because if you don't... you'll just prove me right.

School
* * *

Every child has a calling. Every child is more than we allow him or her to be. They understand what it is they would like to do, and should be allowed to make such a career choice completely by themselves... with some guidance of course from anyone they choose. For many kids it's the dictating of a direction for life long employment that 'turns them off.' A turned off child is a 'dead fish in the water.' And we all know what dead fish do... decompose. That does not mean that all children should not learn the basics, but it does mean that to force a student to preform what he or she cannot, will not, or doesn't want to... is educational rape. Most kids are an empty sponge who are ready, willing and able to accept knowledge about most anything from any source. Although, I feel that every child should have the opportunity to attend any college of their choice... not just what they could afford... money should not be the 'key' to a good education. Rather, desire and the amount thereof should be the only deciding factor.

Let me use a 'real life' example to demonstrate the above statements:

I have known many private school, public school or home schooled students in my life. Guess who is the most rounded, learned and successful student? The home schooled students who chose what they wanted to learn. That does not mean they will be nuclear physicists, nor does it mean they will be the town's trash truck driver; what it does mean is that they have a greater chance of being happy with their choice... and isn't that why we're all here? Not every child will be a sports legend or legend of any sort. But if you have kids, and one parent didn't steal them leaving no forwarding address, then you have the self given responsibility to be a legend to them. And that is very okay.

It's kind of like breast feeding in this way, it brings families closer together. Almost all kids home schooled are taught by their parents. Almost all home schooled students are better test takers according to standardized test scores than most other public school students. Why is that? Well, there are a lot of reasons but the most obvious is, that the school down the street is very busy place where the teachers are underpaid, and the individual student gets lost in the shuffle of the peer pressure jungle. That harsh reality is not the teacher's fault, nor the student's... yet it *is* everyone's fault involved all the way down the food chain (as it were) to the person who pays the taxes that the schools use.

It is just one more 'we let this happen' reality.

J. Elliott Goldwyn

Responsible Reality
* * *

A person is driving down the street, are they responsible for themselves? For their car? How about all the people who are in the car with them? If you say yes, then you are correct. How about all the pollution that their car emits from their exhaust? Or, the oil the leaking engine leaves upon the highway, is that their responsibility? Yes, it is. If someone does not take care of their car when it needs servicing, they are (in effect) needlessly poisoning the air or the lettuce (per ce) that farmer Brown is growing in the field nearby the road... which eventually your child will eat at the beginning or end of dinner that night. Like myself, many people choose to eat the roughage after the meal. Just not too many here in America.

Seemingly (and there are MANY more examples) people don't see the damage they leave behind in their wake. I've come across large oil stains in parking lots due to someone changing their oil and leaving the old oil behind. That same oil spill will eventually reach the water table below the surface of the earth. Sometimes careless people change their antifreeze in the same area, and it will coat the children's (or dog's or cat's) feet when they unknowingly walk right through it... the major problem there is that the dogs or cats (and sometimes limber little laddies) will lick it off or lick it up. Ever seen an animal who has digested antifreeze? No? Well, I'll loan you a shovel... because they are all buried somewhere. Why does that and many other things like that happen? Laziness, stupidity, or just ignorant disrespect... although sometimes they do know what they are doing, but maybe *that* is just their 'cop-out.' Like the woman recently in Michigan who left her 3 year old and 10 month old child

one-of-us

in the car on a 85 degree day in the car with the windows rolled up for a total of four hours. Now she says (after she drove around with the dead kids and their throw up mess all over the seats for almost the entire rest of the day) that she did not know it could kill them.

There is no excuse for not taking responsibility for your actions, especially the horrible one's. But I know it's hard to say you're really that stupid, or addicted, or sick... blah blah blah. If you think it's hard now, wait till later! Because the day will come when you cannot 'record' more on your lifelong video tape, and you have to explain why you did not make the correct choices after your human body had seen how many people it had hurt. Are you ready for that? Over and over, for what could be your "eternity tape" long?

If people did take care of what they did, there may be no need for a police force. No need for courts or (gasp) lawyers. Then we would truly live in a civilized society, but we don't and aren't. Did you make it that way? No? Neither did I! But we both did even if we never do something like the above, by not stopping the other from doing it... we *are* doing it under a different name. What's that I hear? "I'm not my brother's keeper!" Maybe not, but you could be his teacher.

Let's say you decide to take the risk and help your fellow man, and they say no thanks. Then you may rest well knowing that you tried, and you know what sort of animal your fellow man has become. Good time to say, "There but for the grace of God, go I." Please do not accept the notion that I am trying to convey a holier than thou standpoint, for I am not, nor do I wish to be.

What I am is this: Guilty of most every error I've described thus far and to soon follow in this work, it's just

389

that I had a revelation of sorts (White Light) that showed me just how to correct my character flaws on my own. It was school to me, and since I believe that true intelligence comes from watching other people and listening to them about their struggles I hope in some way I might assist you along your way.

There are some other driving topics I would like to discuss: It really pisses me off when a slower driver is minding their own business in front of me driving, and I try to pass. When I'm in the oncoming lane trying to get by safely... the slow guy speeds up. I don't care how fast or slow you drive, but when I'm trying to get by and someone does what I just described... they are putting my life in their hands. (Not a good thing to do!) It's like some other driver is pointing a gun at my head, only I don't know if it's loaded. Let alone if they are going to (or someone going the other way will) pull the trigger.

Is it a power thing? Sure... I guess.

Is it a disrespect thing? Absolutely.
Why else would someone speed up when there is another car trying to pass?

Does it come down to greed again? Indubitably*.

---

* that word is the first word my parents taught me, my mom has said. Except my dad says that I pronounced it in the beginning as: "indoo-ba-bee." I like that word, maybe I'll use it again.

Soul versus Brain
* * *

I'll tell you what it is that makes life so hard for me sometimes. It is when my body cannot agree with it's self. Let me explain with a typical example from my childhood...

This is to be taken literally and figuratively at the same time, or any combination thereof:

I'd get up in the morning and look out the window at the day... gosh darn it, it's raining!

"Oh boy, I really don't wanna go to school on a day like this!" (Or so my brain said)

Then, without missing a beat... "No, you *should* go. There are people waiting for your assistance on the running team at school." (A soft little whisper from my spirit)

So, the competition has begun. Who's in control? Sometimes I feel the power is divided equally, then I look at my life. No way is it equal. Maybe early in my life I listened to my 'softer side' or spirit more often. Now my brain has run the show for so long that it does not pay attention to anything but it's self. Pity, cuz that's how many lives are lost... by lack of communication.

Then my brain says something like... "Oh, they don't really need you."
(Wow, I just put myself down)

"But, don't you remember what happened last time you ditched?" (soul speak)

Then the brain says the words to close the deal...

"Don't worry, you'll get away with it this time!"

Earlier I said that many lives are lost, now let me explain briefly what that means to me:

The communication breakdown I just stated occurs almost every time a crime is perpetrated in my life or your life or any other's life. Could be a misdemeanor or a felony or just a slap on the wrist. Either way, a life is lost to the downward spiral staircase of misbehavior. Jail comes from that and so does prison for that matter, but so does death for you, or someone else. Incarceration, after all, is a death of sorts unless you'd like to be big ole bad boy Bubba's bitch. Or, you are a 'Bubba'*.

---

* I apologize to anyone out there named Bubba, I was just trying to make a very serious point. The state of mind I'm trying to title or convey, is not a state of name.

Love
* * *

There are many types of love, some more powerful than others, some more painful. It seems that we have no decision as to what or how it may come. Love begins before you are even a gleam in your prospective daddy's eyes. Although, I cannot remember such an infatuation, I can remember my first teddy bear that solved so many problems. He became my replacement for something I can not remember. Love is a circle much like life. There are many events in life we have no control of. Love is #1... the rest either center around other people, places or things.

Everything you do is in the name of love... everything you don't do is also. Love is the law, whether you know it or not. Why does a man or woman love? There are lots of reasons, but firstly it's because they want to. Although, we as a people have been mislead into believing what love is. Love is not ownership, although you can love something you own... I love my new vacuum. No, really I do! It's great for our wood floors, it's like an everything machine. (A dyson) In our house, Sara takes care of cooking... I do the floors. I love that arrangement. I honor and respect that household rule, which is one more rule for my body and her body too. Love is honoring and being respectful of anything whatsoever... the sunrise, the power tools, the washing machine, the car, a sporting event, another person and those flowers too. (Please understand the list can go on and on....)

I love my life. Sure, there are some things I'd change if I could... but I am doing that now. Growth, is why I am here.

My life evolves, and I just try to do what is best. This was not always true, so I use what I've learned along the way. I have been gifted with basic intelligence. I see the errors in my path, and I do none of them. That is not to say I don't make errors in judgment, but it does mean I pay attention to the moral lessons involved within said miscalculation. Always paying credence to a lesson is a show of love. I honor and respect my character formulation. I love who I am and what I am and what I'll become.

That does not mean I do everything that has happened to me or around me, rather I now know (because of horrific happenings) what **not** to do. To do something because it happened to me is no excuse for me... or anyone else. In fact, I love the lessons which show to me the way I will **not** behave. To do something again that did not work the last time or the time before, ad. nauseam... is insanity. That is not to say that to try something twice or more is wrong, but you should pay attention to the instructions inherent in immoral, illicit, illegal, illogical, improper, incorrect, ill-advised, in inappropriate investigations. (Whew!)

That's one of the main reasons for just 'repeating history' ad nauseam. We, as a peoplehood, refuse to pay attention. Our need (if I may call it that) of instantaneous gratification serves us poorly with the performance of memory. Although, we (the people thing again) love to call ourselves civilized as a race of animal. Sometimes the animal 'human' is the most precious of creature.

Sometimes not.

one-of-us

I have seen the name of love teach painful lessons with no desired or accomplished end goal being realized... seemingly. Humans have been blasphemous to the meaning truly behind the label 'love.' Love does not mean ownership as I've stated earlier. It is exactly the opposite. Love is freedom. Many of the people whom I surround myself with agree, Love is the Law. The law which supplies one with a true being of freedom... is Love.

An operational example of Love, is labeled 'tough love.' Once an alcoholic (per ce) has decided to drink (per ce) to an inappropriate degree, there is a limit when a person must turn their back upon a needy alcoholic... and the alcoholic's desire to evolve said person into an enabler.

"If it is your choice to drink yourself to death... so mote it be. Just harm no other along the way." That is true love. It is painful, yes. It is also beneficial beyond belief.

A <u>non</u>operational example is thus applied: When person says "love" to another thing whether it be a man, woman, child, animal of any sort, or an inanimate object of any persuasion yet treats it with disdain or disrespect. Or, performs upon it deeds driven dishonorable with the intent of showing that for which love is not... ownership! Or to
lust for effect by doing **anything** to acquire said desired result by means of deceiving any other man, woman or child by saying, "I love you..." is love by name only.

Most everyone has a 'higher self' that is their will which is true. To have 'discussions' with your own 'holy guardian angel' is an expression of Love to the highest degree, concerning the will you were born with and how to accomplish it's responsibilities.

For anything to wish to be with you is admiration, if you desire to return it fully *is* the meaning of Love. Exhibition of one's own true will to be with another of same true will is Magick. There are many other words, but their discovery I'll leave to you... I've got bigger fish to fry.

I, myself, also love my coffee maker. It's made by Bunn. I pour water in it, and after I'm able to turn on the computer... it's done. How do I show it the love I have? I clean it regularly and use only quality coffee bean, filters and very clean water. I want it to stay around for a very long time. That's how I show honor and respect, and it's return for my efforts is to make the best coffee ever.

Responsibilities
* * *

"It is your duty to act civilized!" After all, we *are* a civilized animal! (False!) Not often enough do we act civilized in any manner whatsoever, but you know why that is by now. For no obvious reason do we suffer through the daily onslaught of moralistic hurdles other than to test our moral fibre. Although, that could be the reason. (Hmmm...)

Okay, but now let's look at the really horrible stuff:

Those terrible lessons start somewhere, but surely nothing with possession of a soul could preform such atrocities upon the race of Homo Sapiens. Nope, it's much more serious than that.

For instance, child rapists are a reality (unfortunately) which I feel we could do without.
(Gladly!)
But they keep coming back.

I have had my lifetime's fill of child predators; only one that I know of, but one was more than enough. I have seen how the lowest form of being has crushed many lives other than the child's. I am glad to report that he will serve 30+ years for his actions and I will not waste one more word on him.

I would like to talk about another kind of horrible, an unfortunate reality which is a responsibility in effect: How people drive. Most days are okay, but there are a few worth mentioning:

J. Elliott Goldwyn

On March 31st 1999, a man driving a very big piece of machinery, a heating oil delivery truck, came into my lane and took me and my truck out. I did not die, but my right wrist and driving security (if I could call it that) will forever be damaged. Is driving a life or death match? Or, just another violent 'computer game?' Seems that way sometimes. Although, now Sara and I live in our own home. 25' x 25' very cozy living space. I've had storage rooms that were larger, but I have lived in one much smaller too.

(Oh shit, I'm a home owner.)

On March 27th 2002, three years later almost to the day, it happened again. I was driving on highway 31 heading south (this time) and another truck came into my lane and smacked me head on. This time my truck (that has saved my life two times in all) was totaled. I guess that is to be expected, two head on accidents and I had to say goodbye to my GMC. I loved that truck. She took care of me and I took care of her in return.

I am not saying that either of the other truck drivers were trying to kill me, but they have no business driving with (their lack of control of) the machine they were sitting behind the wheel of. Maybe they should get into a vehicle and have an accident happen to them like what happened to me then I think they might learn. A higher insurance premium teaches nothing, and we can be almost certain of that subsequently. But wait, insurance does teach by proxy. "I can do what I want and take no responsibility whatsoever, other than paying the increased premium and/or fine!"

one-of-us

Because of the head injury involved with my big beautiful green truck being totaled, I now have headaches almost daily which seemingly can be cured by nothing at all. No drug out of the seven or eight prescriptions my brain doctor wrote nor rest or dark surroundings seem to have any effect whatsoever... and sometimes I see spots, I think they call them migraines.

I will not begin again discussing the horrors of tailgating, or how **INSANE** it is to speed up when someone else tries to pass. The responsibility of driving is something I feel very strongly about.

Now I'd like to take a look at the mistreatment of our precious planet earth. Through mankind's need to have it's instantaneous gratification realized, we have been killing this globe. I am not a left wing radical, but we could take a more Godlike overview than we are. We think, on the whole, that we own this planet. Our grandchildren might, but we sadly do not.

I'm not sure about you, but I eat what comes out of the ocean. Major and minor instances of polluting the seas is common. It's like (pardon the language) someone we both don't know comes over to our community garden and pisses and shits right between the peas and carrots and wipes it's self clean with a cob of corn still on the stalk. You would not stand for that, would you?

I didn't think so. Neither am I. And by the way, piss and poop is not the only thing corporations dump daily into our mother sea or lakes, and rivers that eventually feed into them.

Corporations have no business, as we have seen in the news of just such an occurrence recently, except to make money... even if they need to lie about it. Trusting a corporation is like trusting the devil on his 'deal' he made with you not being a dirty trick he'll stick you in the end with.
(That pun should not be excused.)

Although, there are too many more examples of corporate conspiracies for me to even begin, but those instances are not just the sole property of major businesses... individual people do it too. Everything starts with someone.

I think that says enough about the dealing with responsibilities. There are others, this I know... but I've not the patience to mention more meticulously speaking.

Mom and Dad
* * *

I've just spent the last four books using my mom and dad as dental picks so I may examine my daily experiences in relation to themselves, and other 'neighbors' of mine. Today, ten years after I started this work, my relations with my mom and dad are better than they have ever been.

Most of the personality reformation occurred when I reread what I've be writing so far. I've come to discover that in their own way each of them has also grown closer to me, and I in turn, to them. I will not go into details, but now I look for the similarities and not the differences. I understand much more now, and I see that they understand more also. I also couldn't understand, at one time, how they could be the way they were. The way they were was just an affect of our society and their own individual life upon them. And I've come to discover that... I AM JUST LIKE THEM. (Deep down, we are all the same.)

Because that is true; mom, dad and I have had similar situations seemingly my whole life long. The only difficulty began when I was not informed of my parents' less than perfect lives. Now that I've reached adult status, and I've come to expose my life's comedies and tragedies and find that in doing so, I've learned about theirs'. My mom and dad (and every subsequent set of them), are the best for me. I can only hope that they appreciate, love and respect me too.

Everything that happened needed to happen. So, I could be who it is I am today. For that reason, I no longer carry anger. In fact, now they've regained their throne title as

J. Elliott Goldwyn

my God and Goddess whom have risen incarnate. There will never again be another mom and dad in my life. I just wish I would have been made aware of the facts earlier so not too much time was wasted waiting for every 'one of us' to come back together in spirit. We all had to get past the brain and it's need to control, so we can communicate with conscience.

Evil
* * *

There's evil around us everywhere, yea... evil in each and every one of us. Much like the Lord, or any higher power you choose to name. I'll use 'The Lord', because that is most understood by myself as being only the positive entity, whereas it is the devil whom is an antithesis of correctness. I can not prove it without some percentage of disbelievers or doubters whom will disagree with me (only because their employment depends upon the 'god of immorality' or their need for the escape route of 'the devil made me do it' line of malarkey) but it is my life's and my near death's experience (not just an engrossed study of novels) that shows (at least to me) that there is no devil. There is only a circle.

We are as evil as you can imagine, but we were given the power to avoid such by showing simple self-control. That is the only difference between good and evil... willpower. There are those whom have willpower, and those who do not or choose not to exhibit any in anyway, or maybe in ways that I can not see. I'm not sure, but that only means that they (whomever 'they' are) cower away from any 'one of us' who has the will to drive his point through. One only has the right to do one's true will. Now that does not mean any one of 'them' (or you) get to go willy nilly stealing or some such behavior, but rather to find out what one's true will is and follow it's path... while they harm not, or abuse not the other. You have to have a will, before you can have power over it.

The circle of Light, the circle of the Gods, nothing more. There is more great good going on than ever before, therefore

J. Elliott Goldwyn

there is more evil to sway the circle and keep it balanced... pity that the animal 'human' needs balance in extremes.*

Our next very important discovery will be how to have the good without the need for the evil. Or, am I doing that right now? "Time will tell, as it often does." (Thanks Hope!) Hope's favorite quote around the time we were together... way back when.

I got up this morning and just wanted all the stress to be over, but that's not possible... or is it? One more day filled with the godless grey given gladly to anyone whom is alive. Where does it come from if I cannot make it go away? Life is hard you say... I do too, but the grey I spoke on does not come from a person. It's more like a fear from forgone activities not yet realized, or a statement from the soft inner voice we have inside saying, "Be careful, you have to survive in a world where everyone is just as evil as you... some even more!" So, we begin our crusade being careful to become just like those around us in order to win that (rat) race we evolved in to running.

* i.e. good god, bad god - good person, bad person... and no place in-between. (God is, and People are, nothing but in-between.)

one-of-us

Genocide
* * *

As man moves, man should evolve toward being more human in nature... more allowing of other's to be themselves. Well, that's <u>**not**</u> what we have become. We as a peoplehood have systematically dismembered or silenced entire percentages from speaking by giving them NO voice.* That, is genocide to me. No voice, no life either. I was angry as a youth because I had no voice. I think that in this age of computers every man, woman, or child should have a voice to varying degrees concerning voting age limit... and I DO think kids should have a vote concerning the playground layout and equipment for a start. Make them 'part of' rather than just a 'parasite.'

A whole... with a voice! Freedom, but... freedom with a price. Must sign up for a citizenship card, not just a local driver's licence per ce, but a national Id card. With your medical information on it '**if <u>you</u> want**' and **only if you want**. Your photo and driving permit if desired, address and other vital information should be needed so as to make sure of identity since we are a very popular peoplehood, possibly of all time. We should be aware of everybody's voice that we can. By not allowing the 'other's' to have a voice, you are subscribing to the horror of not having a voice for yourself either. But, just because your voice is more popular on a grand scale, does not mean it's more correct for **all** on that same grand scale. We have the technology to support just such an opinion scale vote tabulation on a more individual respect than we do now. I for one, am tired of just having two gosh darn choices of which neither is correct just less

* not necessarily taking their lives... although 'we' as a peoplehood have done that too.

'evil or wrong' than the other choice... and that's not right!

That sort of voting schedule happens about every four years here in the USA, sometimes even more often depending upon where you live. Although, I do feel that we should take back control of the voting process from beginning to end completely. And maybe vote in policies, not politics... or the lying politicians who slander, steal, and subscribe to giving us less freedom than we have now. I think that the whole trust aspect is mute with them, our government bends truth to outfit it's own objectives. Just like the prophets au corporation of late have shown us, "trust no one...!"

No accounting corporation

No managerial corporations

No C.E.O.

No corporate officer

No official anything at anytime or anywhere. (Haven't I said just that before?)

End of story!

No, I cannot let it end there. I wish not to go down in history as just another anarchist... because I'm not!

Even though, my beliefs are not too far away.

one-of-us

Soon we will need no law beyond 'do what thou wilt,' and no storm troopers to guard us from ourselves, but unfortunately that is not how it is now. I've mentioned how it is I feel several times in this novel... it's up to 'us' to bring evolution about. I know there are others who feel like I do. Others whom feel just like they do. Other's just like me, other's nothing like me... and everywhere in between that want to be heard. So, I got an idea...

Your own voice goes into the great computer (per ce) of the people run by the people for the people, and the great computer builds the perfect 'all encompassing' office holder who is a small percentage of you. You are in office, just as much as anyone else whom voted is in office. That could happen when we resign from voting on looks, and vote in policies. Then some dashing movie star type of guy (or girl) could read aloud the print out concerning how it is our 'president' (ourselves really) might feel about ANY decision at a moments notice.

Sounds like more freedom than we have now... maybe more freedom than we've ever known.

Okay, I can end there.

afterthought: I know lots of scary computer stories from the 60's and 70's -2004 so please don't fill my (e)mail box full of 'I'm scared of the computer taking over' crap. Thanks.

skimming off the top
* * *

I don't care who you are or what you do, someone else gets the cream. Nothing worth anything will ever be truly owned by you until you can made that "something" disappear.

If you have that kind of wealth, taxes don't mean anything besides: "Taxes..? That's the accountant's job, he can even sign the checks." But, I'm not one of them, I rent. Year to year, I pay rent. Sometimes it's a month to month arrangement (i.e. storage yard space), most times not. If the arrangement was made between two persons of legal binding age and they agree, then it's just a trade of value for value. Although, your house is not your's. It's owned by the 'system' you pay taxes to. Since the trade is forced like: Money for your very inalienable right to freedom, or to own something, what's that called? Slavery you say? Extortion for certain!

Today I see many people living in fear of something unseen, or maybe it's only an omnipresent overtone that is laid by the guilt of having snuck something behind your proverbial mother's back. It was fun when we were 2-18ish, wasn't it? Well, I'm not 18 no more. Hell, I ain't 38 no more.

It took me a while to try to make sense of the feelings in my heart and spirit and head. Things I will remember from a time long ago in the future when needed and not a moment before. But now I'm just beginning to realize that some of the people I share this planet with have no idea or no desire to live in a copesetic manner with me or other humans. What do we do with these animals? Try to train them to behave justly. Sometimes what we do today works,

one-of-us

but most times not... I'm sure the return to jail percentage is higher than the ones who never go back. Sometimes we are not in control of all our surroundings, and sometimes we fail in our endeavors entirely.

I think we have failed in retraining, we succeed in training criminals to be better criminals though. In most ways jail is a school for the illegal. When I had to go to jail I was wrong, I was bad. I was a scar upon the face of humanity... or so I was told. I was pretty mixed up after a head injury I'd not wish upon anyone, and all the messages from so many different sources... I really did not know what to do. Society tried to tell me. I tried to listen. I wound up behind bars. I slipped through the cracks as it were. I needed to be visited by someone to say, "I know you're not a bad boy Joe, it's just that you're not seeing this whole life/responsibility thing in the correct way." Many I'm sure tried, but they had invalidated their words with their actions. I may have been reduced to the mental age of 6 or 7 for quite sometime in the body of a 22-28 year old man because of the head injury on November 5th in '85, but I was not stupid. I learned from people's actions, not their words. Like most 'children' in life today, I was very confused... only I was a kid in a man's body.

I saw many things as no one else will. I feel this strongly as an adult: We, as the teachers of great societies to come, are doing a very poor job at our framing a world for our great-grandchildren to inherit. Instead of following our founding fathers, we flee from freedom.

We, as a peoplehood, are giving away rights we did not even know we were supposed to have on a daily basis. We may choose to deny the responsibility because it will not effect us (how selfish we are!) but it will directly inflict our future generations with messes both in the ground, in the air and in our very being. Whether or not those poisons are physical, mental, spiritual, emotional, or political... dig?

Things are too big. Too much is lost in the confusion. We have spent far too much time in believing that our government is telling us what it knows, not just telling us what it **wants** us to know.

If, and I use the word 'if' lightly, OJ could get away with any crime at all because of his money, just imagine what a country could do! I digress, for I've covered just such a undesired reality before haven't I? Because we choose to permit today what our forefathers rebelled against bloodily, we live with a blanket of oppression. Sometimes the blanket is real thin like a near nothingness nighty, a satin slip sheet or state tax on a gum ball. But for others it comes down as a far-reaching fire force as in Waco Texas... on that one day, freedom belonged to no one.

Your elected official lives in fear every day. Fear that you'll take his or her job away. So, instead of telling you the truth, they are persuaded by their very selves, with or without the assistance of others, to lie cheat and steal within a system whose very core has been corrupt for years. You should do what you'll say you'll do, or you loose your job. No vote, no discussion. Job's just gone to someone else. "Do your job, or loose your job." Seems so simple to me.

Why we don't swipe the board clean, and start over, is complacency. I guess if we have any gift that is NOT worth giving, is the gift of giving up before you start... but I've spoken about that before too.

Now I'm just repeating myself, see what you've made me do?

one-of-us

Ya know....
* * *

I never met Dr. Phil, but I'd bet he'd be proud of me... although I sure wish he had been around a few crucial times during my life.

J. Elliott Goldwyn

From Iraq to North Korea
* * *

Well, it looks like we might get a chance to meet the Hitler of today's day and age real soon. Now he goes by the name of Saddam Hussain, or something like that. He's not a very nice guy, but this time we will strike first rather than last. ('bout time!) Although it is true he has struck at us before, now we are going to finish it. There are people who drag their feet though, and those people have money to loose. Wow, money again. I see a pattern. DON'T YOU REMEMBER LAST TIME? Oh yeah, we are talking about Germany and France. Germany sure remembers. France, well, we know what France is. The time to "lay down and take it" is over. Now there is too much to loose.

Sometimes I feel as though man as an animal is no more civilized than the troop of ants where food is the wealth they bury deep underground. "Other 'ants' could suffer, but as long as our dollars and cents are not disturbed I really don't care that much." We need to look at the bigger picture. What world will survive a war today? The days of graveyards and craters are over, now its whole areas will be uninhabitable. WHOLE AREAS! Countries and continents. We will really mess it up next time.

Have you ever held a baby?

You tell him or her, I don't have the heart.

"This is what we've built for you."
"Not quite what our founding father's left us, but it's okay... we're complacent."

one-of-us

Think if we come down with an iron fist in Iraq, North Korea will just stop it's problems?
(Rhetorical)

May we all live in interesting times they say.

Indubitably, interesting it is.

p.s. It's Wednesday, that's movie night in my house.

about an hour and a half later...
* * *

To borrow from an enjoyable entertainment experience's ethical ending:

" ...whatever life holds in store for me, I will never forget these words: With great power comes great responsibility. This is my gift, my curse. Who am I? **I am Joseph Elliott Goldwyn."**

(Okay, not a perfect script borrow... after all the man in the movie said "I am Spiderman."

It may mean nothing to you, but it means everything to me. Well, me *and* Spiderman.

Although, swinging on a web would work.... I just don't think I'd do the costume justice!

The correlation mostly ends there... it's just that I've seen most every 'superhero' movie made from the Superman to the Batman to the Ghostbuster flicks, and did not feel the patience to watch another slippery social super-hero sham, saving society's spirituality, such sensually simple somatic slips some souls now require a super-hero to redeem their selves... rather than doing the super-person persona reflection work themselves. Newsflash- the word 'government' doesn't mean: super-hero. (Not by a long shot!) Believing in such will succeed you nothing but eventually higher taxes, and more of the super-hero named 'government' to tell us what we can or cannot do. Mostly, it will be what we can no longer do. There'll be a good reason, there always is... but there's always more than one answer also.

If, and I use the word if almost silently, more people were to act like the 'super-hero' they are is a plausible answer,

one-of-us

and it's a solution we don't even have to wait till our society has a 'black out' before our 'pay taxes super hero' will send in the national guard to disarm everyone! See, we'd be at fault if that were to happen too! So, take away another inalienable right to defend ourselves against what might be a tyranny, or democracy in name only. That's the belief we so dearly need on an individual scale in relation with the world around us.

Let me show through example from the movie which gave me excitement one might feel when one finds someone or something else that feels similarly to yourself.

Please allow me to paraphrase:

Somewhere in the opening scenes 'Spiderman to be' decides to make some money by wrestling for hundreds of dollars, if he should win. He did, and the mean ole man only paid him ten. As Peter is waiting for the elevator some guy who just robbed the mean ole man's money ran by and Peter just let him go. The mean ole man asked, "Why didn't you stop him?"

And Peter answered, "Why should I?"

The future Spiderman got downstairs and found out why. That same robber shot Peter's father figure while stealing "the dad's" car. That's why he should have stopped him:

      Evil you allow, eventually returns.

It's been said that I can only do what I can do. I try to do what I feel is best. I certainly hope you enjoyed the book, but I wager you'll be charmed with the cinematic compendium completely!

J. Elliott Goldwyn

Breaking it down
* * *

Okay, I'll put it to you this way:

No countries, no governments... just neighbors. People who work together. Not to dominate, but to assist others as they assist you. There are no borders, because there are not governments who set them in the first place. Everyone is your neighbor. Neighbors almost certainly should talk to neighbors, neighbors never go to war, governments do. Although, governments are comprised of other neighbors and not aliens... right?

(Well, come to think of it, they do keep to themselves...)

There could still exist battalions of troops (and equipment) to assist with any disaster whatsoever. i.e. earthquakes, floods, etc. Foot soldiers can do other things while in service to his or her grandchild's country, and they should get a raise! **All** people should do years in the service. Building homes for the handicapped, or cleaning up some old corporation's mess left behind. There are no corporations left now, just the workers who own the business entity. When someone is responsible for everything there will be no shield from attachment legally, and that could happen! It has been that way before. The Pyramids were constructed just such a way with very little harmful chemicals. (If any.) And if they could do that then, why do we pollute today at all?

There should be no drapery to do devious deeds in the dark behind, everything's attached to a living breathing person. If any person finds the need to kill the earth, or

one-of-us

it's present or future inhabitants to make a living, then I'll do what I can to help them so they could be self supporting (as I'm sure would others) without the harming of others. Which would allow them to leave <u>no</u> negative trail behind that could harm any 'one of us.' But if they are just lazy, there's a place for them too. There would be a great deal less greed due to the fact that there would be a maximum wage to offset the minimum wage. Although the maximum would be high, there are many people who do great things, school bus drivers, teachers (not just professors), nurses, firemen and too many more to mention. After all is said and done, if the sudsbuster does not supply the chef with clean dishes... no one gets anything and the whole system shuts down. (Analogy time.) It's the little guy the big guy lives off of, I say it's about time that reality became history.

I feel a bank account of 1 million* dollars is enough. All of us could assemble and vote in legislation to make that a law. Know why? I'd bet the majority of 'us' do not have any-where near 1mill cold hard cash. And, majority rules... right?   *or some other number

There are ways we are not looking at so more people could live in happiness. Like voting in important legislation to disrupt the downward spiral of our national state of affairs. Because no matter what they do to us I pray one thing will always be true: Majority Rules.

For instance:

Did you know all of us could get together and vote the National Debt gone. That's right, I said GONE! Didn't know you could do that, did ya? There are fear mongers who live to prey upon what it is 'we as a peoplehood' don't know. We could get together and vote our individual debt to ourselves over. Erase the record books. Germany did just that not long back, but the whole globe needs to do it. One day national debt, next day not.

I wouldn't suffer, would you? Maybe I should run for President? Nah, I'm a Benjamin kind of guy this time, and why should I run for president when I'm already king?

(Tee hee hee!)

Why don't we stand up and demand freedom from our government's problems I ask.

I did not sign up for owning my individual slice of American Debt Pie. The superhero called government did it for me. I think 'all of us' should take the reigns back, and when the tired old gelding (government) resists movement then we should not be fearful in giving the animal new life with the spurs (ideas) it so desperately needs... rather than letting that stable broke animal describe how we'll ride.

(Please examine the following recognition report...)

Two guys, one who seemingly just happened upon that information for the very first time:

"So, I am enslaved from the very beginning?"

"Yes, yes we are."

"Am I scared?"

"Yes, yes we are."

"Should I be?"

"Yes, yes we should."

"Why?"

"Because every small group of people who tried to stand up and say something systematically were destroyed, and I'm not ready to be destroyed like in Waco. Although, that may

one-of-us

be the reason you feel so grey daily. So just shut up, heat up a microwave dinner and watch more of the war on tv."*

Whew, I sure am glad George Washington wasn't here to hear those guys say that. George would have slapped them like the pansy ass bitches they are. Hear me when I say that "**Our great founding father's were not fighting for *their* freedom, they were fighting for our grandchildren's future!** They were that great, they stood that tall."

What are we going to leave, besides a huge national debt? I've seen it for as many years as I've been alive, all of us trying to allow our good natured government to repair it's own self. That doesn't happen if you ignore the vermin, they just multiply. Removing government does not mean chaos. In fact, anarchy means freedom. It did in 1776. Don't allow the mongers who know nothing about how intelligent we are tell us with audacity, that really we're not! When you talk to your neighbor, I'd wager they'd agree... "Why cannot we just have one group of people who live in many different areas in different ways like you and me? "

* I'm not saying David Koresh was a nice guy, I did not know him. But I do know that no one should have died. That was one more time we did not look at other answers to the same problem. Remember, we do call ourselves civilized... but Waco didn't need to burn! Fear monger's were in charge there assuredly so Waco's fate was sealed from the beginning. Gotta spread the fear that there is no answer beyond doing what 'they' say we should do! Talk about a fly and a sledgehammer! (Aren't you ready for the freedom of living in 'no fear?')

We can, could and will decide what the best thing for us is, not someone or something else. Every 'one of us' will decide what is best for ourselves and if you need assistance with deciding, there are people who live to assist, not command. Every system of corruption becomes privatized. There will be fewer and fewer corporate curtains covering up injustices of the greed commanded atrocities of man against fellow man. So, you or your company does a good job, or you (all) look for a job.

If what you decide for yourself does not coincide with the surrounding society, then that group of 'us' will move you where it is acceptable to act in such a way... or just kick you out. If there is no society for whatever you have in mind, no worries...there is a place for just such an animal. It's called a zoo, but only one animal means solitary incarceration.

With all due respect:
* * *

You've been given the rules of coexistence for quite a few pages, and if you cannot play nice then maybe we will no longer play with you; but with a playground for most every action, everyone is sure to fit in somewhere. After all, we are all adults... although acting age appropriate has absolutely aught to do with allowances or age.

one of us
* * *

One new group, and we're the group who will speak up! I'm taking a stand, take a stand with me won't you? We don't have to agree on anything but a desire for improvement! <u>Not</u> in one government worldwide, but <u>**one idea of leadership**</u>. Our founding fathers had some really good ideas. Unfortunately they were written in a far different time than now, but a re-write on a locally mandated level (majority vote) and things will have a real nice place to start. Not by changing the constitution, but returning to it's core when it really meant something.

Let's call us, us. I'm one of us. And, since you've read this far you're probably one too. Today we're just in different bodies, but soon enough, we'll all be one again.

So, let's not worry too much about what your brother or sister (on the other side of the world) gives homage to before they retire for a good night's rest... because that doesn't matter. I know that no matter where he or she lives, there is the slave master called Greed that probably own's their lives by coercion or conscience choice. I believe the days of the marauding masses are over, all we have now are governments who fight with other groups (religious or not) that are some form of leadership based on greed.
There, but for the grace of God...

How the animal human (with all it's inherent individual interpretations) came to live on earth, or where we go when we leave is not as important as living with honor, respect and responsibility while we are here.

one-of-us

Just take care of yourself and those around you. If things get tough for you or him, there are neighbors whom live nearby, who will assist you or him accordingly. Sometimes it's a Geographical association, but there should be teams of mechanical engineers (per ce) from the USA, Mother Russia, England or wherever a team player may live that could look on the 'internet' (I shudder slightly at that word, it's had such 'bad press' lately!) and find a need in whatever his profession is... and just go there. How might he get there? If the company needs a worker, I'm positive they will pay the plane fare. Sounds easy? Sure sounds simply stressless. We'll figure out sooner rather than later I pray: We the people of this earth DO NOT need to be controlled by anything but love. There will always be trouble from the hollow people I've mentioned earlier, but that just needs to become part of the equation (because trying to deny the problem ain't working for me) and understand HP's will always do stupid stuff because they don't know any better. There is no soft voice inside their body telling them not to initiate or participate.

Everyone else has their own way of understanding their relation to their own true will or higher power. My Father doesn't care what name you use. I use 'Father' because that is one way I fathom the greatness. Although, my Father is my Mother because of a direct relation to the circle's path I've spoken about. The Light of both, might and right, are all around us at all times and in all ways. Everything is in relation to it's power. As great and as vast as the universe as we know it is today... it is nothing to our Light of Love and Life.

J. Elliott Goldwyn

Our world is merely a stage you're living on your whole life long.

The pen's mightier than the sword, it is said.

But moreover; mostly the masses are moved by movies.

To be working on an epic is to play with a power greater than atomic fission.

Daily you are writing and living 'the film' you'll remember long after your body is gone.

You will share 'your movie' with other spirits in the Light as they share their's with you.

You might have to explain the choices you allowed your brain to make to the script of your life with your higher self inside.

Never forget who's in charge.

There are many choices, but only a certain amount of video tape... so choose wisely.

Now if you'll please permit me to prepare a pardon, it's time for a scene change.

"...and sleep"
* * *

Don't think of this as the book's end because it's obvious to me that now I'm done... I've really just begun! Besides, it's more of a dramatic pause... like your dreams.